THE
RESTORATION
OF POST-WWII
CARS

THE RESTORATION OF POST-WWII CARS

Peter Wallage

ROBERT BENTLEY, INC.
872 Massachusetts Ave., Cambridge, Mass. 02139

Library of Congress Cataloging in Publication
Data

Wallage, Peter.
The restoration of post-WWII cars.
Includes index.
1. Automobiles — Restoration.   I. Title.
TL152.2.W34 629.28′8′22 77-94368
ISBN 0-8376-0145-2

Acknowledgment

The author thanks the following people and
organisations for help in obtaining information,
illustrations and permission to reproduce them:

> Armaglaze Ltd
> Austin-Morris Ltd
> Chris Goffey, Editor, Motor Trader
> Chrysler (United Kingdom) Ltd
> Ford Motor Company Ltd
> Girling Ltd
> I.C.I. Ltd
> Jaguar-Rover-Triumph Ltd
> Metalok Ltd
> Michael Bowler, Editor, Thoroughbred
>   and Classic Car
> Psimat Ltd
> Spear and Jackson Ltd
> Quinton Hazel Ltd
> Valerie Wallage

Contents

Publisher's Note

While the text of this book was written with an international readership in mind, a choice had to be made between English and American English usage for certain words. The list below is of words and phrases where the difference is more marked, with the English version in the first column.

baulk ring : synchro cone
body sill : body rocker panel
bonnet : hood
boot : trunk
breaker's yard : auto-salvage yard
bush : bushing
choke tube : venturi
circlip : snap ring
clutch release bearing : throwout bearing
coach bolt : carriage bolt
control box : regulator (box)
crown wheel : ring gear ('ring gear' in English is starter only)

decoke : decarbonize
dynamo : generator
earth, chassis earth : ground, chassis ground
estate car : station wagon

float chamber : carburetor bowl
gearbox : transmission
grub screw : dog screw
gudgeon pin : wrist pin
layshaft : countershaft
methylated spirit : denatured alcohol
Mole wrench : self-gripping wrench
overrider : bumper guard, bumperette

panel beating : body repair
paraffin : kerosene
quarter light : vent window (if it opens)
: quarter window (if it does not open)

saloon : sedan
scuttle : cowl
set off : touch dry
set screw : set bolt
spanner : wrench
spigot : pilot
split pin : split cotter
swivel axle : stub axle
trolley : dolly
windscreen : windshield
wing : fender
withdrawal arm/fork : throwout arm

1
FIRST, CATCH YOUR CAR

Before starting to restore a car, you have to find one that is suitable. In this book I am not going to put cars into categories, thoroughbred, classic or otherwise. Now that vintage, post-vintage thoroughbred, classic sports cars and others with their different labels have become investment items, the ordinary car enthusiast looking for something he can restore and take a pride in has turned to the more humble cars of yesteryear as well as the exotic — which are fast pricing themselves out of his reach.

If you like a car, and if in your eyes it has character, then as far as you are concerned it is a car worth restoring. Forget the self-styled purists and experts. Go ahead and enjoy your hobby. For that is what car restoring is, or should be; a hobby. It should not be a serious business of evaluating investment potential. Nor, though sadly some people make it so, should it be a business of faking up an old banger with filler and a quick respray in the hope that some enthusiast with more money than discretion will part with a large amount of hard-earned cash. But such people abound on the fringes of the car trade, so be warned.

Car restoring is a growing hobby. Unfortunately, this very growth has pushed up prices. Almost by definition, a restorable car is an old one, and the normal laws of supply and demand govern prices. But there is no need to pay inflated prices for mediocre examples just to satisfy the sharks. There are still plenty of cars around which are worth restoring, and which can be had at reasonable prices.

Here, though, I feel I should sound a word of warning. Cars which are difficult to work on, often with the most expensive spares, are usually the ones which, in first class condition, fetch high prices. The sadder examples by comparison, are frequently offered at seemingly very low prices.

The '1959 Jaguar, needs some work, suit enthusiast' or the '1949 Daimler, partly stripped for restoration, no time to finish', both at low prices, might well be bargains; but possibly only to the man who has the tools, the place to work, the money, the skill and the knowledge to strip and rebuild a Jaguar engine or a Wilson pre-selector gearbox. If you lack any of these essentials, then cars like these can become expensive white elephants.

As far as a place to work and the money go, you are on your own. But whether you want to restore a car to concours condition, or just make it presentable and reliable, I hope to give you at least part of the knowledge. Skill is largely a combination of knowledge and practice in handling tools, and restoring a car will give you plenty of practice. For tips on the finer points of a particular model, join a one-make enthusiast's club — if one exists for your car.

No doubt you have in mind the sort of car you would like to have in restored condition. It might be a luxury model you could never afford when it was current, the sports car you always fancied but which was never practicable at the time, or maybe a car you once owned and for which you have a nostalgic hankering. Before setting out to look for it, be realistic about your facilities and the time and money you can give to the job.

If all you have is a small, rented lock-up garage with no room for a bench, no electricity and no water, a complete rebuild can become a drudgery, if not an impossibility. You too will become one of the 'no time to finish' advertisers. Far better in this case to pay more for a car in decent running order, with a roadworthiness certificate or vehicle inspection sticker, and put it in the best condition you can without stripping it right down. You will still find plenty to do to keep you happy.

If, on the other hand, you have a reasonably large garage which will take a bench, electric power (even if only an extension cable), and an adjacent source of water — and you do not mind taking a couple of years over the job — then, if you fancy the work, buy the cheapest non-running example of the car you want, and make sure that it is complete, the main parts are sound, and that the price reflects the amount of work that will be necessary.

Perhaps this is the first time you have thought about a complete restoration. If so, and if your previous experience has stopped at cleaning plugs and points, sit down and think seriously before taking on the complete rebuild of a sad, large luxury car, or a sports car of which relatively few were built. Desirable pieces of machinery though these are, and though they fetch high prices when restored, the cost of restoration can be quite enormous. You might be happier with a more humble, once popular model which you will find easier to work on, easier for spares and far less costly.

If you really want to have a go at a Jaguar, Daimler, Alvis or similar high performance luxury car, far be it from me to put you off. But for your first attempt it is better to be successful and driving, than disillusioned with a heap of beautifully made worn out parts. You will have a go at one of the Supermobiles in time, never fear. Once the restoration bug has bitten it seldom lets go.

How much will restoration cost? Anything from £300 to £3000 ($600 to $6000) and upwards, depending on the car you choose, its condition, how much outside help you have to enlist for welding, machining or paint spraying, how fortunate you are at finding spares at reasonable prices — and a large slice of good, old-fashioned luck. On one thing you can be certain. The final cost will be far more than your first estimate.

It sounds a lot of money to spend on a car for which you might pay, perhaps, under £500 ($1000) in the first place, but when the job is finished you will have a car that is as reliable and good looking (if not so modern and fast) as a nearly new car for which you might pay upwards of £2500 ($5000). And yours will not depreciate like the nearly new one — it will probably appreciate.

So, having tempered enthusiasm with a little reality to lessen the chance of becoming both buyer and salesman, perhaps the best way to deal with evaluating a car is to describe, as near as I can remember, some of my trips out to look for likely prospects.

I always take a few hand tools, a tin of hand cleaner, some rags, and old rug or sheet of polythene to lie on, a pair of jumper leads and a couple of flashlights. The flashlights are not for looking at cars in the dark (you can learn very little about a car in the dark!), they are for probing under the chassis of non-runners in dark garages.

My usual approach, while chatting to the owner, is to stand and look at the outside, methodically and for quite a time, before I get distracted by things inside the doors and under the bonnet. Usually I start at the front and work back.

The first prospect was a 10 hp family saloon from the early 1950s described as 'clean body, good runner' in the advert. I found it standing in the owner's drive, and it looked quite presentable.

In this case, the front bumper looked reasonable, discoloured in places, but the chromium plate had not flaked off anywhere, so it would probably come up quite well. The radiator shell and grille was very presentable except for the small plate at the bottom which covered the hole where the starting handle fitted. That looked as if it had been bent and levered out with a blunt instrument, but it would straighten. I always rate the condition of the radiator shell and grille important. They are none too easy to find secondhand, and they are such a focal point that if they are not in top class condition they spoil the look of a restored car.

One wing showed signs of amateur panel beating at the front, and there was a suspicious looking bulge at one side with a semicircle of paint showing brush marks. I ran a hand underneath and, as I suspected, found that the bang in the front had pushed the edge of the wing out and split the beading. There was a hump of glass fibre under there, but that would not hold it for long; it needed welding.

There were bubbles in the paint round the sidelights, but when I tapped lightly the rust did not seem to have broken through. Down at the back of the wings and along the sills the rust had taken more of a hold, and one jacking bracket looked out of alignment. That was not so good, and needed investigating further in case the rot had spread to the chassis. Rust had also broken through along the bottom of one door, and along the bottom of the boot; but these are not structural parts, so I was not so concerned.

The windscreen had a nasty scratch where one wiper arm had gone across without its blade, but it was a flat screen so there would be no difficulty in getting one cut. Had it been a curved screen I would have been more concerned, because curved screens which have been out of production for some time can be difficult to find.

The side windows were all good, except that the chromium plated surrounds were spotty and the chanelling had almost rubbed away, but chanelling is easy to get. Generally, the paintwork was fair, though there were signs of touching up, and abrasive cleaners over the years had rubbed through to the undercoat along the edge of the roof and the top of the bonnet. The hub caps were all there, though one looked as if it had been run over and hammered out again. Three of the tires were

1   You may not find
such a blatant example
of covering up rust as this,
but be wary of hastily
applied touching up

9

2 A very non-standard dashboard, on the author's MG as bought, where some one had tried customizing. In a case such as this a completely new dash is necessary

good, one not so good and the spare was useless. All in all, first impressions were favourable.

While I had been looking I chatted to the owner. He had owned the car eight years and ran it almost daily, which was a good sign, because I get a little sceptical when someone offers a car for sale as 'suitable for restoration' and it turns out that they have had it only a few months. My nasty suspicious mind tells me they have bought a pup and want to unload it. I will still have a close look though. I once bought a car from someone who had owned it just three weeks. It had a vibration that shook your teeth at 40 mph. It took me all of half an hour to take the prop shaft off and turn the universals to their proper angular relationship. The drastic fault that puts one person off might not turn out to be too serious, but extra care is needed. Sometimes an owner will cheerfully tell you about one fault to distract you from another, more serious.

This owner seemed to be a genuine enough chap. He had an idea for some time about making something of the car, but said he had neither the time nor a proper place to work on it. The roadworthiness certificate had expired, and he thought the brakes and steering would want a spot of attention before it passed again. He needed a car on the road, and had bought something more recent with a current certificate. It sounded fair enough, so I looked further.

I opened the doors and lifted each one slightly to test the hinges for wear and the pillars for soundness. The pillars were all right, three hinges were firm but the driver's door showed plenty of play; the striker plate was badly worn and I could see where the bottom had been scraping on the sill. The seats were quite good, with no tears, but the driver's seat was sagging and the stitching had given way in places. The carpets were scruffy and had worn right through on the driver's side. All these pointed to a considerable mileage. The door trims were fair (though scuffed), all the windows wound up and down and the locks worked. Precious little varnish was left on the wooden door rails, and the wooden dash looked as if someone had painted it with brown toffee. All the instruments were present. So far, so good. I asked if I could start her up.

The owner looked a little embarrassed, and said the battery was flat. That probably meant it was at the end of its life, but I hardly expected to get a good one. I brought my car up and got out the jumper leads. The engine fired after a few turns, and sounded quite good — a little tappety, but no immediate signs of bearing trouble. The oil pressure looked good, but I always check that again (if there is a gauge) when the oil is warm. The ammeter showed almost a full charge, so I tried the lights. All worked except for one dip filament. The horn worked, so did the wipers. One semaphore indicator worked, the other refused to budge. The warning lights went out, but these tell you very little because the oil pressure light usually comes on only when the pressure has fallen far into the hazardous region, and the dynamo light will not warn of over-charging caused by a faulty regulator. So about all you can do is make sure that these lights are not burned out and, if you are worried, test the car with temporarily-installed gauges before you decide to do very much driving.

As soon as the engine was warm I pushed in the choke and let it idle. The ammeter started to flicker, so either the dynamo needed attention, or the regulator was out of adjustment; probably both. While she was ticking over I carried on chatting. What was he getting to the gallon? "About 28." That sounded low enough to be genuine; he should have been getting about 34, so probably the carburetter was worn. The mileage read something over 22,500 — possibly second time around from the condition of the driving seat and door, and the wear in the engine.

How much oil did she use? "Quite a bit, I'm afraid, about a pint every 100 miles." Now that the engine had been ticking over for a time I stabbed down on the accelerator. From the cloud of blue smoke that poured from the exhaust I judged he was on the optimistic side with his 100 to the pint. Some of these old long stroke engines can be real oil burners. Special oil control rings might help matters, but more than likely it would need a rebore and new pistons; at a probable 120,000 miles or so I had to expect at least one previous rebore, so I allowed for resleeving in my mental costing. As I revved there was a distinct blow from the exhaust.

I tried the gears and shunted back and forth along his drive. There was just enough room to make sure that all the gears worked and that the back axle drove the car, but I could not tell whether the gears were noisy. Nor could I find out about the state of the synchromesh, but after 120,000 miles, and provided the box did not whine like a banshee, I would be quite happy to double declutch. I pulled up the umbrella handbrake and tried starting off against it. There was no sign of clutch slip, but the handbrake was pretty poor.

Satisfied so far, I switched off, then pressed the starter again without switching on. There

3   After standing for years an engine can look really sad. Check carecully for cracks in the head or block, but do not be too worried about external appearances. Another view of the author's MG before it was stripped down to the chassis.

was just enough in the battery to turn the engine over, but once again I heard a nasty regular grinding sound. Worn teeth on the flywheel ring gear, without a doubt.

Under the bonnet the side valve engine, basically a pre-war design, had the usual oil and dirt over it but no signs of water leaks. Most of the oil seemed to be round the crankcase breather, another sign of worn piston rings — and probably valve guides too.

The ignition leads were none too good, and when I took the distributor cap off I found the rotor camshaft very sloppy in its bearings. Parts of the wiring had been patched with adhesive tape, so a rewire looked desirable, as would be the case with most cars built before non-perishable plastic insulation came in.

The radiator seemed in good condition with no leaks, but when I looked more closely I found solder round the hole in the bottom tank where the starting handle passed through. This rang a bell about the bent front plate, so I found the handle and tried it, but it rubbed on the hole, so I left it in case I started a leak. The radiator would have to come off and be seen to. If the handle had fitted I could have tried the compressions, but I had already found plenty of signs of engine wear, so there was not much point.

While I had the bonnet up I tried the play in the steering and watched the drop arm. Yes, there was some wear in the steering box, but it was an adjustable sort. The ball joints on the track rod looked new, so my guess was the owner had tried to do something about the steering but fought shy of stripping the box. He told me there was some wear in the king pins, so I did not need to check them. If an owner tells you a part is worn, believe him. If he does not mention it, check for yourself. If he had not mentioned the king pins I would have jacked up each side and tried to rock the wheels top to bottom. I would also have spun them to listen for worn bearings, but as these would have to be stripped to do the king pins I assumed they wanted renewing.

Now I got my lying-down rug and crawled underneath as far as I could. I did this without jacking up because I had not brought any axle stands and I do not trust jacks by themselves. With a blunt screwdriver I prodded all along the 'chassis members', actually top-hat sections welded to the floor pan. All seemed sound enough except for the jacking point I had noticed. This was in a bad way, so a new one would have to be made and welded in. The inner sills were also quite badly rusted, but these were not structural.

4 Wolseley Six-Eighties are popular British cars for restoration. They have better internal trim than their Morris brothers, though they share many body panels. This example is in a rally at Biggin Hill air fair in Kent

5 A car that was ahead ▶ of its time, and one which has an enthusiastic owner's club, is the Jowett Javelin

The car stood quite well on its springs, but when I scraped the dirt off one of the rear ones I found a main leaf broken. Levering with a tire lever disclosed wear in the shackles and bushes. With the king pins, steering box and shackles worn, and a broken spring, no wonder the owner found the steering in need of attention. The exhaust was patched with tin plate and asbestos tape, there were no leaks from the back axle, and the petrol tank seemed sound.

There would undoubtedly be other faults I failed to find, but basically the car seemed reasonable. It was a good example of an early post-war family car that could be put in good order and made smart without too much stripping down. Working at weekends I could have got the car on the road in about three months. Then I could run it while I did the other work. To bring it to concours condition would, of course, take much longer.

The price was on the high side, but I could probably have got that down with a little haggling. No-one expects to sell a car for the first asking price. I did not buy this particular car because I preferred another, but it was a pretty fair prospect for restoration.

It might seem I spent a long time examining it, but in fact it took less than twenty minutes.

Even if the price is low I like to find out if the car is restorable or only fit for scrap, and if I am paying a fair amount of money I like to know what I am buying. If I had found anything drastic I would have turned it down there and then and not bothered to look further.

Another I went to see was a 2.2 litre semi-sports saloon from the fifties which made quite a name for itself in rallies. It has an enthusiastic owners' club which is always a help for locating difficult spares. This too looked quite presentable from a distance but when I got closer I found new, rather hurried, hand painting with heavily applied glass fibre along each sill and down the backs of the wings. Whoever painted it forgot to go below the bumpers, and at the back the bottom edge of the body was very poor. It sat a little down on one side at the front, and I was not too impressed.

Inside, someone had tried to customize it with stick-on plastic sheet over the dash, and holes in unlikely places for extra instruments, all missing. The rest of the inside was generally rough. A year-old Silverstone car park pass was still on the screen, presumably to let everyone know the owner was interested in racing, and there were a couple of out of

13

date sports car magazines on the back shelf. The original steering wheel had been replaced with an aluminium one about the size of a tea plate, and it was all a bit obvious and amateur.

Nor did I take overmuch to the owner who sported a rally jacket covered with car makers and oil company badges, and who had a flip line of talk about 'good old motors, these. Collector's car now, you know'. I do; thanks all the same.

He coaxed the engine into somewhat reluctant life, and blipped the accelerator as though he were trying to keep racing plugs clean before the flag fell. To be fair, the engine sounded quite healthy, but I had decided against it and declined with thanks his offer of a run. He had an inflated idea of prices, and there are better, and cheaper, examples of this model about.

So, on to the next. This one was a 3.4 litre sports saloon from the sixties, powerful and, if in good order, a smooth and beautiful car to own. The advertised price was below average, so I looked for the snags.

I went over it as I did the family saloon, but found nothing drastically wrong. The expensive tires were all near the limit, the body showed signs of rust at the back of both front wings, along the sills and the bottom of two doors, but nothing serious. The box sections which support the bumper at the front were rusted — they usually are on this model — but the box chassis itself was sound. A fair amount of work was needed on the body, but not so much as to make it impractical.

The inside was reasonable, and the engine started readily, with good oil pressure which it held when hot. All the electrics worked except the clock. There was a rattle from the engine, partly tappets and partly a rattle which came and went as I revved up. The overhead camshaft tappets are a long and complicated job on this model, and the rattle came from the front timing chain, which is also quite a job to replace. The race-bred engine was a joy to behold with lots of polished aluminium, but it is a highly developed piece of machinery, and stripping down would not be a job for a beginner. This car also had an exhaust blow,

and I found the whole of the double exhaust system in a poor state. Exhaust systems for these cars, as with most spares, come expensive.

The car had a month to go on its roadworthiness certificate, and the owner took me for a run. I could not drive because the insurance was for owner-driver only. It ran very well, and the overdrive was smooth, but the owner seemed to have to work hard at the steering on rough surfaces. It could have been just a case of adjustment, or it could have indicated a need to strip and rebush the complete front suspension.

He drove competently and smoothly without trying to impress me with the car's obvious power. He had owned it four years and agreed it needed a fair amount of work, but pointed out with some justification that it was in better condition than most examples offered at the price. He was getting rid of it because he was not really interested in restoration. He wanted a car in better condition for everyday use.

It would cost quite a lot more to put this car in good order than the family saloon I looked at earlier, but when finished it would be a very nice car indeed. However, had this been my first attempt at restoration I would have weighed the pros and cons carefully before parting with my money.

The last car on my list was a very different story. It was a 1959 2.6 litre solidly built saloon, described as 'stored six years, not running, offers'.

I found the address and learned that the car ran a big end six years before when it was just another oldish car. The owner put it in his garage and left it there. Now he wanted the room, and a friend had told him he ought to get a good price for it, big end or no, because 'people are restoring these sort of cars now'. How many times have I heard that reason for high prices?

When the garage was opened the car looked very sad. One tire was completely flat and the others were well down. The treads were good, but the sidewalls could have been good or bad, probably bad. There was a thick layer of grime all over the body, the paint had gone

◄ 6 Daimler's post-war essay into the sports car field with the Dart, was short lived; but it is a car worth seeking. Some say it died because it offered too much competition to other Leyland sports cars after the formation of the Jaguar-Rover-Triumph group

7 The author's 1964 ► Jaguar Mk 2 3.4 litre. Presentable, but not yet up to class-winning standard in a concours

very dull and the interior smelt like a cellar that had been shut for years.

I had to take his word about the trouble being the big end. No reason why he should be wrong, but big ends go because they get short of oil. This model had a reputation of being an oil burner when the engine was worn, so the rest of the bearings could have been on the way out. Possibly the crankshaft would need regrinding. I had to allow for a complete engine rebuild in my price calculations.

Another thing I had to look at closely was chassis corrosion. There was a separate box section chassis, and though the model was not noted for corrosion, box sections which have been left standing for years can deteriorate badly. I could hardly squeeze along the side of the car to examine it, so I pumped up the tires and tried to push it out into the light of day. The handbrake had seized on, so I had to go underneath and tap the expanders free. Once in the open I went underneath again and prodded every part of the chassis with careful attention to the part where it swept up over the rear axle. This is a favourite corrosion point on a box chassis. If it had been badly corroded it would have meant extensive, and expensive, welding.

I went over the rest of the car as I did the family saloon, and tried the starting handle. The engine refused to budge, but this is not uncommon on engines which have been left standing, and as I would have to strip it down I should be able to free it off without much trouble.

All the cooling system drain taps were open, and the owner told me he had drained off when he put the car away. I checked the oil level, closed the drain taps, begged a can of water and filled the radiator carefully so that any leaks would not be confused with spilling. The owner kept on telling me that the block was sound, but I would have had no come-back if it had been cracked, so I wanted to see for myself.

After ten minutes or so no water had dripped out, so there were no external cracks. I dipped the oil again to see if the level had risen. If it had, it would have indicated an internal crack or a leaking head gasket. I am always pessimistic when buying a car, so I would have gone for the crack, which could have meant finding either another block, or head, or another engine.

The price, considering the possible dangers I had been unable to check, was too high. Remember, I had not been able to try the clutch, gearbox or back axle, and for all I knew they could all be in bad shape. The friend had obviously been looking at advertised prices — advertised prices are not the same as selling prices — of similar cars in good running order. I was interested, so I made an offer, which was turned down. I left my phone number and tried again a week or so later. My guess was that someone would make an even lower bid which would make mine seem good. If, on the other hand, someone paid nearer the asking price, good luck to him. The model was not all that rare.

The four cars I have described are all examples I have been to see over the past year or two and in two cases, a Mk 2 Jaguar and the last one, a Rover 90, I have bought them. The chap with the Rover eventually rang me to accept my bid. At the time of writing the Jaguar is on the road, but needs some more work before it is fit to enter for a concours, and the Rover is still languishing in one of my garages. That sounds very grand, 'one of my garages'; actually I have two prefabricated concrete garages at the bottom of the garden, and the other is full of dismantled 1936 MG, so the Jaguar is in a neighbour's garage. One of these fine days, or years, I shall have them all on the road.

Of course, buying privately is not the only way. You could buy from a dealer, or at an auction. In either case, examine the car carefully and, at an auction, set your top price

8　Morris Minors, and particularly Travellers, are being eagerly sought if they are in good condition. This 1959 example, which belonged to the author, is now beyond economic recall after being given to the children to play with at the bottom of the garden when it was just another old rusting motorcar

and stick to it. It is very easy to be carried away by the bidding, and most annoying to pay dearly for a car only to see the same model in as good, or even better, condition on sale a little later. Never be embarrassed about taking your time over examining a car. Even at a low price a car can be dear if it is corroded to the point where it is fit only for scrap or spares. Remember, there are always more cars to look at. I have turned down more cars than I have bought, and I have owned 21 in the past 25 years.

Now to the tools you will need. If you buy a car in reasonable mechanical condition and intend to make it presentable, or indeed very smart, without stripping it down, you will be able to tackle most of the work with a kit of hand tools and an electric drill. If you are going for a complete strip and rebuild you will naturally want more.

Always buy good quality tools. They are cheapest in the long run and save many a rounded nut and much bad language. You will want a set of open ended spanners and preferably a set of ring spanners as well. Depending on the car they will be Whitworth sizes or A/F — that is the size of the bolt head across the flats — and, for many cars of the fifties, a mixture of both. For a continental car you will of course want metric sizes, and you will find metric bolts on some later British cars.

If you contemplate more extensive mechanical overhaul, a socket set is almost essential. I say almost, because mechanics coped in the days before socket sets were around, but they had a tougher time and less complicated cars.

The smaller socket sets lack a few accessories I find most useful. These are a long bar handle with a swivel at the business end, a universal joint, without which you will need universally jointed arms for some jobs, and a socket or set of sockets which take either plain or cross-head screwdriver bits. I prefer these to an impact driver for stubborn screws. My experience is that on bodywork which is at all weakened by rust the impact driver sends the screw straight through the panel.

I know a great many people manage without a torque wrench, but I would put it high on your buying list if you are going to have the head off the engine or renew the bearings. It saves a great deal of worry as to whether or not you have tightened head or bearing cap bolts sufficiently, and avoids that last half turn for luck which invariably shears off the bolt.

Another tool, broadening the definition somewhat, that too many restorers attempt to do without is a service manual or workshop manual for the car. Without a manual, it is difficult to detect non-standard parts installed by former owners or to assemble or install new or reconditioned parts correctly. Examples are: setting the valve-timing on a Jaguar; there is only one correct way to install new kingpin bushes in a 1949 Cadillac. Without a manual they can present numerous problems. The manual from the manufacturer may be well out of print, but specialist publishers are reprinting or rewriting original manuals. You may be able to pick up an original manual at an autojumble or swap-meet.

You will want an assortment of screwdrivers, pliers, hammers, a wire brush, oil can and a decent lever-type grease gun. I could go on and on — indeed a walk round a well stocked tool shop almost convinces you that you need to spend as much on tools as you paid for the car. I have no intention of making a list. My experience is that no-one goes out and buys all the tools on those nice tidy lists drawn up by motoring writers. They add to their kit as and when they need extra tools, as I am sure you will.

I would list a few pieces of garage equipment as desirable if not essential. The first is a decent quality jack to replace the cheap and cheerful one you may, if you are lucky, get with the car. Second are four axle stands so you can get the car off the ground with all the wheels off. Third is a sturdy bench and a decent vice, not one of those fiddly handyman's efforts which is supposed to hold onto the bench with a thumbscrew.

Unless you are a masochist who enjoys the aches and back pains which result from lying on a cold concrete floor, you will find a mechanic's cradle, or crawler as it is sometimes called, a great comfort when you spend long hours under the car.

So, having found a car and assembled a fair kit of tools, you can get down to the really interesting part: actually working on the thing. Try to find out all you can about the model you have bought. Read old road tests and descriptions, and if you can get a workshop manual it is really worth having.

9   Autojumbles and swap meets offer a chance to pick up elusive spares at bargain prices, but take a notebook with the exact specification of the parts you want. Here, the author is trying to decide if a carburettor is really the one he wants

=2=
MAKING IT PRESENTABLE

Having got the car home you will no doubt be itching to get the tools out and start work. Enthusiasm to get on with the job is a fine thing, but if you can curb it for just a while to get to know the car and find out just what you have bought before you start tearing it about, you will save yourself a great deal of frustration and probably time and money as well.

Whether the car is a runner or not, a really good clean is the best way to find out what sort of a state it is in. It does not matter whether it is lightly dirty or covered with the dirt and muck of years of storage, there is only one way to start a cleaning job. You want a garden hose and a copious flow of water with either a flat brush to fit on the end of the hose or a big soft sponge. Real sponges come expensive these days, but I have found modern plastic ones do the job just as well and last longer.

Even if you feel sure you are going to have to repaint the car, resist the temptation to brush the dirt off dry. Flood the body with plenty of water and use the sponge or the brush to float the dirt away. You can put a spot of detergent such as washing up liquid on the body and rub it in with the sponge, or if you want to be more sophisticated, buy an attachment to go on the hose which dispenses detergent when you press a trigger.

At this stage you are not looking for a showroom shine, even on perfect paintwork, so there is no need to use an expensive chamois leather to dry off. I find old squares of towelling ideal for this, and it does not matter if you tear them on the edges of bumpers and similarly awkward places.

When you get down to the wheels, especially spoke wheels, you will find that the brush on the end of the pipe and the sponge are not much use. You can still buy old-fashioned spoke brushes which look like a Christmas tree, and these made the job much easier, as they get most of the dirt off; but for getting into the crevices around the spoke nipples and hubs an old paint brush is ideal. Magnesium or aluminium alloy wheels come up well with one of the proprietary brighteners, but keep these off the paintwork because some of them take out the colour.

If you can get the car up on four axle stands so you can take the wheels off, so much the better. Then you can tackle the caked mud underneath. Garages clean down undersides with a power cleaner and a hot water lance, and if there is a tool store near you from which one can be hired it will turn a dirty, messy job into a much more pleasant one. Alternatively, if the car is a runner you can take it along to

10 Power washers such as this Psimat take all the hard work out of cleaning the grime off the body as well as the underside. Sometimes portable ones can be hired but if not, many garages offer a power cleaning service

a garage and get them to do the job for you.

If, however, you have to do it the hard way, make things less hard by making yourself a washing lance to go on the end of your hose. Get a piece of ½ in (13 mm) copper pipe about 3 ft (1 m) long, fix it in the end of the hose with a clip and bend the other end slightly about 1 ft (30 cm) from the end. If you hammer the business end to a fan shape you will get a good hard jet which, though not as powerful as a power cleaner, will shift almost all the mud without getting you wet.

Inside the engine compartment, and probably along the underside of the floor as well, there will be a mixture of old oil and mud that will resist cold water for days. You can use a cleaner (such as 'Gunk') to shift it, but with heavy deposits you will need gallons of the stuff, which can be expensive. It is much cheaper to start with a tin of paraffin and a stiff bristle brush, then hose down and let the car dry before you use a degreaser. You will finish up with the engine compartment sparkling. Do not worry about getting the electrics wet as they will dry out, but do take the battery off and, if there are signs of acid corrosion, clean off with soda or ammonia.

When you come to the inside, have all the seats and carpets out, brush out the worst of the dirt and finish with a vacuum cleaner hose to get in all the nooks and crannies.

Then, when everything is dry, you are ready to start more thorough cleaning and examining. I always like to start with the underside first because it is the dirtiest job, and I am always glad to get it out of the way. The hosing and degreasing will have got rid of most of the loose muck, but when you get under there with a scraper and wire brush you will find plenty more. If the car has one of the older bitumen underbody coatings it may look quite sound till you start scraping. Then you will find large portions of it peeling away where rust has got in and worked its way along under the coating.

All the coating which is not properly bonded to the floor must come off. If you leave it you are only laying up trouble for yourself later when the rust it hides starts to come through. You will get covered in dirt and grime doing this job, so wear an old beret and goggles, and a handkerchief over your nose and mouth. You might look like a cross between a nineteenth century coal miner and the Lone Ranger, but that is better than spending hours getting dirt out of your hair, eyes and nose.

A circular wire brush, or a sanding disc on a drill or on a flexible lead, speeds things along, but unless the car is on a hoist or over a pit you will be working in cramped conditions, and it is easy to catch your clothing in the brush and have a nasty accident. Most accidents which happen on ear restoring are avoidable, and in this case I always go for arm ache rather than injury.

While cleaning you will find all sorts of jobs that need doing underneath. There will be rust, of course, and you will find things like corroded brake pipes, worn mechanical brake linkages and bushes, clips missing from wiring and pipe runs, and so on. Make a note of what needs doing before going on to cleaning other parts of the car. Memory is fickle, and out of sight under the car is often out of mind.

I will deal with tackling rust in the next chapter, so having got the underside clean carry on with the more visible parts. If you are going for a complete respray there is not much point in polishing the old paint, but it is a good idea to go over all the chromium plated parts so that you can decide which will come up shining again and which will have to go to the platers.

Most of the dull brown colour on otherwise good chromium plate comes from thousands of tiny pin holes in the chromium. The plating itself is porous, and it depends for its long-lasting shine on the quality of the coating between it and the steel. On the best plating the steel is covered first in copper, then in nickel, and finally in chromium. But on cheaper jobs, common on bumpers and grilles of American cars, there is only one under-plating, either copper or nickel, and it peels off when the rust gets going. On the cheapest of cheap jobs, often from back-street replaters, the chromium is put straight on the steel and has a very short life.

The only real answer to bad chromium plate is to take the parts to be replated, but in many cases I have cleaned dull and brown plating so effectively that it needed a very close look to tell that it was ever in poor condition. Chromium is quite a hard metal, and will withstand mild abrasives. This does not mean that you can go at it with wet or dry rubbing down paper, but one of the cleaners for restoring dull paint, or cellulose rubbing down compound, will fetch most of the brown off. On large areas such as bumpers and hub caps, one can almost work magic with a power buff and buffing compound. Use a fairly large rag buffing wheel, either in a drill or on a flexible lead, and the least coarse buffing compound you can get. This will probably be red or pink. The coarse yellow and grey buffing compounds will cut too deeply into the plating.

Start with the fastest speed of your drill and go over the surface with a light touch. For finishing off, and for getting into corners where the buff tried to run away with you, slow the speed down — an electronic speed controller is useful here — and use a heavier pressure. Buffing compound will leave the

11 For a shine that reflects like a mirror there is nothing to beat a lambswool bonnet on a power polisher

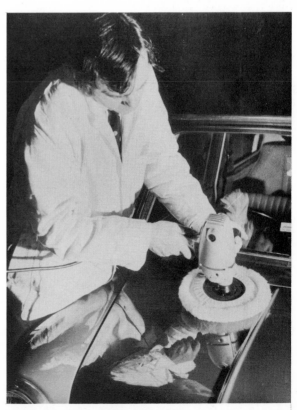

surface smeary, and it is difficult to rub off with a rag, but a going over with liquid chromium cleaner will lift the smears and bring up a final shine. You can use a power polishing mop with a lambswool bonnet, but these tend to have a short life on the edges of bumpers.

To make a proper job of cleaning behind bumpers and decorative fittings you will have to take them off. Take a few moments to investigate how they are fixed before you start levering with a screwdriver. In most cases, name plates and trim strips are held by clips at the back, but some have nuts on studs, and some strips are held by a mixture of clips and self tapping screws. Always take the clips off. You can get the strips off by levering from the front, but you will probably dent the bodywork. Some clips can be very awkward to reach, and I have found one of the old-fashioned vee-ended nail lifters a great help. Even if you are not repainting, it pays to take all the trim strips off since you will probably find rust starting underneath them. After killing it, bed the strips and name plates back in wax polish to protect the underside.

If you are sending parts to be replated you can often save yourself money by buffing them first. You pay at least as much at the platers for cleaning and preparing as you do for plating, and if the parts are presented in a clean smooth condition your plater will like you.

Buffing is made a good deal easier with a high speed bench-mounted buffing motor. It will take a larger mop than the average home electric drill, and generally speaking it is easier to hold the part in both hands and present it to the wheel than to hold a drill-mounted mop against it. You can use a coarse buffing compound if you are having the parts replated. Wear a pair of heavy industrial gloves because the mop can be very unkind to your fingers, and the parts get very hot. It is also advisable to wear goggles to protect the eyes.

What you are aiming for is a totally smooth surface with all traces of rust pitting removed. If the pitting is so deep that buffing it out leaves the surface uneven, it would be advisable to try and get a part in better condition. If this is impossible, take the part along to the plater and ask his advice. A good plater can often suggest solutions to problems which would be beyond the scope of a home workshop.

Before the parts can be replated some repair may be necessary. Dents or distortions are best left to the plater to take out on his rolling machine. If you try to knock them out with a hammer you may end up with a series of humps which can be more difficult for the plater to remove.

Parts which have come loose, such as grille slats in a radiator shell, should be carefully marked to show their position so that there is no chance of the plater brazing them back in the wrong place. A china clay crayon is handy for this. If you have the equipment for brazing at home you can do the job before you send the parts, but I would advise against soft solder repairs if the part is being replated. Plating will take well enough over the right grade of soft solder, but brazing or silver soldering will make a stronger job less likely to come apart when the plater buffs the part after it comes out of the plating vat.

If, on the other hand, a slat has come loose in a grille that does not need replating, soft soldering is perhaps the better way to fix it back in place. It needs less heat than either brazing or silver soldering so there is less chance of permanently discolouring the plating. Make sure both parts to be joined are absolutely clean, coat them with resin flux, tin them with an even coating of solder, clamp them together and heat with a flame till the solder fuses. In most cases a butane torch (such as Ronson) will give enough heat for this. If the heat runs away too quickly, lay the parts on a bed of sand covered with a sheet of soft

12 An elegant radiator
and grille is the focal
point of the car. Slight
dents and scratches
which might be unnoticed
in other places will shout
at you here

asbestos to reflect the heat back.

I always use resin-cored solder and resin flux. A killed-spirits flux (such as Baker's Fluid) is very corrosive and you need to scrub the parts with detergent afterwards to get it off. Unless every trace is removed it will make its presence known by a spreading green stain which is even harder to remove, and may lift the plating.

Hardest of all chromium plated parts to deal with are the ones cast from mazac, or zamac as it is sometimes called. In either case the word is derived from the alloy of zinc, aluminium, magnesium and copper.

These parts are cheap to produce because the alloy leaves a beautifully clean and precise shape when it is cast, but they are the despair of restorers and platers when they start pitting. This pitting will not buff out, and if the part is irreplaceable you are left with the choice of having it replated, pits and all, or trying to fill the pits yourself. I have not found platers any too keen to take on plating these parts in a pitted state because the plating does not last, and none that I know of will attempt to fill the pit marks because of the high labour cost and a degree of uncertainty about the quality of the finished job.

You may, however, find a plater who will co-operate with you in doing the job. He will probably not give you a guarantee, because the success of the finished job depends more on your workmanship than his. The first step is to buff the part as smooth as possible to get rid of the rough surface, then take it to the plater for it to be put into a chemical cleaning bath to remove the corrosion from the pitted craters. When you get it back, go over the pits with a countersink bit to enlarge the craters slightly, smooth down again on the buff and take the part back to the plater to have it coated with copper.

The copper plating gives a much better surface on which to use soft solder to fill the craters and helps to spread the heat, so there is less chance of local overheating crystallizing the casting. Use a soft solder that will take plating – the plater can advise you here. You need one that melts at a sufficiently low temperature to allow a margin before the casting itself starts to melt. Some solders melt at a temperature of a match flame, but as most zinc-based die castings melt at around 381°C (750°F) you will be safe with a solder that flows around 232°C (450°F).

Try to get resin-cored solder in a thin wire and use a flame, rather than an iron which localises the heat too much. A butane torch will give plenty of heat. Use a non-corrosive resin flux, and play the flame over the casting, touching it from time to time with the solder wire till it flows. Then pass the flame back and forth over the job a few times to make sure the solder is flowing and not just plastic, and leave it to cool. Do not cool it in water or there is a possibility of surface cracks or distortions. When the solder is hard, dress it down with a fine file and emery cloth and take it back to the plater for him to copper plate it again, nickel plate it and, finally, chromium plate. It will not be a cheap job, but provided all the corrosion in the pitting is removed, the new plating will probably last longer than the original.

Contrary to popular belief, zinc based die castings can be straightened and welded, but it is a highly skilled job. I have seen it done, and done very successfully, but I must admit the only time I tried it the result was not neat enough to pass unnoticed after plating.

If you want to have a go, practice on some old castings from the breaker's yard before you tackle an irreplaceable one. For straightening, the technique is to heat the part frequently and beat it gently into shape with dozens of light hammer blows, rather than trying to make it in one go which will only fracture it.

Welding calls for a solder rod of pure zinc, and a suitable flux, on which the shop that supplies the zinc rod can advise you. You need a welding torch with a very fine nozzle, finer than most in a commercial kit, because the heat must be kept localised.

Heat the part and the end of the zinc rod together until the zinc melts. Use plenty of flux but keep the flame more on the zinc rod than the casting. Then use a brass wire to stir the puddle of molten zinc into the join, scrubbing it with the wire and flux to make sure it fuses properly to the casting. You will be working very close to disaster temperature, and at your first few attempts do not be surprised if the edges of the casting melt away before your horrified eyes. But practice gives confidence, and it can be done.

Now back to the paintwork. Even if this is in good condition it will probably dry out dull and lifeless after the wash, and though wax polish is a fine protector of paint it will not bring back the deep shine where the surface of the paint has died. This top surface of dead paint has to be cleaned off.

There are quite a few preparations on the market that will do this (Color-Bak, T-Cut and Simoniz Kleener are examples). I have not found much to choose between them, but some seem to suit different colours better than others, so when you have found one which works well on your car, don't change it for another. To keep old paint in pristine condition you will probably have to use the preparation every couple of years or so, depending on the part of the country in which you live. City atmospheres are better than they

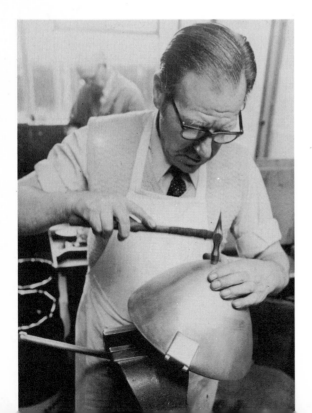

13   If all else fails, there are specialist craftsmen who can make new parts, such as this lamp shell, by hand, and who can often work wonders in restoring a dented example — provided you haven't made it worse by clumsy attempts at dent removing

used to be, but sea air is most unkind to the older fugitive greens and maroons.

These cleaners, or surface restorers, are not abrasive (or they should not be). They work with a chemical action, and sometimes smell of ammonia. Rub the cleaner into the surface till it starts to go tacky, and leave it to dry. It helps to avoid a patchy look if you work in straight lines along the bonnet and down the doors rather than in circles. Some colours, and paint that has been neglected for years, may need going over two or three times.

When finished the paint should be gleaming with a full depth of colour, ready to take the protecting wax polish. On some older paints you may find areas where, no matter what you do, the surface stays dull. Some of the early post-war paints seem to suffer a change right through when exposed to heat either from the sun or, on older lift-up bonnets, from the heat of the exhaust where it ran close. It is difficult to match the colour exactly on some of these older paints, and respraying just one panel always stands out. In some cases I have found that after cleaning and cutting back lightly with rubbing compound, the paint can be improved if one sprays on a light coat of thinners or even a clear lacquer, which I will talk about in Chapter 5 on painting. If you try a thinners, make sure it is compatible with the paint. Try it in an out-of-the-way spot first because some modern thinners tend to curdle old paints.

After cleaning, the surface needs protecting, and I have found nothing better than old-fashioned hard carnauba wax. (I use Simoniz because I have more or less grown up with it and am used to it, but I have no doubt there are others just as good.)

There are plenty of car polishes on the market — a bewildering display in most accessory shops — many of them promising to give you a deep shine without hard work. Most of them do what they claim, and I have nothing against them, but I have yet to find one which

lasts as long as plain wax. These polishes are usually a mixture of soft waxes and an emulsifier, whipped up into a cream. You take your choice between more frequent waxing with less work each time, or less frequent waxing with more work each time. Wax polish is also good for protecting the chromium plate that took so much trouble to clean. It seals the tiny pin holes in the chromium so there is less chance of corrosive road dirt getting to the base metal.

If restoring a wood-trimmed or wood-framed estate car, you will be very lucky indeed if the varnish on the wood is still in good condition. It is more likely to be discoloured and missing in places, and the exposed wood will have turned a grey colour. However much this silvery grey is prized on cedar shingled houses, it looks terrible on a restored car.

Possibly the worst case to deal with is where some misguided previous owner has painted the wood. I once had to tackle one which had been undercoated and painted so well it was almost a shame to scrape it off. But that is what you have to do — go over it slowly and painstakingly with a hand scraper. If you are stripping the metal panels as well you can use a chemical stripper to get the varnish off, but you will still have to scrape to get that clean-grained finish. A power tool with an orbital sanding head will help on long straight runs, but I am not too keen on using a rotary disc sander because it tends to dig in and mark the wood. In the corners there is no alternative to hand scraping.

When the wood is finally clean and sanded, go over it with a tack rag to get rid of the dust and give it four coats of best quality yacht varnish. The first two coats should be thinned down with 50 per cent thinners to get right into the pores of the wood. I have found yacht varnish is the only one to stand up to the rigours of winter and the grit blasting the wood will get every time another car passes in the wet. Finish the varnish and mask it off before you spray or paint the metal panels. If you get colour paint on the varnish you can sand it off and give another coat, but if you get colour paint on the bare wood it sinks into the grain and is most difficult to get out.

In some places you might find that the grey colour goes so deep into the wood you cannot scrape it out. Try bleaching it out with a commercial wood bleach or a strong solution of oxalic acid crystals in hot water but be careful of splashing your paintwork. This may not remove the grey entirely, but it will make it less noticeable. As an alternative, try neat household chlorine bleach. Use plenty of water afterwards to get rid of the oxalic acid or the bleach before putting on new varnish.

Moving on to the interior, the best cleaners I have found for upholstery and carpets are the ones made for the job. Whatever your grand-mother used to clean her carpets I doubt that it was as good as modern preparations. Read the instructions carefully if dealing with leather upholstery. Not all cleaners designed to deal with PVC upholstery are suitable for leather, and some of the really powerful industrial cleaners which contain strong sul-phonated alcohols can lift the dye right out of leather.

A good old standby for cleaning leather is saddle soap which can be got from a shop which caters for horsy people. It also softens leather to some extent, but better still for this is a proper hide food. Think twice before you use the standard softener offered by harness and saddle shops, which is neat's foot oil. It softens leather beautifully, but will stain any part where the surface dressing has worn off.

Almost all the leather for upholstery on British cars was supplied by Connolly Brothers in London. They still supply hides, and are most helpful when it comes to restoring. They run a restoration service from Chalton Street, Euston Road, London, and will supply leather dyes and resurfacing lacquers for you to do the job at home; all you need to do is to send them a snippet of leather from behind the rear seat or somewhere where it will not be missed, and on which the colour has not faded. In the USA the above mentioned Connolly leathers and refurbishing kits are available from Bill Hirsch, 396 Littleton Avenue, Newark, New Jersey 07103. This is also a source for other Scottish, English, Scandinavian and American hides and for automotive carpet, convertible top materials, and a great many other items for the restorer.

For restoring PVC upholstery there are a number of dyes on the market. (One I have found very good is packed in aerosol cans by Sperex.) You can even change the colour of PVC upholstery with this provided you do not want to go from a very dark to a very light colour. It is not suitable, though, for leather.

Plastic headlinings are easily cleaned with the same cleaner used on PVC seats, but cloth ones are a little more of a problem. Most of them are a dyed woolcloth, which can go streaky if washed with detergents. Sometimes it is best just to go over them with a vacuum cleaner hose. The awkward part is rinsing the dirt out, but if it is a case of clean or replace you have little to lose, so try working up a light foam with a sponge and carpet cleaner, and wiping it off with a wrung-out cloth to avoid getting the lining sopping wet. If it does get wet it may pick up dirt from the roof bows or even the metal roof itself.

The clean upholstery and carpets will show up any shabbiness in wooden dash panels or window trim. If the surface has gone dull but is still in good condition, you can bring back the shine by rubbing down lightly with a pad of steel wool and detergent and finishing with metal polish. Only try metal polish if the varnish is unbroken; if it gets on bare wood it stains and is a job to get out. Where the varnish is in a bad way, the only remedy is to strip it and revarnish. I will deal with this in Chapter 6 on a complete retrim.

=3=
DEALING WITH RUST

The greatest enemy of anyone restoring a post-war car is rust. In many cases it is a more serious problem than for the man restoring a car from the twenties or thirties, because after

14 This is what you often find when starting to rub down blisters on the paintwork. Fortunately this is not structural rot, so there is a choice between welding and lead filling, or repairing with glass fibre

the war design moved quite swiftly from an open channel section with a separate body, to unitary construction with just the vestiges of a chassis left as box sections welded to the underside of the body shell. There was an intermediate stage, where open channel chassis gave way to a box section, still with a separate body, but these too are more subject to rust than older designs.

It is not just a question of thinner metal on post-war cars, or inferior steel, though the thickness certainly was reduced. Designers went for lighter, stiffer structures which

could be produced more easily on mass production lines. This meant large numbers of folded and welded pieces of thin sheet metal which gave a tremendously strong and stiff structure, but which depended for their strength on being welded together with many closed or semi-closed box sections.

In their enthusiasm to get stiffer and lighter structures, which undoubtedly improved the roadholding of the car, designers tended to forget all about rust traps. On cars up to the late sixties, and even beyond, these abound all over the body. They are found in particular under the front wings round the headlamps, across the floor pan where outriggers and sills of closed sections are welded to the sheet floor to stiffen it, under the rear wheel arches, across the floor of the boot and, much more seriously, where the suspension and steering are mounted.

In these areas the metal rusts from the outside where mud collects (often saturated with salt that local authorities put on the roads in icy weather), and from the inside where condensation of corrosive moist air settles and goes on eating its way through year after year.

Where this rusting has weakened the structural parts of a body shell to the point where they are unsafe, the only thing to do is to have them cut out and new sections welded in their place. No amount of filling will put back structural strength, and welding extra plates on the outside is at best only a temporary measure. The corroded sections underneath will go on rusting, and in time will eat through the extra plates.

Where the rust has not bitten so deeply that it weakens the metal to any extent, it can be neutralised and kept at bay in the future. It is a long and tiresome process, but if you want your car to last it is essential.

There are a number of rust killers on the market, and they all work on the principle of changing the rust into an inert compound which will no longer attack the base metal. Most of them contain phosphoric acid or tannic acid, or compounds of these.

They work, and they work well, but despite what it might say on the tins they are not magic compounds you can just brush on and expect all your troubles to be over. Some of the early ones contained hydrochloric acid, which is a fine rust eater, but unless it is completely washed away afterwards it is also a fine corroder of steel. Most of these types have disappeared from the shops but they are still used in industry, so be careful of any that have to be washed down afterwards with water, which is the usual way of getting rid of the hydrochloric.

On plain panels, or parts that can be taken off the car and washed down afterwards, these rust killers are fine. But on structures with welded seams and crevices it is difficult to wash all the acid away, and even if you do you are left with the problem of drying out the water. Any left behind will, given time, rust the metal under the nice new paintwork and you will be back where you started.

Much better are the phosphoric or tannic acid rust killers which do not need neutralising afterwards. These are the ones which turn the rust a deep blue-black. On the tin or plastic bottle there are often instructions to brush off the loose rust and brush on the liquid, but if you are going to kill the rust once and for all you have to go further than this.

The trouble is that the blue compound into which the acids turn the rust seals off the surface before the acids have a chance to work right down to the clean metal. You can prove this for yourself by brushing some on, leaving it for 48 hours or so to do its job, and then scratching around on the surface with a screwdriver. In many cases you will find traces of rust under the blue, and in time this rust will come up again through the surface. You have to scrub away with a wire brush or sanding

15 This sort of rot is much more serious. The whole wheel arch structure is in danger of collapsing. The only cure is to have it cut out and new metal welded in place. Glass fibre in a place such as this is not safe

disc till only the colour of the rust is left, if the acids are to have a chance of getting right down to good metal.

A much easier way of doing the job than brushing and sanding is to have the whole underside of the car grit blasted. This is not so expensive as one might think, and will clean off rust in places you will find difficult to reach by hand. You can sometimes hire portable blasting machines to use at home, but take care how you use them. Wear the protective hood and gloves, and do the job out in the open. If you try using a grit blaster in the garage the air will be so thick with fine grit it will be impossible to avoid breathing it. Even in the open you have to watch where you do the job or the neighbours will start complaining.

Even grit blasting will not reach into box sections and door pillars, so you have to get a chemical inside. You could inject rust killer, but there is no way you can clean the rust off first, and the coating will use up the killer before it does its job properly. One answer would be to strip the shell and have it treated in a large industrial phosphating tank, but few companies which have these will take in outside work. In America there are companies such as Redi-Strip with plants in various states which handle outside work, but unfortunately I know of none in England, so there the work will need to be done at home.

Fortunately, chemical technology has caught up with the problem and there are a number of compounds on the market which, unlike acid rust killers, do not change the rust chemically but work their way under the rust down to clean metal, and set up a physical barrier to stop further rusting. They do their job by a combination of soaking and electrolytic action, and as they are not themselves chemically changed they will penetrate through loose and flaking rust.

Probably the most well known in England is Waxoyl made by Finnigan's Speciality Paints Ltd., at Prudhoe in Northumberland. I have talked to Finnigan's about their product and they definitely say it will stop further rusting. Under the conditions of the Trades Descriptions Act, Finnigan's must be pretty sure of their ground to make such a categorical statement.

As an alternative to Waxoyl you can inject one of the grades of Tectyl made by the Valvoline Oil Co. Ltd., at Birkenhead, on Merseyside. This retards further rusting by sealing the surface off from the air. It also penetrates through the rust to some extent, but Valvoline do not make the same sweeping claims as Finnigan's. I have used both compounds, and after two years there was no sign of further rusting, but this is a relatively short time in the life of a restored car, so only time

29

will prove whether rusting has really stopped. I am cautious, but hopeful.

Companies which let out franchises to garages for anti-rust treatment (such as Ziebart) inject the sections with a compound which is guaranteed to stop rust coming through on new cars for up to ten years, but the guarantee is given only on cars which are less than three months old, which rules out restoration projects. I have talked to some of these companies, and while they say their treatment will undoubtedly retard the spread of existing rust, they do not claim it will neutralise it. Their business is to stop it starting on new cars.

Whichever compound you decide to put in your box sections, you have to find some means of getting it there. Ziebart, for example, use high pressure lances to inject their compound, but these are far too expensive for home use. An alternative is a syringe with a long plastic pipe on the end. These are often supplied in kits together with the compound. Finnigan's do a complete pack of compound and syringe, and so do Sound Services Ltd., of Witney, in Oxfordshire, whose compound smells as if it is Tectyl based.

For the last car I treated I used a pressure spray intended for spraying insecticides in the garden. It has a plastic pressure container which you pump up with a handle like an old fashioned tire pump, and a pipe with a nozzle at the end. This nozzle, I found, was too fine for spraying Tectyl, so I enlarged the hole in it and fitted a length of plastic tubing. I blocked the end of this tubing with a plug, and drilled a series of radial holes in the last three inches to give an all-round spray.

To use something like this, poke it into the box section, turn the pressure on and spray while you withdraw the tube. Long sections can be treated from each end. Often you can work through existing holes, and on door pillars you can work through the holes for the courtesy light switches, but if the section is fully closed you will have to drill a hole. Be careful where you drill it. Never drill structural chassis box sections at top or bottom. This will weaken them and possibly lead to fracture. The only permissible place to drill a hole is in the side, midway between the top and bottom flanges. This is the neutral axis of the section and a hole here will weaken it least in bending. Close the hole afterwards with a plastic or wooden bung.

When it comes to dealing with rusty panels where you can get to both sides, the job is much easier. After cleaning off as much rust as possible, treat the area with a rust killing liquid or a rust killing paint (such as Kingston's Kurust). These paints dry only where the rust killing agent has acted. Over good metal you have to wash them off with methylated spirit. Be sure to follow the directions on the bottle. The makers naturally want you to get good results so you will buy their paint again. If the instructions say paint over with a primer after 48 hours, paint after 48 hours; not after a couple of hours, nor wait till next week. Half the disappointments with chemical rust killers come from not using them properly.

Rust killing paints have earned themselves a good reputation, but one or two paint makers have tried to jump on the bandwaggon by adding just a little rust inhibitor to their ordinary primers. These are usually labelled as 'helping to stop the formation of rust' or some similar wording, but any primer does that. They are also much cheaper than true rust killing paints, but as always you get only what you pay for. A small sum saved on paint is negligible compared with the cost of restoration.

No doubt when you cleaned down the paintwork you found a number of areas where the paint was starting to bubble, but the skin was unbroken. This bubbling is the start of rust under the paint, and if ignored will soon develop into an unsightly rust patch. Rust always travels further under the paint than shows from the outside, so to make a good job you have to rub these areas down till you reach clean metal. You might finish with a piebald car, and what started as a retouching job might end as a complete respray, but that is better than having a car where rust is constantly breaking through.

I have known people make an excellent job of killing the rust on the outside, and forget all about the interior where the rust does not show because it is hidden by the trim. To make a thorough job of the car you need to take out all the trim panels and carpets. It is surprising how much rust can form from condensation. Pay particular attention to treating it inside the doors, at the sides of the scuttle panel where it joins the floor, under the rear seat where the suspension brackets are welded

16   A line of rust pimples along the bottom of a boot lid or door is less serious than it looks. Once again, lead filling or glass fibre can be used

to the floor and on the inside sill plates.

When you have got rid of the rust you want to stop it coming back. On the outside the paint will do this, but underneath I like to give two coats of a good polyurethane paint and cover this with a non-setting sealer. Underbody sealers can be bought in most accessory shops, but make sure to get a non-setting one. The cheaper ones which set rock hard often chip off. I like to get the underside painted before I treat the box sections, because Waxoyl and Tectyl take over paint but paint will not take over them.

It is a good idea to use a sealer inside under the carpets and inside the doors, but take care to keep the drain holes at the bottom of the doors clear. If there are none, make some to let out the water which finds its way down past the window seal in the wet. It is not a bad idea to lay some sheet polythene over the sealer on the floor inside to save the underfelt sticking to it. This sticking can be most annoying if you want to get at plates in the floor to top up the back axle or service the master cylinder.

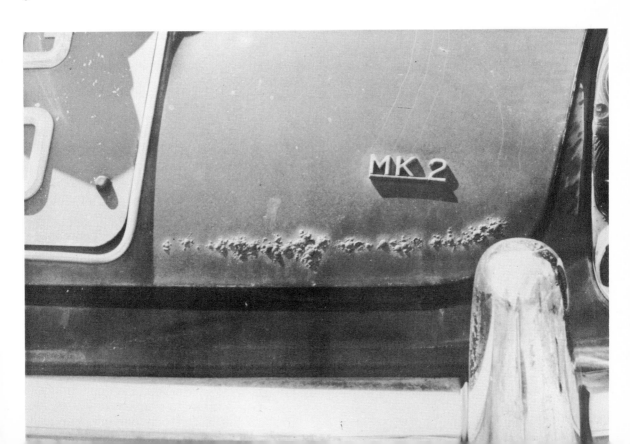

=4=
BODY REPAIRS

You will be fortunate indeed if the body of your car is completely free from dents and gouges. Straightening bodywork which is badly distorted from accident damage will call for the use of professional equipment such as pulling jigs and body jacks and, if the distortion extends to suspension or steering mountings, an alignment frame, all of which are far too expensive pieces of equipment to keep in the home garage. This work should be left to the professional bodyshop.

Minor dents, gouges and bumps can, however, be successfully taken out at home using hand tools and a portable source of heat, an oxy-acetylene set for preference. Some tool hire shops will be able to supply a complete body working kit of hammers, dollies, spoons and pry bars of different shapes and sizes all of which have specific applications. But if you are buying there is no need to go to this expense. When I worked in a garage many years ago I watched almost in awe as our elderly and very skilled body repair man coaxed dents out of body panels with a minimum of heavy hitting. He used many light blows, and at times he sounded like a rivetting machine. Most of his work was done with two or three favourite hammers and dollies and a couple of spoons.

Body repairing tools fall broadly into three groups: hammers, dollies and spoons, pry bars and body files. Body hammers come in different sizes with different shaped heads. The most useful ones for the home restorer are a general purpose bumping hammer with one flat and one curved face, a cross-pein finishing hammer with one end in a blunt chisel shape and the other in a large round flat, and if you master the use of it, a shrinking hammer with cross-milled serrations on its face.

Like hammers, dollies come in different shapes. Two useful ones are a general purpose, which has a variety of curved surfaces, and a thin-toed dolly which is a flat slab of metal thinned down at one end where the surface is curved. This is most handy for getting behind awkward corners.

Spoons are used in a similar way to dollies, and look rather like tire levers with curved and polished ends. A general purpose double-ended spoon is probably the one used most, but you should have two spoons, because for finishing it is often useful to use one as a hammer. Pry bars, sometimes called levering bars or bending irons in tool catalogues, are also like large tire levers but with flat hooked ends for levering panels back into position while they are being hammered.

Body files, like ordinary files, come in a variety of patterns. The basic kit should have

17 Using a spoon (with a dolly inside the wing) to shape the final contour after a dent has been taken out with a hammer and dolly

one large smooth cut, one coarser single-cut for taking down body solder or resin filler, and a file which takes rubbing-down paper on its surface for finishing.

Panel beating tools are not cheap so, for a minimum basic kit, start with a general purpose bumping hammer weighing about 10½oz (300 g), a general purpose dolly of about 2¾lb (1.2 kg) and a general purpose spoon of about 2½ lb (1.1 kg). These will deal with about 80% of the dents. Later you can make other spoons from old spring leaves. A rubber faced hammer is often useful for springing back panels which have 'oil-canned' without stretching. With luck, these can be bumped back without even breaking the paint.

Broadly speaking, removing dents from body panels can be divided into three parts: bumping out, which is bringing the panel back to its proper contour, levelling, to produce a smooth surface, and finishing. Before starting bumping out, have a good look at the dent to see how it was caused, how the blow has distorted the shape and how far the distortion spreads. For example, a blow on the side of a front

wing will have pushed in a dent at the point of impact, and it may also have strained the bottom of the wing away from the front skirt or grille panel. A blow on the front of a bonnet may have produced only a small dent at the front, but it may have humped the bonnet panel up some distance backwards and distorted the side flanges.

In most cases the best way to bring a panel back into shape is with a combination of pulling and bumping out. Sometimes you can get a helper to grip the end of, say, a wing and pull it while you straighten the flange and bump out the dent. Better still, use a clamp, a chain and tensioner, and a pulling post. You can buy body clamps, complete with a shackle for attaching to a chain, or in many cases you can use a large G-cramp and the lifting tackle from an engine hoist as a tensioner. A garage will have a sturdy pulling post concreted into the floor, but at home you can sometimes make an anchor by driving a piece of steel scaffolding into the ground. I have even seen a heavy garden roller and chocks used. It depends on how strong a pull is needed.

33

With the handbrake on and the wheels firmly chocked, start by applying a light tension to see how the panel tries to resist. It is usually obvious which distorted flange or dent is holding it, so bump these out so that the tension on the puller slackens. Then apply a little more tension and carry on till the panel stays in shape when the tension is taken off.

The bumping out is done with the hammer and dolly. There are two methods of using these, bumping on and bumping off. Bumping on is when you hold the dolly directly under the part you are hitting with the hammer, and bumping off is when you hold the dolly slightly to one side.

Bumping on is used when you are taking out a dent. The dolly is held up against the underside of the panel with a fairly hard pressure and the panel is struck with the hammer immediately over the dolly. The force of the blow should not be enough to make the dolly bounce back sharply, though it will bounce a little. The hammer should be swung with a loose wrist so it bounces sharply back. Start at the edge of the dent, and with a rhythmic even tapping work round the dent in decreasing circles. The pressure on the dolly, combined with the slight bounce back will gradually push the dent out. If you bang the dent from underneath you will only stretch the panel.

Bumping off is used when you want to take down high spots on the outside of a panel. In this case the method is similar, but the dolly is held slightly to one side of the hammer blows to support the panel while the hammer beats down on the raised part. The dolly should be only about a quarter of an inch from the blows and it should not bounce at all, so it must be held very firmly. Once again work round the damage, gradually coming to the centre.

A spoon is used in a similar way to a dolly, but where the dolly puts pressure on a small area the spoon has a much larger contact area and spreads the force of the hammer blow more. Spoons are used with a large faced hammer to level the surface after it has been brought to contour with a hammer and dolly or, in awkward places, where it is difficult to hold a dolly. Sometimes two spoons are used, one in place of the hammer.

The big difference between bumping out with a dolly and levelling with a spoon is that the spoon is held fairly lightly, so that it follows the contour of the panel. If it is held too tightly the edge of the spoon will raise lines. Keep the hammer blows, or the blows from the outside spoon, fairly light, so that the inside spoon bounces about 1/16 in (1 or 2 mm), let the hammer bounce lightly as well, and keep a steady rhythm as you move them across the surface of the panel.

It sounds easier said than done, and to some extent it is, but practice will give you confidence. Try to get hold of a scrap wing to practice on before tackling your car. At first you will finish with a surface like a moonscape, but gradually, like riding a bike, you get a feel for the job. The easiest parts to deal with are those with a gentle curve, and the hardest are the flat ones like a door, where the slightest wave shows up as a distorted reflection when the paintwork is polished.

The bumping and levelling might stretch the metal, so that it cannot be got back to a level contour. To shrink the metal back one has to apply local heat and quenching. An experienced body man will often do this with a flame and a wet sponge, but this seemingly simple technique requires a great deal of skill and practice. It is easy to finish with a panel that is so twisted it refuses to go into shape.

A safer method for the less skilled is to cover the stretched area with a flat pancake of wet shredded asbestos. Press it well down to get rid of air bubbles, and poke a series of holes through it with your finger. Then use a flame to bring the metal exposed by the holes up to bright cherry red, and immediately push the asbestos down in the holes to cool it. As with taking out a dent, start at the edges and work round in a spiral to the centre. If you happen to shrink the metal a little too much so that it puckers, you can take this out by planishing lightly with a pair of spoons to stretch it out again.

An alternative method used by many body men is to heat the stretched panel to just below cherry red and use a dolly and a shrinking hammer. This shrinking hammer has serrations on its face like a coarse file, and with skillful use the metal is actually compressed back into shape. It is a fast and effective method and, if you can master it, it is easier in that you can see what you are doing. On balance, though, the asbestos method is probably safer for the amateur because there is less chance of permanent damage to the panel. A carelessly wielded shrinking hammer can make a real mess of the surface.

When the surface of the panel is as level as you can get it, go over it lightly with a large body file using just enough pressure to mark the surface without taking off much in the way of filings. This will show up the high spots as islands of bright metal and the hollows as dark patches. Go over again with a pair of spoons using lighter and lighter blows till the surface is as smooth and level as possible.

Final levelling is done with a body file which is really a holder for rubbing down paper. Use a medium grade paper, dry, and work in long strokes to give a final smooth surface. With exceptional skill a craftsman can leave the surface almost ready for painting, but most professional body men will be happy to leave a surface that can be given its final levelling with a coat of plastic surface filler. These fillers are made to take direct on to bare metal after it has been degreased. They are not intended to fill large depressions or seam joints but are ideal for taking out the last waves on a panel so that it gives a smooth

reflection. Precise instructions will be on the tin, but the principle is that you brush it on, leave it to dry, and rub down with a body file and rubbing paper till it is almost rubbed right off, leaving only the depressions in the surface filled. It is not to be confused with a surfacer, which is used as part of the painting stage.

Gas welding, and the general use of an oxy-acetylene torch, is such a useful skill for the restorer that once you have learned it you will wonder how on earth you managed before. Gas welding is much more easily taught by demonstration than by words, and it pays to go to welding classes. Many local authorities run them as evening classes, and though they are really intended as vocational courses for metal workers, most colleges welcome people who want to learn the skill for a hobby such as car restoration. The only usual proviso is that you have to wait for your place on the course to be confirmed till those who want to learn as a trade with which to earn their living have been allocated places. The classes are not often fully booked, however, and in most areas you will get a place.

There are, however, certain techniques which can be learned from a book. The first is the size of jet to use on the torch and the type of flame for a particular job. The first is easy because there will be a table printed inside the lid of the welding kit. The jet nozzles are numbered, and the table will give the number to use as well as the pressures of oxygen and acetylene for different thicknesses of metal. If the table is missing, any welding shop can supply you with a booklet (often free) setting them out.

There are three types of flame: carburizing, with more acetylene than oxygen, neutral, with equal quantities of both, and oxidizing, with more oxygen than acetylene. For the majority of welding jobs on steel a neutral flame is used. The torch is lit by turning on only the acetylene, which burns with a wavy yellow flame. When the oxygen is added a bluish white cone forms gradually at the base of the flame next to the nozzle. As the amount of oxygen is increased, the edges of this cone get sharper, and the neutral point is reached when the feather edges of the cone just disappear.

Be careful not to go too far with the oxygen or you will get a flame which is oxidizing and tends to burn the work and form hard slag. The flame is oxidizing when the inner cone is more pointed and slightly smaller than with a neutral flame, and you can usually hear a pronounced hiss. This flame is used for welding brass, but seldom for car body repairs.

For welding aluminium and for putting a hard facing on steel, such as when building up rocker faces, a slightly carburizing flame is necessary. This is the flame you get when the oxygen is turned down till the edges of the inner cone start to feather, and the cone grows larger than with a neutral flame.

The amount of gas passing through the pipe needs to be adjusted to suit the size nozzle you are using. If there is too great a flow you get a harsh flame which is difficult to control, because it tends to blow the molten metal away from the join. If the flow is too low, you get backfiring and popping, with the flame sometimes going out. This can also happen if the nozzle is loose.

If anything goes wrong with the flame, turn it off and start again. The safe way to turn off a torch is to turn off the acetylene first to put the flame out, and then to turn off the oxygen.

Free oxygen floating around a workshop can be dangerous because it mixes with oil and grease to form an explosive mixture. Free acetylene is dangerous because it is highly flammable. Remember these points, and also that you have a searing hot flame at the end of the torch, and you will avoid the accidents which can happen. Treated properly, an oxyacetylene set is a very useful servant. Let

familiarity breed contempt, and it can become a killing master. The other vital safety point is that you must always wear goggles, even when you are just heating a piece of metal to bend it or free a seized bush. Goggles protect your eyes from possible welding slag and splatter as well as from the fierce light of the flame.

The basic process of welding two pieces of metal is to bring the edges up to melting point, add a filler, and fuse the whole lot together. The weld should stand only slightly proud of the surface. Most beginners use too much filler rod so that it looks like a mound along the surface. On the other hand, too little rod leaves a depression along the join. Only practice will teach the right amount of rod to use, which is governed by the speed with which the torch and rod are moved along the join.

There are two methods of welding: leftwards, starting at the right hand end of the work and moving towards the left, and rightwards, starting at the left and moving towards the right. With leftward welding the filler rod goes in front of the torch and with rightward welding the torch goes in front of the filler rod. If you happen to be left handed, the directions are reversed. Leftward welding is used for metal up to about 1/8 in (3 mm) thick which covers most jobs on car restoring. Rightward is for thicker metal.

The best way to get used to manipulating a torch is to fuse a line across a plain piece of sheet steel about 20 gauge. Scribe a line on the steel, and with a neutral flame start at the left and move the flame across so that the steel is melted in a thin line. It should fuse together again behind the torch without using a filler rod. Hold the tip of the nozzle abour 1/8 in (3 mm) from the steel at an angle of about 60° and work slowly across the steel in a series of tiny circles about 1/8 in (3 mm) across. When you turn the panel over, the fusing line should be even along the back as well as the front. If it has not gone through to the back you have either moved the torch along too fast or held it at too shallow an angle. If you burn holes in the metal you are either moving too slow or holding the torch too near the vertical.

After a few successful runs try joining two pieces together using the filler rod. An experienced welder will often start at one end and run straight across, but people who use a torch less find it easier to tack the edges together first every 4 or 5 in (10 or 13 cm) before making the run. On a long run there is more chance of the panel distorting with tacking, particularly when welding a long narrow piece to a large piece, such as putting a new base in a door. The small piece expands more because it becomes hot all over, and an experienced welder will allow for this as he works. With tacking first there might be a slight puckering at the tacks when you make the long run to join them, but you do not have to worry about holding the edges together. The puckering is usually easier to hammer down and perhaps fill afterwards than dealing with a twist from differential expansion.

The holding welds need only be tiny, and after tacking you can go along with a hammer and dolly to make sure the edges are nicely in contact. Then go along with one uninterrupted weld to lay an even bead.

With body restoration you will often want to weld new sheet steel to thin metal that has been pocked with rust. A skilled man who is welding all day can almost weld rusty air together, but us jacks of all restoring trades have to cut back to find stronger metal. Even so, it is easy to burn holes in existing bodywork when bringing the edge of the new metal piece up to fusing point.

For this reason I prefer to bronze weld on old bodies rather than use a mild steel filler rod. Bronze welding is not the same as brazing, which is more akin to soldering. With a bronze welding rod you work in much the same way as with a mild steel rod, but instead of bringing the two edges of the steel panel to fusing point you fuse the bronze rod to each. This means using a slightly lower temperature (bright orange instead of white heat), and there is less chance of burning the edge of old body panels. The bronze bead also hammers down more easily afterwards.

Unlike welding with steel filler rods, you have to use a flux with bronze rods and a flame which is just, but only just, on the oxidizing side of neutral. Warm the end of the rod in the flame and dip it into the tin of flux powder to get a coating on it. Then carry on in much the same way as with a steel rod.

The flux will burn to a slight slag, but this should float to the surface of the molten bronze. If it stays buried in the puddle and hardens so that the bead is full of dark slag holes, you are probably using too much oxygen. One of the other advantages of bronze welding is that you can use the flame rather like a brush to flow the pool of molten bronze along the join. With steel rod the bead hardens almost as soon as the flame passes.

Most welding shops keep bronze rod as well as steel. The ones I like to use are made by Sifbronze. This company makes a large selection of rods for different materials. I have found their Sifalumin one of the easiest processes I have tried for gas welding aluminium.

Welding aluminium is very different from welding steel. It is possible to fusion weld it with a torch, but the trouble is that the edges of the aluminium oxidize almost before you can take the torch away. Also, the difference in temperature between fusion and melting into a hole is so small that it is easy to melt the edges of the join away.

Most professional body shops use an inert gas welding process for aluminium where the part being welded is surrounded by a pocket of inert gas, but the equipment is costly and the technique is critical.

With Sifbronze's Process 36, many of the

difficulties disappear. It is not really welding, it is low temperature brazing, but for all except structural work it is adequately strong. The technique is similar to welding, except that instead of moving the torch along the join in a series of tiny circles you wave the flame along the join. You have to watch what you are doing and not stay too long in one place, or the flux used will burn instead of melting and you will have to clean it all off and start again. The idea is to work while the flux is flowing freely.

The same rod and flux can be used on sheet aluminium and castings, but on a casting you have to vee-out the join so that the filler rod has somewhere to go. Be careful not to get your face too near aluminium castings when working, because some of them have trapped air pockets which can spit when they get hot. The flux for Process 36 is very corrosive and has to be scrubbed off afterwards in boiling water. If you cannot get a brush to it it has to be neutralised in weak nitric acid and washed off afterwards.

If you write to Sifbronze at Gipping Works, Stowmarket, Suffolk, they will send you a leaflet on Process 36. Most other makers of rods offer a process for joining aluminium, and your local supplier of welding rods will be able to tell you what is available.

Till recently, gas welding equipment was bulky and costly, and home restorers had great difficulty getting supplies of the large gas cylinders, or bottles as the trade calls them. Then the British Oxygen Company brought out their Portapak. This is a complete gas welding set that will do anything a large set will do. The only real difference is that the bottles are smaller and packed on a handy trolley that will go in the boot of most cars. BOC's idea was to produce a set that maintenance engineers could carry with them, but the chance for the home restorer was too good to miss, and provided you meet certain safeguards about the fire resistance of your garage

and its security, you can buy a Portapak from any of BOC's 50 depots in the UK. Some tool hire shops may have them. You cannot buy the bottles outright because they are classed as pressure vessels and by law have to be inspected at regular intervals. It is an offence to use bottles with an out of date stamp. With all its bottles BOC retains legal ownership, and the price of a Portapak includes indefinite rental of in-date bottles. (If you have trouble getting a Portapak, write to BOC Ltd., Gas Equipment Division, 2 Peel Road, Pimbo, Skelmersdale, Lancashire.)

Electric arc welding is usually reserved for thicker metal than that used on car bodywork, but in the past few years home arc welding kits which run off car batteries have appeared on the market. These are very different from the ordinary small industrial arc welder, which packs too much punch for sheet metal work and would burn the panel. I have tried a couple of these home battery kits, and while they are not professional tools they can, with care and patience, produce a passable weld on car bodywork.

The main trouble most people encounter is that the intense local heat of the arc buckles the panel. If you are not careful the piece you are welding in can resemble the strip you get when you open a tin of corned beef. The whole secret is to tack weld. Unlike gas welding where the tacks are just points, the best tacks with low power arc welders are about 1 in (2.5 cm) long. When welding, say, a new sill to the body, space the tack welds about 8 or 9 in (20-23 cm) apart. Then go back and join them up in the reverse direction, tack two to tack one, tack three to tack two and so on. You will still get some local buckling, but this is easier to hammer out than a long twist.

You can also use this type of welder for brazing by putting a carbon rod in place of the fluxed welding rod. Strike an arc with the carbon till the metal glows red hot and then feed in a flux coated brazing rod. Brazing is useful for patching an unstressed and unseen part, such as a boot floor, where you do not wish to go to the trouble of accurately cutting and welding in a new floor.

Cut the patch to overlap the weak part, and make a series of holes about ½ inch (13 mm) or so diameter all round the edge. Then clean up the underside of the patch and the top of the floor to bright metal, coat them both with flux, clamp the patch in place and fill the holes with braze. It is known as plug brazing. To make a good job the patch and the floor must be in good contact, and one way to do this, if you cannot get a clamp in place, is to hold the patch down with self-tapping screws. You can take them out afterwards and fill the holes with braze.

It is possible with first class welding, and hammering and dressing afterwards, to leave a join almost invisible, but only an experienced welder can guarantee it. Most of us rely on the weld for strength, and use a filler to restore the surface after grinding and rubbing down. There are two sorts of filler you can use, metal or plastic. Plastic filler has got itself a bad name because so many home repairers either use it wrongly or use it to try to restore strength when they should have welded first. Properly used, plastic filler can do a good job, but filling with body solder, or body lead as it is usually called, is the method most professional restorers use.

Though body lead is more difficult to use than plastic filler, it is not so difficult that you need fight shy of it. Most failures come from using the wrong sort of solder — body lead is really a solder, so you cannot use any old piece of lead pipe — or because of failure to clean the body panel properly and tin it.

Two sorts of solder are used by body men: tinman's solder, which is usually 60% lead and 40% tin (though it is possible to find some which is 50% of each), and body filling solder also known as plumber's solder) which has more lead, usually 70% lead to 30% tin. The more lead there is in a solder the easier it is to shape, but the more difficult it is to bond it properly to steel. Body solder will not bond easily, so you have to tin the surface with tinman's solder first.

The idea is to get a thin even coating. You cannot build up with tinman's solder because it passes very quickly from a solid to a liquid state as it is heated, and runs off the panel. Body solder starts to go soft around 180°C (356°F) and goes from a solid state to a liquid state around 250°C (482°F). When it is in its soft state you can spread it in much the same way as you spread plastic filler.

Before you start the panel has to be clean — really clean. Go over it with a wire brush in an electric drill and a sander till every trace of dirt and rust has gone. Then wipe over the surface with methylated spirit to make sure there is no grease left. Even the grease from fingermarks will stop the solder tinning properly. You can tin either with a stick of tinman's solder and flux, or with one of the proprietary tinning paints; these are a liquid flux containing solder powder.

A butane torch will give enough heat for soldering, and you want the flame shield that gives you a fairly large spread of flame. If you are using a welding torch, use the nozzle which gives you a fan shaped flame without intense heat. Instructions for using a tinning compound vary from make to make. If you are using tinman's solder and flux you heat the panel gently to drive off any moisture, then brush on either a paste or a liquid flux. Continue heating, and rub the stick of solder on the panel till it melts. The solder should melt from the heat of the panel, not the heat of the flame.

Now spread the solder over the area you want to tin using either a folded rag with flux on it or a ball of industrial steel wool coated with flux and held in a pair of tongs. Pass the flame lightly over the solder from time to time to keep it liquid and if it drags add more flux. Finish off with light even strokes so the surface looks as if it is painted with solder.

Put on more flux, heat it with the flame and put on the body solder. This time push the stick of solder against the panel and heat it just behind the end so that you melt off a small lump and leave it sticking to the panel. Make several lumps of solder over the area you want to fill. At this stage you do not want the body solder to flow, so hold the flame on it till it goes bright and give the stick a twist to break off the soft end.

So far the job is dead easy. Now we come to the part that makes most people say that lead filling is difficult. It is not if you go about it the right way. To spread the solder you use a hardwood paddle, usually made of beech. The solder would stick to the bare wood so the paddle has to be well soaked in flux. In many body shops you will find paddles left standing in the flux so that it sinks right into the grain, and most body men prefer a paddle that has been well used. Almost every body repair man you talk to has his favourite flux. Some swear by a proprietary brand, some use tallow, some palm oil, some beeswax, some boiled linseed oil and some ordinary lard. I usually use one from the welding supply shop. I have tried several brands, and they all seem to do the same job.

Whichever flux you choose, coat the paddle with it, heat the lumps of solder till they are plastic and spread them over the panel. It sounds very easy, and so it is when you get the hang of it. The secret, if there is one, is to keep the solder just plastic without melting it, and tilt the paddle slightly as if you were spreading butter on bread. Some fluxes tend to splatter a little, so wear goggles and keep your face back from the job.

Horizontal panels are easier than vertical ones, and the first time you try a vertical panel quite a lot of the solder will probably run off and fall on the floor. It is quite expensive, so put a clean piece of hardboard down to catch it. You can melt it together and use it again. That is about all there is to body leading except practice.

It is very little use trying to bridge large holes with body solder, though a row of small pepperpot holes will usually fill. Where the hole is continuous, say along the bottom of a door, the proper way to make a repair is to cut the bottom of the panel off, weld in a new section and fill the join with body solder. But not everybody wants to do this for just a couple of holes, and if the panel is a double curved one and a replacement door skin is not available, it takes a great deal of skill to shape a piece up and weld it in to be invisible — or a great deal of money if you put the job out to someone else. In a case like this I would sooner see the job done with plastic resin than left as bubbly blistering paint. If the job is done properly it will never show.

You need to clean the panel down thoroughly, treat it with a rust killer on both sides to make sure rust does not spread again under your filler. Then you have to provide a backing to stop the filler falling through the holes. Filler is just that — filler. It is not intended to bridge over holes and not intended to restore strength.

If you can get to the back the job is easy. Coat round the hole with glass fibre resin, push a piece of perforated aluminium or zinc over the back of the hole and cover it with glass fibre matting. In the case of a closed section, fold the perforated sheet to push it through the hole and then open it out again with a piece of hooked wire. Work through the hole to coat the perforated sheet with resin, and hold it up against the hole with the wire till the resin sets enough to hold it. A few minutes is enough.

When it has thoroughly set off check that none of the patch nor the edges of the holes stand proud of the surface. To make sure, tap the edges lightly with a cross-pein hammer

18   Where the grinding has revealed rust pinholes they should be indented lightly with a hammer to give the filler room to lay on the surface

to leave a slight depression. Now fill the front of the panel with a plastic filler. There are a number of these on the market, but make sure you get one which stays flexible after it sets off. The ones which set hard will crack and fall out. Secondly, also make sure that you get one with a high proportion of resin. Some of the cheap ones are bulked out with French chalk.

Fillers I have used successfully are Plastic Padding Flexible, Bondaflex and Isopon P38. With all of them the secret is to mix the resin and catalyst hardener in the correct proportions and mix them well. The resin will not stick to polythene, so use a polythene bowl to mix it in and a polythene spreader to spread it across the surface.

With either plastic filler or body solder, leave the filler just a little proud of the surface and cut it back level after it has set. Some chalk rubbed on a steel body file will help to stop body solder sticking to the teeth. Use a single-cut body file such as the one made by the tool division of Firth Brown, and called a Trimatool. Alternatively you can use one of the cheese cutter types of open file, such as a Surform.

With either type of filler you will probably have to finish off with cellulose stopping to get a completely smooth surface. I will deal with that in the next chapter.

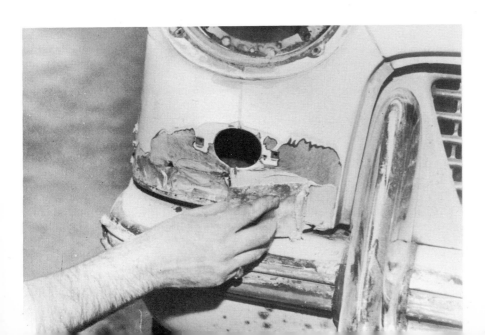

19   Plastic resin filler is best applied with a piece of flat plastic sheet. It will not stick to poly-thene

=5=

A COMPLETE PAINT JOB

No matter how carefully you faded in the patches left by all the rust removal, there comes a time when you have to consider a complete repaint job. This may have been evident from the start, and if you have been keeping the car off the road, the patches will still be in primer. Either way you have to decide whether the old finish is sound enough to provide a good base when it is rubbed down or whether the whole body needs to be stripped.

If the paint work is original and the car has been reasonably well looked after, the large areas such as the roof and bonnet may be sound even though the paint film has deteriorated on the surface. One can usually tell by rubbing down part of it with a medium wet or dry paper, using plenty of water. If the paint rubs down easily to a flat and hard film it will be a good base for refinishing. If, as is often the case, there are signs of paint cracking, which refinishers call Chinese writing, you will never get a good lasting finish. The old paint will have to come off for a lasting job.

I also think it is worth stripping off if the car has been hand painted. The old finish underneath may have been good, but there is no means of telling, and on most amateur hand-painted work the brush marks never quite rub down. You might have a car which has been resprayed properly, in which case

a good rub down may prepare it for new paint. If, however, there are signs that it has been smartened with what the trade calls a quick blow over, there will be signs. I have even found cases where the respray can be scratched off with a fingernail. In all cases, rubbing down will soon tell.

Start by giving the car a hose down to get rid of any grit, and start rubbing down with a medium paper and plenty of water. Keep dipping the paper in a bucket of water containing a generous squirt of washing up liquid, which helps to keep the dead paint you are rubbing off floating instead of clogging your paper. Keep a saturated sponge in the other hand so that you can constantly flood the surface as you rub down.

Wet or dry papers are graded by the size of their grit particles; the higher the number the finer the grade. The most used grades in a body shop are 180, 240, 320 and 400. The coarsest grade, 180, is used only for cutting down really rough surfaces, or used dry to cut down to bare metal to get rid of rust. For rubbing down old paint to be refinished, start with a 240 paper and finish with a 320.

Rubbing down is, without doubt, the most tedious arm and finger aching job in the whole business of refinishing, but it must be done properly because it is the basis of getting a good finish. Unlike house paints which will hide a multitude of sins, automotive refinishing paints are the most unforgiving in the world. The better the final shine, the more ruthlessly they will show up poor workmanship in preparation.

It helps to save your fingers if you wrap the paper round a block of very hard plastic foam or a block of hard rubber. This also helps you to follow the contours of the body and avoid over-rubbing in some places and under-rubbing in others.

Keep going with the 240 grade paper till the surface is completely dull and even. At the front and back there are areas where the paint has suffered from road grit and looks as if someone has fired a charge of buckshot at it. If it is too bad, save your fingers and energy and strip off to the nearest panel break line. But there is no need to strip off because of a few pock marks in an otherwise sound panel. Leave them for the moment and fill them later.

By the time you have been over the whole car you will have decided which panels are sound and which need to be stripped. If it has been obvious from the start that the whole car needs stripping, and there is a firm near by which will do it by sand blasting, it will save hours of work but, as with most time saving things, there is the inevitable snag. The drawback to having the body sand or grit blasted is that unless you are stripping the car down to a completely bare body shell you will be finding grit and dust for days. If you do not get rid of it all it will pop up again while you are painting — just when you need it least. For stripping without dismantling everything a chemical paint stripper might be quicker in the long run.

Unlike stripping old varnish off wood panels inside the car, you do not have to be careful about choosing a stripper that will not change the colour; you can use the most powerful stripper you can find. The main choice will be between one which needs neutralising with white spirit or turpentine and one which can be washed down with water. Two or even three applications of stripper are needed to bring all the paint off, and a wire brush can be very handy for getting into crevices where the scraper will not go. I have found that most strippers have little effect on rubber window surrounds, but I cannot vouch for all of them, so try a little first. Some strippers may make plastic wing piping go sticky, so be prepared if necessary to take the wings off and renew the piping. If the piping is badly rubbed you will be doing this anyway.

Stripping the paint will reveal more surface rust, so treat this with coarse paper and rust killer. A disc sander will help on the more open areas, and I find it helpful to have a speed reducing control and to use quite a slow speed, so that the disc does not take charge and run along the panel to make a score mark.

When the body is stripped, give it a final wash off and leave it to dry before starting on the painting. There is a choice between brush or spray painting, but to my mind there is only one method for a post-war car — to spray it. Hand painting and varnishing, as done in the twenties, gave a superb finish, but it is not the same as a spray finish and, though it looks in place on a veteran, it stands out on a more modern car. Nevertheless, not everyone wants to spray, so I will go through the technique of brush painting first.

Paints for brushing are different from those for spraying, and while it is possible to spray many paints made for brushing, the other way round is seldom satisfactory. It is mainly a question of drying time and the ability of the paint to set off slowly enough for the brush marks to flow out. Coach enamels for brushing are not so easy to come by these days, and you may have to order them through a paint supplier. Do not accept anyone's word that putting dopes or extra thinners in a paint compounded for spraying will make it suitable for brushing; they help but they are not the answer.

With any painting, spray or brush, the final finish depends on the trouble taken with the ground coats. First of all, if you have gone down to bare metal, you need a primer. These are compounded to bond properly to bare metal and in some cases have an etching action, which gives a first class key. An etching primer is essential for aluminium. Primers are generally put on quite thinly and cover well so there is generally no need to rub down afterwards unless there are any runs. If there are, let them dry hard before rubbing down.

Old-time coach painters used to follow the primer with several undercoats, each one rubbed down, to build up a solid layer of paint like an egg shell all over the body. The principle still holds good, but modern paint technology has saved us a great deal of time and effort by producing surfacer paints. These are compounded with heavy pigments to fill the surface imperfections left by wire brushes and sanders that the primer coat cannot fill. Most surfacers are made for spray application. Some are called primer-surfacers and are intended on production lines to be sprayed straight on to the metal. Perhaps I am old fashioned, but I always feel happier using a separate primer.

This is one case where you can brush a spraying paint. You will find the surfacer drags as you brush it, and you will be better off with two thin coats rather than one thick one. When the surfacer has set rock hard, go over it with 240 grade paper and plenty of water, and finish off with a finer grade paper till all the brush marks and imperfections have gone.

Secondly there is the undercoating. Always use the shade of undercoat intended for the final colour you want to use because many top colour coats are slightly translucent, and the final depth of colour depends on the reflection of the undercoat. Flat the surface down after each undercoat. With the first one you will find you rub through to the surfacer in places, so with the successive coats use a finer paper and plenty of water. Flood the surface with water and rub down lightly with a circular motion. Be careful at the edges because it is very easy to rub right through the paint. New paint is nothing like so hard as old paint. You should finish with a flat surface which is dull, but which has a sheen and hardly any scratch marks.

Wash down and leave the body to dry before starting on the colour coats. However dust free your garage seems there will be a light film of dust over the body when it is dry. Dusting with a dry rag is not much use because the dust rises and settles on the body again. Use a tack rag, which can be got from any paint supplier. It feels slightly sticky, and when passed lightly over the body it picks up the dust instead of just distributing it. Go over the whole car, and then go over each section again just before you paint it.

With any paint it is important to stir it thoroughly, and however careful you are there will be slight lumps and possibly some dust in it, so it needs straining. You can buy strainers, but just as good, and much cheaper, are old nylon stockings. Get a clean, dry container, stretch two or three thicknesses of stocking over the top and strain off just enough paint to finish the panel being worked on. Keep the tin of paint tightly closed so that there is less chance of dust settling in it.

Most paints have to be thinned from the consistency in the tin. Different painters like different consistencies of paint, and I have found the best to be paint that is thin enough to run freely from the brush when it is dipped in, with just enough paint left on the bristles to need a light wipe on the wiping bar to stop dripping. The wiping bar is a piece of wire across the top of the kettle, as painters call their container, and it is much better than

20 After masking and dusting off, the whole area to be sprayed should be gone over with a tack rag to get rid of the final specks of dust which would mar the finished surface. This has to be done after each rubbing down

using the side of the container.

Opinions differ as to the best order in which to paint a car body. It does not matter a great deal as far as I can see, except that you should try to work so that you do not have to reach across a freshly painted area to get to an unpainted one. If you start on the roof with a long broad band of paint down the middle and work to each side you will be able to cover the roof evenly before the paint starts to drag. Finish each section at a natural break line such as the base of the screen pillars and the line where the rear quarter-panels come down to the boot.

I have watched skilled coach painters working on veteran cars and old horse-drawn coaches, and most of them work the same way. They lay a fairly full coat with even brush strokes, lay it off with lighter strokes at right angles, and finish with even lighter strokes in the original direction. The direction depends on the panel. A roof should be finished along

the line of the car, so should the bonnet and wings, but doors and the boot lid are generally finished vertically.

If you have been careful with the tack rag, and finished off with light strokes, the finish should dry with hardly any brush marks or dust spots. There are bound to be some, however careful you are, but let the last top coat dry and harden for several days before trying to get them out. Then rub down with one of the proprietary rubbing compounds. Brush painting will never give the same surface that spraying will, but with care you will get a finish vastly superior to the average amateur look that spoils so many home-painted cars.

A word about brushes; always buy the best you can afford. Cheap brushes may look similar to expensive ones, but they do not have the same spring in the bristles, and the bristles often come out, which is most annoying. This sometimes happens with good brushes the first time they are used, and most painters like to work in a new brush on an old panel for five minutes or so. Brushes should be cleaned and dried after use, not just left standing in a tin of thinners. The first clean can be in thinners, but after that use one of the special cleaners, such as Polyclens, which are rinsed out with water. Smooth the bristles down afterwards, dry them, and keep the brushes in a plastic bag to save them collecting dust.

Even though it is possible to get an excellent finish with a brush, post-war cars were originally sprayed, so the restoration should be done the same way. Spray-painting equipment is not cheap, but most tool hire shops keep it. There are two main types: high pressure and high volume. High pressure is the type most used, so I will deal with that first.

The set you hire, or buy, will probably have the compressor and filters mounted on a trolley, and apart from following the instructions about filter cleaning there is little that needs doing. With the gun there is a selection of needles, jets and air discs, and it is here that many home spray painters get in a muddle. The jets and needles are chosen to suit the type of paint being sprayed, and its viscosity. The discs vary the spray pattern. If there is not a book or chart with the set, ask for it and make sure you get it before you start wasting paint by learning the hard way. Some guns do not have air discs; they have either a knob which turns to vary the air pattern, or the whole of the head turns.

Most instruction booklets have a chart which says which needle and jet to use for the particular air pressure and paint viscosity. The best viscosity for the paint will be in the paint-maker's leaflet. Some people recommend thinning the paint 50/50 with thinners, or some other empirical proportion, and even some professional painters work by rule of thumb and experience to judge the best viscosity. You may or may not (usually not) get a good spray this way. The proper way to measure it is to use a viscosity cup.

There are various viscosity cups, of different sizes and grades. The most well known are the BSS series and the Ford series. Most paint leaflets quote a viscosity time for both types. For example, the leaflet may say: Viscosity 28 to 30 seconds, BSS B cup. The cups look like small funnels, and you hold a finger over the bottom while you fill them, either to the brim or to a marked line. Then take your finger off and measure the time it takes for the paint to flow through the cup. Count only the flow time, that is, until the flow from the bottom breaks from a continuous flow to a series of drops. This method is accurate because it takes into account the temperature as well as the amount of thinners you have put in.

With paint of the correct viscosity in the gun, try the spray pattern on a spare piece of panel or a board. The gun should be held about a foot or so away from the panel and moved across in an even sweep, keeping it at right angles to the panel. If you wave it across by flexing your wrist you will get more paint in the middle than at the end of each stroke. the correct way is to hold your forearm and the gun at right angles to the work, and to move across with your upper arm and shoulder so that your forearm and the gun stay in a straight line. It is not a natural movement, and takes time to become easy. Your arm will ache at first, but you will soon get over that, and you will get an even spray pattern.

With many guns the amount of paint which comes from the nozzle depends on how far back the trigger is pulled. Triggers are usually fitted with a stop, and an experienced painter will wind this right back and vary the amount of paint passing through the gun by how far back he pulls the trigger. When you are experienced you can do the same. It is a useful skill for dealing with odd areas such as door rebates, where it is impossible to keep the gun always the same distance from the work when making a pass. To start with, though, I would advise adjusting the stop to give a nice even coat with the trigger hard back and a fairly slow pass across the work. Do not try to put too much paint on with each pass or you will get runs. Start the pass just before the work and finish just after it. That way you will get an even covering with a minimum of overspray.

For most panels on a car body it will be easiest to work with a vertical spray pattern of a flat fan so that your arm is moving horizontally. Exceptions are under a wing where it is easier to work vertically with a horizontal fan pattern, and round the edges of door, bonnet and boot rebates where a fine cone pattern is easiest.

You will need to mask off the parts of the car you do not want to cover with paint. Use masking tape and brown paper to cover the windows, hang old cloths over the brake drums and hubs, and tuck another old cloth round the engine while you spray the bonnet rebates. Where there are holes in panels where you have taken off decorative trim, put some masking tape over the inside if you do not want paint on the inside of the panel.

There is a pattern most sprayers use to paint a body. Start on the roof with a fairly broad pass along the centre from front to back. Work to one gutter, then go round the other side and work to that gutter. Unless you take too long over it the band down the middle will not have started to set off and will blend in nicely. Then, whether you are working with the doors off or on, change to a cone spray pattern and come down the windscreen pillars and round the door rebates and door edges. Many sprayers keep the cone pattern while they go across the scuttle, round the bonnet rebates and the boot rebate. Then go back to a vertical fan for the doors, the rest of the panels and the wings. It does not matter much in which order you do them except that you should always try to end a panel at a natural break.

Because you will not be working as fast as a professional sprayer (they often work in pairs on a large vehicle) there are bound to be places where the joins in your spraying show because one part has started to set off

21 Even for a partial respray the masking should extend well beyond the panel to catch the overspray. Note the distance the gun is being held from the work and note also that the operator was so keen to co-operate with the photographer he forgot to put on his face mask!

before the paint next to it is applied, and it is impossible to avoid a certain amount of overlap. Do not try to correct this by spraying more paint on; that will only make it worse. Leave it to dry and, if it is on intermediate coats, paper it down lightly or, on the final coat, cut it back with rubbing compound. If it still shows, you can fade in a light spray over it after it is dry.

Generally speaking at least two, preferably three, colour coats will be necessary. All except the final one should be rubbed down with the finest wet and dry paper, grade 400 or even 650, with plenty of water. Make sure the body is absolutely dry in all the seams before spraying on another coat. Some types of enamel are known as wet on wet. These do not need rubbing down between coats; they are made so that you can spray on a second coat before the first is dry. This does not mean you can spray away happily to get a thick coating; that would cause runs the same as with any other paint. By 'wet on wet' the paint maker means that a second coat can be sprayed on after the solvent has evaporated from the first so that it is almost, but not quite, touch dry. It is a quicker method, and I prefer it because there is no chance of water in the seams of the body when you spray, as there is when you rub down between coats. You should be able, with a wet on wet paint, to finish the colour coating in an afternoon. The final coat should be left for 24 hours, or even longer, before being rubbed down lightly with compound to get the final gloss.

Some paints are advertised as 'high gloss straight from the gun without compounding'. They are formulated to have excellent flow properties, but I have yet to find one that is not improved by giving a gentle rub with compound after it is hard. The thermosetting reflow paints should not be used for home spraying; they are used with a low temperature oven. You need air drying paint.

Another paint process you will come across is known as c.o.b., which stands for clear over base. With this system the top colour coat is sprayed on, and then, when it is dry but not set hard, a coat of clear lacquer. It gives a depth of gloss, like looking at the paint through glass, that cannot be got with any other method. The final clear coat can be lightly buffed with compound after it is hard to give an extra glass-like gloss.

Clear over base paints were introduced when metallic finish paints became popular, because the aluminium flakes in metallic paints often rise near the surface and, without a clear coat over the top, might show up as metal pips in the paint with normal cleaning. You can, however, use the clear over base technique with almost any spraying paint. I have had good results with a half-hour synthetic lacquer colour coat followed by an acrylic clear lacquer. It gives a very hard and durable finish, but be careful; the synthetic and the acrylic have completely different thinners which do not like each other. Make sure the gun is cleaned thoroughly after the synthetic; blow it dry with compressed air and run some acrylic thinners through it before putting the clear lacquer in. If the colour coat solvents have not evaporated sufficiently the thinners in the acrylic will turn the colour coat slightly milky, so make sure the synthetic is touch dry before putting the acrylic on. It is safer to use a colour and a clear lacquer which are compatible. If in doubt, ask the paint maker.

So far, I have mentioned only high-pressure spraying equipment. If you are using this there are precautions you must take. The amount of paint mist in the air round a car which is being sprayed has to be seen to be believed. To avoid wind and dust you will want to spray in the garage (you will get complaints from the neighbours if you try it in the garden) and paint spray is nasty stuff to breathe. Wear a proper respirator and eye mask which can be bought from any supplier of spray equipment.

Do not rely on an old hankerchief tied round your face like a Wild Western bandit. It will not save your lungs from paint spray any more than it saved him from a .45 bullet.

In recent years there have appeared on the market several high air volume, low-pressure spray outfits. These are similar in a way to the do-it-yourself guns that go on the end of a vacuum cleaner hose, but unlike those they are not cheap amateur outfits. The guns are high-precision jobs, and the air comes from a high-speed turbine blower.

The only one I have tried is made in France by Volumair, who have agents and concession-aires in most countries. The big advantage with this outfit is that it only needs an electric supply. You are free from trailing air hoses. Just plug in, hook the turbine over your shoulder, and away you go. I borrowed one from the makers on trial, and was so impressed with it that I bought it. It copes with synthetics, celluloses and acrylics as efficiently as any high pressure gun I have tried.

There is a difference in operation in that the air comes through the gun all the time the blower is switched on. The paint is released into the air stream when you pull the trigger. The air from the blower is warm, and this tends to evaporate the solvents in the paint more quickly than a cold air spray. I have found I get better results with the viscosity just a little thinner than the paint maker specifies. This is no drawback once you get it right, which is best done by trial.

Another big advantage is that there is very little over-spray or mist in the air. I would not say you could go on spraying for hours without a respirator, but the atmosphere is certainly much cleaner than with a high-pressure gun.

Trouble shooting chart for spraying

———— Fault ————	———— Cause ————
Fan spray heavy at top or bottom	Air cap horn partly blocked or paint collected on jet
Fan spray banana shaped	One side of air horn blocked
Fan too heavy in centre	Air pressure too low, or jet too large, or paint too thick
Fan split into figure of eight	Air and paint not mixing properly; could be pressure too high or jet too small
Orange peel	Air pressure too low, or gun held too near or too far from work, or wrong type of thinners
Paint coverage streaky	Gun held tilted, or incorrect overlap on passes
Runs or sags	Paint applied too heavily
White cloudy film	Humidity too high, or cold draught, or wrong thinners, or reaction between two types of paint on c.o.b. system
Blisters or bubbles or pinholes	Moisture or oil, or both, coming through air line. Clean the filters and both oil and water traps

=6=

A COMPLETE RETRIM

I dealt briefly with cleaning the interior in Chapter 2, but cleaning will not restore head-linings and upholstery which is torn, nor carpets which are frayed. Here you have to make up your mind whether to renew, or repair by patching to preserve as much as possible of the original.

Perhaps patching gives the wrong impression. No one wants to see upholstery that looks like Charlie Chaplin's trousers, with patches cobbled on the top, though I have seen this. Sometimes it is possible to repair a straight tear with a patch stuck on or ironed on the underside and, if it is done carefully, the repair is almost in-visible. The alternative is to renew individual upholstery panels.

Whichever method is chosen you have to take the trim off the car. The seats will come out easily enough and should be stored some-where safe while you deal with the body trim and headlining.

Before you can get at the fastenings for the headlinings, quite a lot of the side trim and the finishers will have to be removed. As soon as a part is taken off, mark the back of it with a felt tip pen so you know where it goes. Some cars have so many small trim panels that when putting them all back it is like trying to do a jigsaw puzzle without the picture for guidance. It is also wise to number them in the order in which they were taken off. This avoids the annoyance of having to take off parts you have replaced to get some other part on. If you can, it is helpful to take as many photographs of the interior as necessary, to help with fold lines and seams. After old trim is undone and repaired many of the natural folds dis-appear.

Methods of fixing headlinings are as numer-ous as there are models of car, so it is impossible to give detailed instructions for taking them out and replacing them. But there are guidelines which apply to most makes. For the first eight or so years after the war most makers of quality cars stayed faithful to the pre-war wool cloth for headlinings and the traditional methods of fixing them. When the trim strips are off you will find the sides of the lining tacked to the body, either direct to the framing in the case of a wood-framed coachbuilt body, or to wooden insets in the case of a steel body. A variation on this might be a fibreboard strip holding the edge of the lining, which is screwed to the body with self-tapping screws. Later, when production engin-eers started counting minutes saved on each car in terms of hours saved a day on produc-tion, headlinings were often held to the body with adhesive and the pressure of the trim strip.

Whichever method you find, go all round the lining and release the edges before starting to take it from the roof panel. If you come across a hard taut edge on the headlining that does not want to come away from the side, but which does not seem to be fixed, investigate for a tension cord or wire. These were sometimes sewn into the edge of the lining, anchored at the rear and run down the inside of the windscreen pillars, to a bolt round which the wire could be wound to tension it and hold the lining taut. This bolt is often hidden right up behind the dash, so you might have to take out the glove box, or even half the instrument panel, to get at it. Things were often planned for ease of assembly in a set order — and hard luck on the man who had to repair things.

By now the headlining should be hanging down like a curtain all round the inside of the car, and you can investigate how it is held up to the roof. On most cars it is held where the seams in the lining make it easy to provide hanging tapes in the best quality work, or just an extended fold in the seam where production speed overruled craftsmanship. Sewn-in tapes are better because they spread the strain, and are better able to take tacks or adhesive than wool cloth. They tended to die out with the introduction of plastic headlinings because the strength of these compared with wool cloth made tapes less necessary.

Whichever method is used, the principle will be the same. The seams of the lining are held to wood bows, metal frames or, in some cases, even lengths of heavy gauge wire bridged across the roof and either screwed or sprung in clips at the sides. There might be a combination of all three methods on the same car.

Make sure you know exactly how the lining is fixed before you rip it off, even if it is torn and rotted. If you walk into a body-retrimming shop you will see trimmers just grab an old lining and rip it off, but they know how to put the new one in. You have to find out by taking the old one out carefully, one stage at a time, and making notes if necessary.

You might end up by taking the lining out in one piece, though often round the rear quarters or round a sunshine roof you might have a number of separate panels. Once the lining is out you can commandeer the living room floor to mark out the new lining.

This is where the experienced trimmer allows for stretch, and many home restorers end up with wrinkles after a month or so. All headlining materials have to be stretched when they are put in, the degree of stretch depending on the material. A tightly woven plastic cloth needs less than a loosely woven wool cloth. On the average car, with perhaps three bows across the roof, the stretch will be between ¼ and ½ in (6 and 13 mm) for each foot (30 cm) run between the bows, so you space the seams a little closer than those on the old lining.

If the tapes are tacked to wooden roof bows you can err safely a little on the tight side, because if you leave your tapes long, and the seam does not quite line up with the bow, the tapes will make up the difference and no one will know. Leave a fairly generous length at the front and back, and at the sides, to pull well down when you fasten these.

Make sure all the panels are cut the same way of the grain. Some materials have a slight nap, like velvet, and show a difference in colour one way from the other.

When the new lining is seamed and ready to go back in the car, offer it up and fasten it to the middle roof bow first, then work alternately towards the front and rear pulling it taut as you go. When you come to fasten down the sides, tack them, or put blobs of adhesive on, lightly and well spaced at first. Then go back and take in the slack between the first tackings. As you get nearer to finishing you will probably find your first tackings are too slack, or perhaps, in the corners, too tight, so if you leave them a little proud they can be lifted out with pincers without damaging the cloth. If the sides are tensioned by a draw wire, tighten each side a little at a time till the tension is even.

Even with careful tacking and pulling you might find there are a few sags and wrinkles that refuse to come out no matter what. This is where the experienced trimmer gets the kettle out, not to make a cup of tea, but to steam the lining to its final stretch. This works with almost all linings. I say almost, because though I have never found one which fails to respond I have not tried some of the latest plastic materials so, just in case, try the material first. Take an off-cut about 1 ft (30 cm) square, tack it tightly over any old frame, such as a wooden box, and start the kettle going. An electric kettle is much better than a gas kettle for this. Put a length of rubber pipe on the spout, and when it is boiling merrily send a jet of steam under one corner of the lining and play it on the underside. There is no need to soak it. Then leave it to dry to see if the material tightens.

If it does, and if the steam does not make the dye run, or pucker the cloth, or anything else peculiar, take the kettle in to the car and do the same with the headlining. Make sure all the tacking is tight, and that any adhesive used is dry (or else when the lining dries it will pull more wrinkles). You can generally find somewhere convenient to poke the rubber tube under the lining, such as the interior light hole but, if not, loosen one tack at each side and tack up again before the lining dries. (Check the kettle from time to time to make sure it is not boiling dry!)

After the headlining is in, and before you tackle the seats, do anything that is necessary to the side and door trims. Most of these will be PVC or leathercloth, stretched over panels of fibreboard held in place by chromium plated screws and cup washers, or by spring clips that push into holes in the steel.

In many places, particularly where the rain has seeped in the doors, the old fibreboard will have warped and bellied out and generally deteriorated. It is a waste of time trying to straighten it. Make new panels from thin resin-bonded plywood or thin hardboard. Alternatively, it is often possible to buy new compressed fibreboard of the original sort from trim suppliers.

On the highest quality bodies the side and door trims will be in hide, the same as the seats, but in most cases they will be leathercloth or PVC. Old leathercloth often goes brittle and tears, so replace it with modern PVC cloth which matches the seats. Some of the modern vinyl upholstery cloths are so good that people will think you have spent a fortune on hide to match the seats. Even if you are aiming at 100% originality, and can still find the old leathercloth, it is much inferior to modern trim material.

If you are fortunate enough to have a really top quality body with hide side trims of which some are torn, replace the torn panels with new hide. Though the modern vinyls are good, they are not that good, and they always stand out when sewn next to leather.

On lesser breeds of car the panels will most likely be plain, so they offer little trouble, but if the car had even slight pretensions towards luxury there will be fluted panels, piping and arm rests to deal with. I will deal with fluted panels when we come to the seats, but if you have to take the old covering off arm rests or door pockets, watch carefully how it comes apart and make notes. With doors you are fortunate because one side can be left in the original condition while you tackle the other; but make sure everything matches the original design. Watch particularly how any elastic tapes are fixed to hold the gathered tops of door pockets.

Whatever material is being used for covering the trim panels, it will look hard and austere if you put it straight on the panel. To give it that plump luxury look, cover the panel first with a thin layer of wadding. You can buy this wadding from upholsterers, where it goes under the name of linter's felt. Because most household upholstery these days is done with plastic foam, you may have to search a little for linter's felt, but if you have difficulty try an antique furniture restorer. If he does not do traditional upholstery, he will know someone who does.

Hold the linter's felt in place with a few dabs of adhesive, lay the trim cloth face down on a clean table, put the panel on the back and pull the edges over. Start at the centre of each side and work to each corner, pulling the material tight as you go. When you get to the corners you may have to make a series of vee nicks when folding the material over to avoid too much bunching. On many production cars the material is fixed to the back of the panel solely with adhesive. This works fine with a hot press or something similar, but with most cold setting upholstery adhesives I find the adhesive tends to creep after a time and the material goes slack.

I like to reinforce the adhesive with a few strategically placed staples. You can buy a staple gun in most do-it-yourself shops but be careful about the length of staples. The ones packed with the gun are often too long for this job and there is a danger they will go right through and mark the face of the material. In the better-stocked shops you can buy staples in various lengths.

With the seats still out of the way, it is time to have a look at the carpets. The front carpet is likely to be badly worn and tatty, but the rear might be almost unused. This is a pity in a way, because it goes against the grain to do away with perfectly good carpet, but you will be very lucky if you find new carpet that exactly matches the rear, so it is usually a case of new carpets throughout.

Older-type carpets, excellent quality though they were, could be devils to work on, because no sooner had you cut an edge than it un-ravelled. Modern car carpet has the great advantage that it has a layer of adhesive on the back to seal the threads. You can cut it to your heart's content, and the edge stays firm. I would use this modern carpet every time, even though the older type is still available. There is the slight drawback that it is difficult to get it in the older-style straight pile, like the bristles of a broom, that was a feature of luxury cars of the fifties. If you are a purist, and insist on using the older type of carpet, brush a generous line of carpet adhesive, such as Copydex, on the underside along the lines of the cuts before you make them. This will help to stop the threads coming adrift, but you will still have to take care and bind the edges.

Even with modern carpet that does not really need it, you might like to bind the edges if the original carpet was bound. The edge binding is a strip of PVC or leathercloth — or hide, on top-class jobs — and it used to be sewn in one of two ways. It was either just folded over the edge and sewn through, or the top was blind sewn first and then the binding was folded over the edge of the carpet and hand sewn with a curved needle to the underside.

Blind sewing, in case you haven't come across it, is the method where the binding is laid face down on the top of the carpet, level with the edge, and a line of stitching is run down about ¼ in (6 mm) in from the edge. When the binding is folded over so that its right side is uppermost, the stitching is hidden. Hand sewing to the back with a curved needle was quite easy on old-style carpet, but with a modern adhesive-backed carpet you will find your fingers getting sore after a few feet of pushing the needle through the closely-stuck-together threads. With foam-backed carpet it is almost impossible.

In a few cases, on the highest-class work, old-time perfectionists used to shave down the edge of the carpet pile where the binding went, so that it lay flush with the pile instead of standing proud. There were even small hand planes to do this. It is a nice touch of perfection, and the sort of thing from which legends are made, but I hardly think it is worth the trouble on restoration, because unless it is done perfectly the end result can look worse than binding over the pile. In any case, the number of people who could spot the difference, even on a national concours, is small.

The only place where there is likely to be trouble fitting the carpet is over the gearbox hump. Sometimes this is a separate piece of carpet, and the floor carpet just butts up to it. Sometimes it is sewn into the front carpet. Depending on the shape of the gearbox cover, the hump might be made in one piece with a vee cut out and sewn, or it might be a number of pieces sewn together. In either case, copy the original faithfully, except that if you do not feel you can tackle the sometimes complicated hand sewing, butt the edges together with a thin line of carpet adhesive, and reinforce the join underneath by sticking on a layer of webbing.

If you want to put a rubber heel mat in front of the pedals, try to get the proper thing, which has a rebate round it so that it fits from the underside into a hole cut in the carpet, and leaves a flange underneath which is sewn or stuck to the carpet. This looks much more professional than just sewing a rectangle of rubber over the top.

Now we get to the seats. Whether these are in cloth, PVC, leathercloth or hide they will be upholstered on the same principles. The top cover, with its panels and flutes, will have a layer of linen sewn under it to hold the stuffing in place, and this will come away from the frame and springs as a self contained part. In a few cases there might be another layer of stuffing underneath, but usually there is just a layer of hessian or canvas to protect the linen from the springs. On cheaper production cars even this layer of canvas might not be used, but it is worth putting one in,

otherwise the slight movement between the springs and the linen will tear it.

The method of taking the covering off the frame will usually be obvious. Some cars have a wooden base so that the cover is tacked on, but more often the frame is metal and the cover is held by clips, with sometimes a dab or two of adhesive. Take the cover off and put it to one side while you deal with the spring unit.

This will either be a series of tubular tension springs or a complete built up unit of coil springs woven into a wire mesh. Some automotive upholstery suppliers keep a range of spring units, and a few will make up a new unit to pattern. If the seat has seen a great deal of use, and the springs are sagging badly, it is well worth while trying to get a new unit.

The other alternative is to put new coil springs in the old unit. This is often more difficult than it sounds. Most traditional upholstery suppliers can find you suitable springs, but originally the springs were wound into the mesh in a jig. Putting them in by hand is possible, but it needs strong wrists, two hefty pairs of pliers and a great deal of patience. Even so, one way or another you have to get the springs in good shape or the seat will never be comfortable and never look quite right.

When tackling the covering you will find that all the fluting and panelling is made up of separate pieces of material, with the linen undercover sewn to the seams to hold the rolls and pads of stuffing in place. Whether you want to insert a new panel or just get to the underside of the top cover to stick a patch on, the linen has to come off. The old linen tears easily — in some cases it just falls apart in your fingers — so do not waste time trying to save it. Run a pair of scissors down each flute and lift the rolls and pads of stuffing out. Lay these out somewhere where they will not be disturbed, and lay them out in order, so that you know where they go back.

An experienced upholsterer will throw the lot into his carding machine where they will be teased out into good-as-new stuffing. He knows from experience just how much to put back in each flute and panel. Lesser mortals like us usually end up with stuffing left over and flutes which are too flat, or not enough stuffing and flutes which are too plump.

With the stuffing out you can make any repairs with stuck-on patches, or replace any panels if necessary. If you have to make a new cover take the old one apart by cutting the stitches so that you can use the panels as patterns to cut new ones. Once again it is a good plan to draw a diagram of the panels, to number each one and put the same number on the old panels as they are taken off. If you leave it to memory you had better be good at puzzles.

When the covers are repaired, or new ones made up, new linen has to be sewn on the underside and the stuffing put back. This sounds easy and straightforward, but unless you know the right way to do it you will end up with a seat with more bumps and ruts than a country lane.

It is completely useless trying to hold each pad or roll of stuffing in place while you sew the linen over the top. That way lies disaster. Sew the linen to the cover first, then put the stuffing in.

This needs a little care and forethought. To get the seat even each flute has to hump up just the right amount. If you make the humps too tall the cover will not be wide enough to reach across the seat frame. Make them too low and the cover will be too wide, so that the edge piping falls over the side instead of sitting nicely along it. I know this from bitter experience, so I evolved a method of getting it right. Whether experienced upholsterers use it or not, I have no idea; probably not, but it works.

Lay the linen over the bare seat springs, and mark the edges all round. Then sew the outside edges of the top cover to the marks on your linen and arrange the flutes evenly across the linen before you sew them down. For the moment, sew only the side edges. You will need the ends open to get the stuffing in.

Now cut a piece of thin plywood about half an inch narrower than the narrowest flute, and six inches or so longer than the longest one. Sand off the edges, and staple a piece of webbing to one end so that it lays out in line with the wood like the thong of a whip. Now lay the roll of stuffing on the wood, fold the webbing back along the top to hold it in place and push the whole thing through the flute in the cover. When it comes out the other end, put a hand on top of the cover to hold things steady and ease the webbing right through. With a little luck you will leave the roll of stuffing in place and the wood can be pulled out.

If the stuffing does not lay quite even it can be eased into place with a long needle, working through the linen. You can buy a special tool for this in upholstery shops. It is a strong steel pointer with a handle on the end; upholsterers call them regulators. With all the rolls of stuffing in place you are ready to sew the ends up, sew on the side panels and put the cover back on the frame.

In most cases the rolls of stuffing will have flattened, which is why a professional will tease them out in his carding machine. You and I can take the easier way out and put a thin layer of linter's felt over each one before it goes back. This gives it just that little extra fullness that makes the seat look plump and luxurious instead of flat and sad.

Upholstery and interior trimming is a skilled trade, and the number of hours you will spend on the interior would probably make you uneconomic to employ in a trim shop, but take your time. With care and patience, and planning each step, there is no reason why you should finish up with

22   A plumpness to the
seats, which you can get
with linter's felt, gives an
air of luxury, as on this
Humber Sceptre

anything you need be ashamed of.

Bringing the headlining, carpets and seats up to scratch is going to make the dash and window finishers look rather sad and unloved. These will be either varnished wood, metal grained to look like wood, plain painted metal or, on later cars, hard plastic foam covered with PVC.

Taking the real wood ones first, these were originally finished in spray cellulose or lacquer. People talk about French polished woodwork, but you have to go back to the twenties to find real French polish. Excellent though this may be on antique furniture, it was a poor finish for cars. The alternation of heat and cold, and the roasting the dash capping rail gets through the screen in summer, give it a short life. Early spray-on finishes were not a great deal better, just quicker to put on, but as the chemistry of resin based lacquers advanced so did the lasting qualities of the varnish on dash panels and door finishers.

If the lacquer is original, and the surface

has gone dull without cracking, it is possible to bring it up like new with the same cutting compound used on external paint finishes. A final high gloss can be brought up with liquid metal polish. If, however, the surface looks like crazy paving, or if there is any bare wood showing or if, in a fit of misguided enthusiasm, someone has painted the whole lot over with what looks like liquid toffee, there is nothing for it but to strip down to bare wood and start again.

The best way to strip the old varnish is with a chemical stripper, but choose your brand carefully. Some of the most effective and powerful strippers contain the chemical lye, which is an excellent stripper but which has the unfortunate property of turning some mahoganies and walnuts purple. I like to use Polystrippa, made by Polycell Products, which I have found quite safe in this respect, and which is neutralised by washing off with water.

In the United States, Formby's Furniture Refinisher is available and is quite unlike ordinary paint and varnish strippers. It is expensive, retailing for almost $10 per quart, and is suitable only for varnish and lacquer. I haven't tried it but American friends tell me it is extremely easy to use, simply by sponging and scrubbing the surface with a soaked pad of steel wool. There is never any need for scraping or sandpapering, the old finish seems to melt away almost instantly and disappear instead of turning into a nasty sludge, and no residues are left that will interfere with the application of a new finish. Something of the nature of a Triumph instrument panel can be totally stripped and prepared for refinishing in less than fifteen minutes.

23 Polished woodwork suffers badly where the sun beats on it through the screen. In this condition it spoils an impressive instrument display. This is the author's Jaguar as bought

24 If you have to strip ▶ and rub down beautifully grained burr walnut, be careful. The veneer is often literally paper thin

After the wood is dry it needs rubbing down with the finest grade of glass paper or steel wool you can get. If you can get garnet paper, which is even finer, so much the better. Always rub with the grain. Rubbing across it will produce scratches. These hardly show when the wood is bare, but they will stand out like tramlines when it is varnished. Be careful with veneered panels. The beautifully figured burr walnut is literally paper thin, and it is possible to go through it with the greatest of ease if you are too enthusiastic.

If you are unlucky enough to have pieces of the veneer damaged or missing, replace them with veneer from a craft shop that goes in for marquetry. These shops stock veneer in shades to match anything.

The worst patch to put in is one in the middle of a panel. If you cut the ends of the patch square across the grain the lines will show badly. The way to tackle this is to cut a veneer patch in the shape of a long thin diamond. For a blemish about ¼ in (6 mm) across the diamond should be at least 3 in (8 cm) long so that the sloping sides are as nearly along the grain as possible. Cut the patch first, then lay it in on the panel and scribe round it with a craft knife or a razor blade. It is easier to cut a hole to fit a patch than the other way round. Glue the patch in and wait till it is thoroughly set before sanding it down level.

When sanding down the stripped wood you will have found that the original makers were nothing like as careful as you thought about choosing pieces of wood with matching colours. (If you have used Formby's Refinisher, you will not have needed to use sandpaper, and the colour of the original varnish will have been retained in the wood — a desirable characteristic.) The final shading was done with tinted varnish. You have to do the same. Start off by giving the wood a couple of sealing coats of varnish thinned down till it is almost like water. Use whatever brand of varnish you fancy, either plain or tinted. I like to use a polyurethane varnish which I find lasts well in direct sunlight through the screen, and I like one slightly tinted yellow, which gives the wood a little extra richness. Water-clear varnishes, I think, leave the wood looking slightly clinical.

The first coat of well-thinned varnish will sink so far into the wood that you will hardly see where it has been, but the second will show an eggshell gloss. It will also raise the grain slightly, so that it will need sanding down with worn glasspaper. Then use tinting coat. Mix some stain with the next batch of thinned varnish. Make sure to use a stain which is compatible with the varnish. Some seem to mix all right at first but separate out when the varnish settles, so do not be content with just stirring the stain in. Try some on a spare piece of wood and let it dry to make sure the stain dries evenly with the varnish.

Use the tinted varnish to touch up the sections of wood which are too light. The original will have been tinted by spraying to fade in the edges, but with a brush you can fade in well if you do it carefully, and before the tinting coat has quite dried go over the whole panel with plain thinned varnish so that the tinted parts fuse into the rest without a hard line. After this has dried you can carry on building up coat after coat of varnish till you get a high gloss. Leave it for at least three times as long as the maker says it takes to dry, then take off the nibs and the dust spots with a pad of steel wood dipped in liquid metal polish. Go very lightly so you flat the surface slightly without making scratches. After that, bring up the final mirror-like gloss with a pad and plain metal polish. Do not be tempted to use a mechanical buffer. It will generate so much heat it will spoil the varnish surface.

Plain painted metal is easy enough to deal with, but metal painted and grained to look like wood is a different ball game altogether. In some cases the grain was painted on by

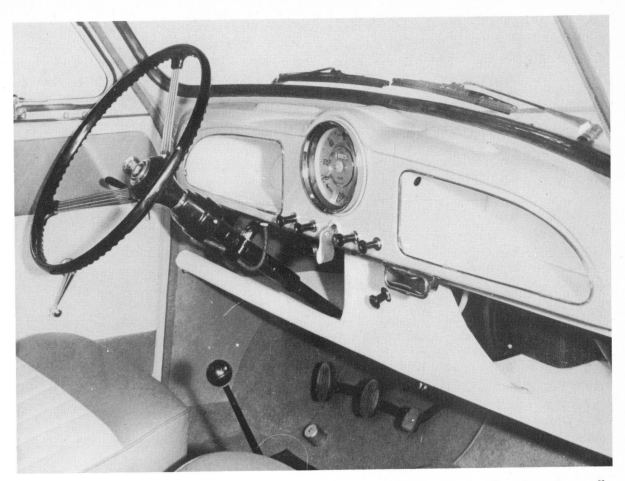

25 Even a plain painted dash (this is a Morris Minor) will get top marks at a concours if it is as carefully rubbed down and resprayed as the outside of the car. Note, too, that the steering column and all the small accesory trim strips are in faultless condition

hand and in others it was photo-printed on the steel sheet before it went into the press former. With properly designed press dies it is amazing how little the delicate photo-printed film suffered, and after varnishing it was quite hard wearing. Unfortunately it was not hard wearing enough to resist fingers round switches

and elbows on window sills, where it usually rubbed down to the undercoating of plain brown.

If you have a car like this you are faced with three choices. You can either repaint in a plain colour which will look smart but will lose marks in a concours because it is not original, you can try to touch up the graining where it is worn, or you can rub the whole lot down and try to grain it afresh.

If you watch a skilled painter graining a panel he goes over it with such a deft touch and so surely and quickly that you feel you can do the same with ease. You realize your mistake when you try. I must admit here and now that I have never been much of a hand at graining, but it won't quite be a case of the blind leading the blind because I have watched a skilled painter at work and asked a lot of questions, so if you want to have a go it will be a case of do as I say, not as I do.

The first thing my painter friend impressed on me was that no one can produce a first class grained finish unless the ground work is absolutely sound. The metal must be rubbed down, undercoated and rubbed down again till it looks like smooth satin. Then the ground coat is laid on. In the case I watched this was a sort of murky yellow colour with slight leanings towards cream. This ground coat can be any hard-drying paint. In this case it was cellulose, because the top coat was going to be cellulose. An oil based or synthetic paint can be grained on top of cellulose ground paint, but not the other way round because the cellulose will curdle the paint underneath.

When the ground coat is dry the work is given a quick coat over of scumble. In the old days when woodwork inside houses was grained to look what it was not, this scumble was a thick, slow-drying, oil-bound paint, but you can use any fairly slow-setting paint. The painter I watched used a quick-drying cellulose, but this was for professional speed. He suggested a slower-drying paint for anyone trying graining for the first time.

He used two shades of scumble, one a medium brown and the other a dark brown slightly tinged with red. They were laid on with broad brushes in what looked a fairly haphazard way, the medium brown going over everything and the darker shade in a few dabs here and there. Then, working quickly before the scumble dried, the painter used a graining comb, which was like an ordinary hair comb but made of rubber with teeth about half an inch long, together with a tool of his own, an ordinary inch-wide paint brush with the bristles cut down to a stiff stubble. With these he went over the scumble coat quite firmly so that the scumble was spread in slight ridges leaving the ground coat to show through in streaks. On a window finisher he went right round in one sweep of the comb, swaying it slightly from side to side once or twice so that the graining lines were not dead straight. This, he told me, was the whole secret of graining. It looks all wrong if it is regular because trees do not grow regularly, so neither is the grain pattern.

On the dash he made what looked like a few squiggles with the stubble brush over the parts where he had put the darker scumble, then went over the whole panel with the comb. His movements left a beautiful irregular grained pattern that left me looking in sheer admiration. I tried several times on scrap panels, using his tools and under his direction, but I am afraid I came nowhere near qualifying as a grainer, even though after half an hour or so I was getting a finish that was not too awful to look at.

He was very understanding and told me that if I practised I should, in a year or so, be able to produce a good pattern. Anyone wanting to have a go should be able to get a graining comb from the more arty type of interior decorators' supply shop, or from a craft shop. The stubble brush you can make yourself. After that it is a matter of practice till you feel confident enough to tackle the car. There is one consolation; if you mess it up you can clean if off and start again.

That leaves only the dash which is finished in PVC over hard foam crash-padding. If this is badly damaged there is little you can do except replace it. The PVC is hot-formed over the moulded foam and it is usually in shapes that, however much you try to stretch and pull, you can never recover without the odd wrinkle or two. The covering is also much thicker than the PVC used on upholstery, so unless you know someone in a car or trim manufacturers who can get offcuts, it is very difficult to let in a patch. Fortunately the process is fairly recent, so there should not be much trouble in finding either a new or good condition replacement.

=7=
TAKING ON
A COMPLETE REBUILD

So far I have been talking about taking on a car which is basically a runner, or at least one which is not going to be rebuilt from the chassis up. Sooner or later, though, you are going to come across a desirable piece of machinery which has been badly neglected and has not turned a wheel for years, but which asks to be put back on the roat in its former glory. The only way to restore a car like this is to take it all apart and rebuild it as near to new as possible, restoring each part as you go along.

If you can, get it into a rolling chassis state where you buy it so it can be loaded on to a trailer and can at least be pushed in and out of the garage. I have known one or two quite reasonable restoration jobs that were made much more difficult after they were bought — and much more costly — by the unsympathetic attentions of a crane and winch operated by a gorilla who was much more at home working in a breaker's yard than operating a recovery truck.

Even when the car will roll on its wheels, try to be there when it is winched up on to the trailer to make sure the hawser is attached to a part of the car where it will not do any damage. Bumper bars and suspension units are not the ideal places to attach a hawser, but I have seen it done — and by people who

should have known better.

To tackle a complete strip-down rebuild you need plenty of storage space, because a car in pieces takes up a great deal more room than when it is in one piece. Ideally you want two garages, one to store the bits and one to work on them, and reassemble the car as each part is restored.

Before you start taking anything to pieces, as I said before, take as many photos as you can from all angles. As you take off parts to expose more parts take photos of these as well. The pictures will be absolutely invaluable when you come to put things together again. The idea is to reduce the car to the least number of complete sub-assemblies and work on each of these as its turn comes in the rebuilding programme. Try to resist the temptation to jump from one thing to another unless you are really held up for spare parts. You can get in a terrible muddle because a car is made up literally of thousands of pieces, and the old joke about having enough pieces left over to start building a second car is too close to the truth to be comfortable.

A surprisingly large number of small bits and pieces will have to come off as it is, and it pays to label these and put them in groups in cardboard boxes. It is a mistake to be too cryptic in your labels. You might know when

26   Open channel chassis generally suffer less from corrosion than box sections, but rust can get a hold under closely bolted panels such as the front apron, as on the author's MG

you take a part off what 'NSF 3rd hole back' means, but in two or even three years' time it can be as puzzling as a top secret code.

Make plenty of notes while taking things apart and transfer these from the oily bits of paper in the garage to a decent work book when you have cleaned up. Not only will it help you when putting things together, but you will have a complete journal of your car and everything you have done to it. I was given this advice many years ago when I first became interested in old cars, and I wish I had followed it. The books would be fascinating, and nostalgic, to read now.

Inevitably when you start to take things apart you are going to find nuts and bolts that have rusted up solid. Penetrating oil and freeing agents (such as Plus Gas or WD 40), and the patience to wait while they do their job, help a great deal. I have also found diesel fuel to be a good freeing agent. But there are always the few that just will not yield. The head of the bolt, or the nut, rounds off so that even a pair of Stilsons or a Mole wrench will not get a grip. Sometimes applying heat from a butane torch helps, provided you do not set the whole thing alight. Keep the flame well away from fuel lines and carburetters as well as from the petrol tank. Even if these seem empty, and have been empty for a long time, there might still be enough vapour left

to make a mighty big bang. Keep a fire extinguisher handy and make sure everything is out and not smouldering before packing up. Being hauled out of bed to be told that your garage and precious car is going up in flames can give you that well known sinking feeling.

When all else fails the parts have to be cut apart. An easy way, if you can get to the nut, is to use a pair of nut splitters. Some of these use a screw action and some work like a substantial pair of pincers. They are most useful tools, and no restorer should be without one, but there will be some cases where there is no room to get the tool to the nut. You have to resort to a hacksaw or cold chisel.

Your first thoughts will probably turn to hacksawing the bolt through just under the nut, but unless the bolt is so loose that you can slide the hacksaw blade under it, this is not the best way. It is difficult to avoid twisting the hacksaw blade, and it is ten to one that unsightly saw marks will be left on one of the components just where they are not wanted. You might also inadvertently saw through a stud or a welded-in bolt, and find yourself in even greater trouble.

The best way is to saw down through the nut alongside the bolt or, if it is definitely a replaceable bolt, saw down through the centre of the bolt and nut to cut the nut in half. Do make sure that the bolt is replaceable. I once sawed happily down through what I thought was a standard bolt only to find it had a stepped diameter. A replacement bolt was quite unobtainable so I had to go to all the trouble of turning one down on a lathe and rethreading it.

Resort to a chisel only if the bolt goes through something really substantial. Try to split the nut if possible because this is almost always softer than the bolt. If this is impossible lay the chisel flat against the component and shear off the bolt with a couple of hefty blows. Always use a good heavy hammer and chisel and a few heavy blows, rather than tapping away as if you were rivetting. If the blade of your chisel is blunt, sharpen it, and if the top looks like a battered mushroom grind it back to its proper shape. It is not a bad idea to wear a heavy industrial glove on the hand that holds the chisel, and a very good idea to wear eye protectors. When cutting with a chisel pieces tend to fly.

When dismantling, try to put the nuts and bolts back in their holes. If you have to cut through them make a note of their sizes and lengths and get new ones as soon as possible. Put the new nuts and bolts with the components; then you avoid the annoyance of starting to put something together and finding yourself a bolt or two short.

The number of sub-assemblies to which the car is reduced depends on the model. Start by taking off all the parts which are most likely to get damaged or which will get in the way, like the bonnet, lamps, radiator and grille, bumpers and so on. They will not be needed for a long time, so put them away carefully somewhere where they will not get kicked or knocked over. Take out the seats and carpets and put these away too. Even if the carpets are tatty you will need them later for patterns.

An older style bonnet which lifts up from each side can be a very awkward thing to store. Standing it up on end may be fine for a day or so while doing a decoke, but on a rebuild it is going to get knocked over and damaged. The best way is to take out the hinge rods and store the bonnet flat; but hinge rods usually put up quite a struggle before they let go. You will need penetrating oil, a drift and a Mole wrench. While the penetrating oil is soaking in run a couple of pieces of rope under the folds and hang the bonnet up from the garage roof like a flying M, well out of the way.

As you take each component off make a note of the new pieces that will be needed when it goes back. Things like radiator hoses, bonnet tapes, mounting rubbers and the like can cost a great deal of money if bought all at once, even if you can get them from the agents. If you have to search it can hold you up a long time. If you buy them as you find you need them it builds up your stock and spreads the financial drain; it's like doing the restoration on hire purchase. It also gives you time to search for elusive parts at autojumbles and swap-meets.

I prefer to leave the axles and wheels on as long as I can so that the chassis is mobile. Dismantling is a dirty business, and it is handy to be able to wheel the car out once in a while to sweep the garage. If you have the older type of car with a side lift-up bonnet and separate wings and radiator grille take all these off but, unless you have a hoist, leave the engine in place for a time. The chassis makes a handy engine stand, and the block will be lighter than a complete engine when you come to lift it out.

On later cars, where the engine is buried deep down in a tin box, it is best to have it out in one piece. Sometimes it is possible to take the gearbox off first and lift the engine out through the top, sometimes the engine and gearbox lift out through the top as one unit, and sometimes they drop down underneath. If you have not managed to get a manual take a little time to investigate, because it can be awkward to have the engine and gearbox on the hoist and have to jack up the chassis to get it out underneath because it will not come out the bonnet aperture.

With some cars (Jaguars are a case in point) the whole front suspension has to come off as a unit before the engine can be lowered out. With others, like some Austins and Morrises, the engine is bolted on to the front suspension sub-assembly, so that if the body is lifted high enough the suspension, complete with the engine and gearbox, can be wheeled out from underneath. In cases like these it is better to leave the engine in place till most of the other parts are off and you have the chassis up on stands.

If the car has a separate chassis, and there is sufficient room, take the body right off. If it is old enough to have wooden floorboards they will be rotten in places, but save them as patterns and make new ones from resin-bonded outdoor grade chipboard, or resin-bonded plywood. There will also be the remains of felt or rubber strips which once kept the floorboards watertight. Measure up now for new ones.

Take off the petrol tank, boot lid, spare wheel carrier, running boards, wings and any other bits and pieces that hang on the body, and undo as many of the body mounting bolts as you can find. These may go through rubber bushes on brackets from the chassis side-members — make a note of any that want renewing — or, on some coach-built bodies, the bottom rail of the body might sit straight on top of the chassis with rubber or canvas strips in between.

If this is the case, the chances are the body is held down by coach bolts — the sort with a domed head and a square underneath that is supposed to stop the bolt turning in the wood. Every one I have tried to undo on an old car has turned in the wood, and in some cases the nut could not be reached to split it. Sometimes it is possible to mount a hacksaw blade in a pad handle and slide it between body and frame, but most times it is not. I have seen some horrible examples of wood rails hacked about where someone has cut into the wood to try to get a spanner on the square. There is really no need for this. All you have to do is drill down the centre of the bolt and use an Easyout or similar stud remover; these are hardened taper taps with very coarse left hand threads. With the right sized drill they bite into the bolt like self-tapping screws. With the square on the top of the Easyout held in a tap wrench you can hold the bolt firmly enough to shear it off if the nut fails to move. Easyouts are also invaluable for their proper job of getting broken studs and screws out of castings without damage.

Most post war cars have the scuttle panel and firewall integral with the body, but there were one or two small production sports cars built in the vintage tradition with the firewall held on brackets to the chassis and the body

27 When tackling a complete rebuild invest in a good quality socket set such as this one by Spear and Jackson. It will pay for itself over again and, if taken care of, will last a lifetime

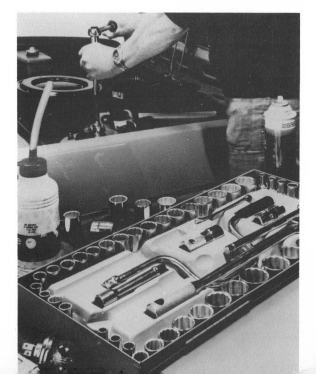

bolted to it. On a few the steering column and the instrument panel may be mounted on the firewall independent of the body. Whether you leave this on the chassis and unbolt the body from it, or unbolt the brackets and take the firewall off with the body, is a moot point.

It is very convenient to have the firewall on the chassis at the rebuilding stage, but old bodies tend to be on the weak side without it. My advice would be to leave it on while dismantling, and take it off the body later if you want it on the chassis while rebuilding. The more support you can give an old coachbuilt body at this stage the better, otherwise there is a very real danger that it will collapse like a house of cards when you lift it off.

Some people take the doors off before lifting the body. On a steel body in good condition it is a matter of choice, though I think it better, and essential on an old wood-framed body or an open one, to keep them on and shut during the lifting to help support the body frame. Unless you have facilities for lifting the body really high, take out the steering column, handbrake and gear lever if they stick up very much. The old electric wiring will be useless if it is rubber insulated, as it probably will be, so do not waste time and effort taking it off. Cut straight through the loom between the body and chassis. The cables inside the loom will be colour coded to help trace them if you need to, and when the body is off you can photograph the looms on the chassis as guide to rewiring.

Check that the body is quite free of the chassis by using a crowbar to ease it up ½ in (13 mm) or so at each mounting point. If all seems free it is ready to come off, but if it does not want to lift anywhere stop and find out why. You have probably forgotten a holding bolt somewhere. Make certain that all the linkages to the handbrake, the pipes on hydraulic brakes and all the wiring are undone and then you are ready to go.

In a commercial garage bodies are lifted off — or were when this type of car was common in commerical garages — by passing some ropes under them, or through the windows, and lifting with an overhead crane. The average domestic garage has neither the headroom nor a strong enough beam to take an overhead hoist, so a different method will have to be used.

Get hold of a couple of hefty lengths of timber, at least 4in x 3in (10cm x 8 cm) cross section, or a couple of steel scaffold poles. If the garage is wide enough these should be at least 4ft (1.2 m) longer than the body is wide. Then, because bodies without their chassis are awkward things to move about, take the car to the place where the body is going to sit till it is put back on the chassis. Use jacks and levers to lift each side of the body a couple of inches (about 5 cm) and run two more lengths of timber, about 4in (10cm) wide by 1in (2.5 cm) thick, under the body side rails along the chassis and tie them to the body. These will avoid a point loading on the body rails when you use the lifting poles.

Now jack the body up a little further and run the lifting poles across the chassis under the body, one just behind the windscreen pillar and one just at the front of the rear wheel arches.

You now want four good supports — old five gallon oil drums ballasted with sand or earth are quite good — and several strong helpers. Get your helpers to lift the body, one pole at a time — but not one side at a time — while you position the supports under the poles so that the body is held clear of the chassis. Provided the supports are far enough apart to clear the wheels you can now pull the chassis out from underneath; cover the body and leave it in peace till you have finished the chassis.

The first job on a chassis is a filthy dirty one, so wheel it out of the garage for its first clean down. If you can put it on a trailer and take it to a commerical garage for power cleaning so much the better. If you have to do the job yourself you will be doing battle with up to thirty years of accumulated oil, rust and general muck. Get some heavy industrial gloves, a stiff wire brush, a scraper, a couple of stiff bristle brushes, a couple of gallons of paraffin and set to. At this stage hand brushing and scraping is more effective than using a power wire brush. Paraffin is much cheaper than degreasing fluids so get as much muck off as possible at this first clean. Then clear away the mess, go over the chassis with 'Gunk' or similar degreaser, hose it down and dry it.

Now you are ready to knock out the shackle pins and wheel the axles away, leaving the bare chassis up on stands (or more ballasted oil drums) so that you can check it, get rid of the rust, and paint it. If you can find somewhere to work on the bare chassis, even if it is only an awning at the side of the garage, this is the best way to deal with it. If not, you will have to do as I did before I had two garages; leave the axles and wheels on, push the chassis out in the open to work on it and push it back under the body every time you pack up — or every time it rains.

If you are reasonably lucky the chassis will never have been in an accident bad enough to distort it, but it is possible that this has happened and you were unable to spot it when buying the car. On cars with separate front wings a previous owner may have repaired the obvious signs of a crash by fitting a new wing without having the chassis checked. The most usual form of distortion comes from a bang on one corner, usually the front, which either pushes one side-member back relative to the other so that the frame is lozenged, or bends the whole of the front of the frame over to one side. Even a skilled chassis straightener usually leaves some signs, and home attempts at straightening are more obvious. Look for ripples or waves in the top or bottom flanges of open channel frames and for the same things in the side walls of box sections.

If the chassis was straightened professionally it should still be true. The odd wave or ripple is not serious, provided the straightening has been done properly to get the suspension points true and none of the flanges or walls is actually buckled.

Even if your chassis does not appear to have been in an accident, it is worth checking the alignment while you have it stripped down. If you have a chassis alignment drawing in the manual it will give a horizontal datum line. You may not be able to set your chassis exactly in its horizontal datum, but get it as near as possible. Without a chassis repairer's jig frame you will not be able to take all the manufacturer's checking figures, but you will be looking for symmetry. Only if you find something wrong do the actual figures become important.

The first check is for twist. Use a spirit level to bring the front and rear crossmembers transversely horizontal, and try lifting each corner with a spring balance. The weight at each side at the front as the corner justs lifts clear of the support should be the same, and so should the weight at each rear corner. They will not be the same to within fractions and it is difficult to give an acceptable tolerance, but if there is a difference of, say, 10 lb (4.5 kg) or more it is worth checking further.

Most chassis twists come from distorted crossmembers. Open chassis frames of ladder construction are usually flexible enough to lie flat with slightly distorted crossmembers, but the weight check should show them up. Look for buckles in the flanges, or possibly a fractured weld on the end plate where the crossmember meets the side frame. If the crossmember is bolted or riveted to the side frame, take it out and check the weights again. If they are now acceptable, straighten the crossmember so that it fits without strain.

With a welded channel section crossmember try using a hammer and dolly to take out any flange buckling, and again check the weights. A box section chassis, particularly one with cruciform bracing, is much stiffer in torsion, and if there are serious weight discrepancies it is wise to get a professional to check it on his chassis jig.

The next checks, for longitudinal alignment, are quite critical. If they are seriously out the front and rear wheels will never run true to each other. You will get poor handling and short tire life. First establish a centre line down the middle of the frame. Mark the middle of each crossmember with a dab of white emulsion paint so that scribed marks will show, then measure carefully at the front and rear to mark the exact centre of these crossmembers. Measure from a definite point on the chassis, such as a suspension mounting, rather than just from the side of the frame, because the relationship between the front and rear suspensions is the important thing. What the ironwork does between them is less critical. Stretch a line tightly between these two centre marks and scribe the centre of the other crossmembers. Weight the line at each end, or tie it, so that there is a central datum line.

Now measure from the offside front suspension mounting to the front spring hanger of the rear spring on the nearside. Then repeat the measurement on the other side, front nearside to rear offside. The two measurements should be the same to within 3/8in (9.5 mm). I am not saying the frame is all right if there is exactly that difference, and all wrong if the difference is 13/32in (10.3 mm). Measurement with a steel tape over this sort of distance is not all that accurate, but the nearer the two measurements are the better, and 3/8in (9.5 mm) is a reasonable tolerance.

Then repeat the diagonal measurements across the rear spring mountings, front offside to rear nearside and front nearside to rear offside. The discrepancy between these two should be less, and they should agree to within ¼in (6.4 mm). In each case, the diagonals should cross on or very near to the centre line you established. In the case of a car with leaf springs at the front, repeat the measurements across the front spring mountings.

If these dimensions are within tolerance, it is a pretty safe bet that the chassis is true. If the readings do not agree, it could be that your measurement is suspect — within the limits of experimental error, is the let-out phrase — and the most likely place for error is sag in the tape where it was stretched between the measuring points. Make a second check by dropping a plumb line to the floor at the measuring points and marking the floor directly beneath them. Then measure with your tape lying flat on the floor. If the measurements are still way out it is time to call in the specialist with his alignment jig.

Assuming all is well you can carry on with the general inspection of the chassis. On a welded chassis check carefully round all the welds where the crossmembers join the side members to make sure none of the welds is starting to crack. If the car has been used heavily laden on uneven ground, e.g. on a farm, weld cracking is more likely than you might think.

On a riveted chassis check all the rivets for tightness. There are two ways of doing this, visually and with a hammer. In a visual check look for signs of movement between the chassis members. This will show up as a distinct mark round the flange where it has moved. As well as the frame members, check all the spring hangers and body mounting brackets.

Even if there is no sign of movement, go along with a hammer and tap each rivet in turn. If they are tight they will give a solid 'ding'. A loose one will give a 'dunk' sound. It is quite useless to try to tighten a loose rivet, and not very practical to try re-riveting in a home garage. If any are loose, drill them out and replace them with tight fitting high tensile bolts and nuts. There is no need to use engineers' fitted bolts, which are made to close tolerance on diameter. Ordinary high tensile bolts are fine, but they must be a good snug fit in the holes. If you cannot get a bolt which is a good fit, ream the hole out to the next size up.

Use a plain washer, not a spring washer, under the nut, tighten it firmly and cut the bolt off about a quarter of an inch from the nut. Use a ball pein hammer to peen over the end of the bolt like a rivet head and the nut will stay there for all time.

When you are satisfied the frame is true carry on with the cleaning and scraping. A wire brush or a sanding disc in a drill makes life a great deal easier here. Then treat the frame with rust killer, prime it and give it three coats of good quality paint. If any parts of the chassis show when the car is reassembled, use body filler to give a good surface. It is worth taking trouble with the chassis even though most of it will not show. It is the heart of the car, but once out of sight it is often out of mind. If you make a good job at this stage it will last for years without further attention other than hosing down.

Cars with integral chassis and bodies need a slightly different approach. Strip just about everything off the body shell so that you can get at every part to check for corrosion.

Working on the underside of a body shell when it is close to the floor is a miserable job. It is worthwhile making, or having a carpenter make, a pair of strong trestles, so that you can get the body up to a reasonable working height. The alternative is to mount the body on lower supports over a pit. If you have a pit in your garage it is a luxury you will bless time and time again, but few of us have, so the body trestles make a good substitute. They need not be too high; 2½ft — 3ft (80 cm or so) is about right. This will allow you to sit on the floor underneath instead of lying flat on your back, but leave the body low enough for you to climb in. Please make sure the trestles are strong enough to hold the body with a good safety margin, and as an extra precaution rope or chain the body to them.

Make the same diagonal checks as on a bare chassis. Here you will have to drop plumb lines down to the floor, because trying to measure along the underside of an integral body shell is almost impossible. If there are discrepancies it is most unlikely that the body shell is twisted. They are immensely stiff. It is more likely that a bump at some time has pushed one of the suspension mountings out of line. Check very carefully for any signs of ripples along the floor of the body at the rear, down the inner front wings and on the main

◄ 28   After checking and cleaning down, the chassis should be primed and undercoated and given several top coats of a good quality enamel, not the cheap paint often sold as chassis black

29   With a separate   ►
chassis check measurements can be made direct, but with an integral chassis and body you have to drop plumb lines to a level floor to check the major suspension mountings for distortion

front crossmember.

Accident repair on integral bodies is carried out by pulling the shell back into line with powerful hydraulic pullers. Provided the suspension and steering mountings are all in the correct position relative to each other, odd ripples across the floor do not matter. The repairer has done his job properly, and he cannot get rid of them all. But ripples combined with discrepancies in measurements calls for more accurate checking on a jig.

If your measurements do not agree and there are no signs of bent metal having been pulled back into shape, search carefully for any peculiar weld lines where there should not be any. It is possible — just possible — that you have bought a 'cut and shut' job made up from two halves of different body shells, each of which has been in an accident but at different ends.

If you are unlucky enough to find this, and it is a practice very much frowned upon in the repair trade, it is definitely a case for checking by a competent repairer both for alignment and for structural strength. It does not necessarily mean that your car cannot be used, but it needs very careful checking.

Once again, assuming all is well, carry on with the scraping and brushing and rust killing. If you find parts rusted too thin for comfort, this is the time to cut them out and weld in new sections. For many cars you can get pre-shaped body sections either from the makers or from specialist firms, but if not you will have to make them or get a good sheet metal worker to make them for you.

It is going to take a long, long time. If you can get the shell grit blasted it saves you literally days, but if not you will just have to persevere. It is the most important job you will ever do in the restoration of a chassis-less car and it has got to last. Persevere, and at last you will be able to spray it with primer, breathe a sigh of relief, and start on the job of restoring the individual components.

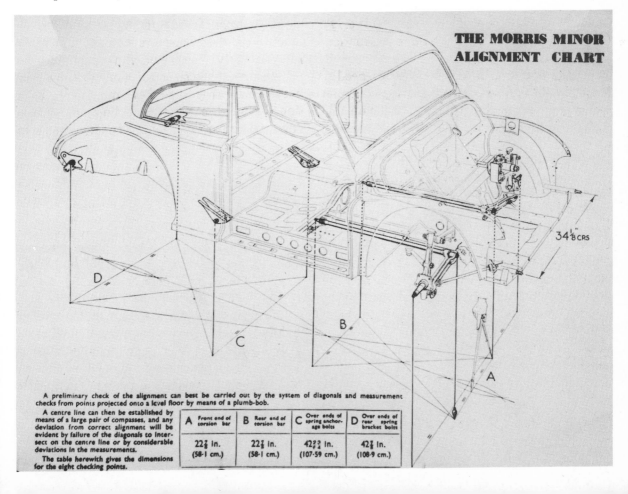

THE MORRIS MINOR ALIGNMENT CHART

A preliminary check of the alignment can best be carried out by the system of diagonals and measurement checks from points projected onto a level floor by means of a plumb-bob.

A centre line can then be established by means of a large pair of compasses, and any deviation from correct alignment will be evident by failure of the diagonals to intersect on the centre line or by considerable deviations in the measurements.

The table herewith gives the dimensions for the eight checking points.

A Front end of torsion bar	B Rear end of torsion bar	C Over ends of spring anchorage bolts	D Over ends of rear spring bracket bolts
22⅞ In. (58·1 cm.)	22⅞ In. (58·1 cm.)	42¾ In. (107·59 cm.)	42⅞ In. (108·9 cm.)

=8=
OVERHAULING THE SUSPENSION

When the chassis frame is completed (or, in the case of an integral body, when you have finished any underside repairs), has been painted and given a coat of good sealer, it is a good time to make the car mobile again by overhauling and fitting the suspension.

Taking leaf springs first, you will have noticed, or should have, if any were on the weak side when you bought the car. If they were, do not waste time on them. Clean them down and send them to a spring specialist. He will reset the leaves to their proper camber, fit new clips and send them back as good as new.

Spring firms which specialise in restoration work will probably have all the data necessary to overhaul your springs if you give them the car make, model and year. But just in case, it does no harm to find the figures from the car maker or, if the maker is no longer in business, from the appropriate one-make club. Quote these figures when sending the springs away and then there is no chance of getting them set wrongly. The necessary figures are the free camber i.e. the curve of the spring when it is off the car, usually given as the distance between the spring base and a line joining the eyes, and the rate per inch or centimetre of deflection.

If the springs do not appear to have settled to any extent, take them apart yourself and give them a good clean. The leaves are held together by a centre bolt and by two or more clips along the length. It is best to finish one of a pair of springs before taking them both apart; then you have a pattern as to how many leaves go each side of the main leaf. It is easy to get some of the little stub leaves of some springs in the wrong position.

With most springs the individual leaves are cambered more than the finished spring when it is all bolted together, and the centre bolt is under considerable tension. Never attempt to undo it without having the spring clamped in a vice to hold the leaves while the bolt tension is released.

The clips also hold several of the leaves together, so take them off first. In most cases the U-shaped body of the clip is joined by a rivetted rod, sometimes with a roller. You cannot salvage this rod, so take it out by cutting or grinding off one end, and replace it with a high tensile bolt and nut when you rebuild. The body of the clip is usually rivetted to one of the leaves, and it should be firm. If it is not, peen the flat side of the rivet to tighten it.

When the nut is off the centre bolt, release the vice slowly to let the pack of leaves expand, and keep your feet out of the way. Very often at least one leaf drops to the floor when you undo the vice and it can give your toes a nasty bang.

In some springs there is zinc, rubber or plastic interleaving. This can often be saved and used again but, if the clips have been loose and the leaves fretting, the ends of the interleaving will probably be chewed. Most spring specialists will be able to supply new interleaving, or at least the material from which to cut it.

Nearly all the old springs I have taken apart needed a new centre bolt. Even if it was perfectly tight to start with it will have stretched over the years, or the interleaving will have compressed so that the leaves will have moved slightly. The slightest sign of ridging in the shank of the bolt means it needs replacing. You may be able to get a replacement from a spring specialist, but if not get a local engineering works to turn you one to pattern from a standard fitted bolt that has a close tolerance on diameter and is high tensile. The head, usually a plain cheese head, must be a snug fit in the hole in the spring pad on the axle. If this seating hole has worn because the U bolts have been slack, drill it out to the next size up.

Give all the leaves a clean with a power wire brush and examine them for signs of digging in from the ends of adjacent leaves. There is almost certain to be some, but a little is of no consequence unless there are sharp ridges. These could be stress raisers, so smooth them down with a grinder. If the wear is too deep there is nothing that can be done except to replace the leaf or spring. Grinding out deep wear only thins the spring and makes it more liable to break. The only leaf of vital concern here is the main one. It locates the axle on most designs, and any sharp indentations could lead to fracture with the result that the axle would be free to wander. The stress on the other leaves where adjacent leaf ends touch is not very high unless the spring goes into violent rebound.

One place where there might be trouble from worn leaves is on slipper mounted springs where the ends bear in bronze bushes instead of finishing in a normal eye. With some designs you can dress the ends of the leaves with a grinder and let the two halves of the bush together to get a good fit. With others a new main leaf and bushes may be needed.

The fit of the bearing where it locates the spring sideways is important. On rear axles which are located on Panhard rods and radius arms, the only duty of the slipper end is to take the weight, and a good fit in the bush is less important.

On more usual eye-ended springs the bushes will be either rubber Silentblock type, or bronze with hardened steel shackle pins. New rubber bushes are obtainable in a wide range of sizes from Silentbloc and Metalastik, but if bronze bushes and steel pins are worn and replacements are not available, they will have to be made. The pins should be made from a good quality tough case hardening steel. Some shackles were a forged U shape, and these are difficult and costly to have forged, but they can be replaced by separate pins and plates.

The sideways fit of the spring is important if you want the car to have good roadholding. The locating end of the spring, usually the front end, should be shimmed to a close fit in its bracket. The shackle plates, where they hang on the chassis, should be free to move without any side play. Then the springs should be mounted on the axle and lifted between the shackle plates, where they should be shimmed to good sideways fit.

Most longitudinal leaf springs will go up without much effort, but transverse leaf springs, like those on early post-war Fords, need a spring spreader to take them off and put them back. Make an effort to get a proper spreader. Makeshift arrangements of clamps and levers can be dangerous, because there is a great deal of energy wrapped up in a spring which is under tension. On this type of suspension make sure the bearings of the A-frame, or links, which locate the axle are in good condition. Even a little free play here can give the car peculiar road habits.

Rear suspension dampers, or shock absorbers as they always used to be called, were not called upon to contribute to the roadholding on early post-war cars so much as they were later. Even so, the car will still fail its roadworthiness test if they are not in good working order. On later cars with softer, longer travel springs, poor shock absorbers can make it wander as well as roll. Nowadays most dampers are telescopic, but in the fifties and early sixties there was a variety of vane and piston designs. A few telescopics take apart for rebushing, but the majority are sealed and the only cure is to replace. Vane and piston types nearly always take apart for repair. There is a fair chance the pistons and bores will be in serviceable condition unless they have been operating without fluid for years, but the bushes for the arms often wear and the valves become clogged and seized. Some designs have replaceable bushes for the arms, but other arms bear directly in the body of the damper. If this is worn, the damper is useless.

If the bearing surface of the arm pin is worn, it can be built up by welding or metal spraying, but this is only worth while if the unit is a rare one and replacements are not available. There are several companies which specialise in reconditioning dampers, and it is worth while trying them before going to the trouble and expense of reconditioning them yourself. Many offer units on an exchange basis.

If the damper is almost unworn, and the seals are in good condition, it may only need

cleaning out. You will have to disturb the valve setting to clean it, so mark the valve position and count the number of turns necessary to unscrew it. The actual pressure rate can sometimes be found in a manual, but it really needs a special jig to set it properly. The actual setting is relatively unimportant provided it controls the suspension movement. Many designs of damper could have the rate varied by a tele-control on the road to suit the car's load. Other types are adjustable, by using a screwdriver through the filling hole. When the car is on the road adjust them to give good control, and make sure that the damping rate is the same, as near as you can judge, on either side of the axle. If it is different you will have a different rate of roll left and right, which makes the car tiring to drive as well as a possible danger.

When it comes to dealing with independent suspensions there was such a variety of designs in the fifties and sixties that to try to go through them all would be impossible here. A workshop manual is invaluable both for checking for worn parts and setting up the suspension geometry.

However, there are some general points on which I can give guidance on checking whether or not the suspension is in serviceable condition. The first thing to check is for wear, and this is not always as simple as it might seem. The coil spring, leaf spring, torsion bar or whatever is often under either compression or tension or torsion, even when the suspension is unloaded by jacking up the chassis, and this

30   Torsion bars are sometimes set up by altering the position of the arm on splines or, as on this Morris, by a vernier-plate fixing for the arm

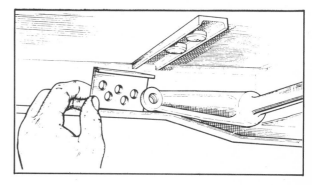

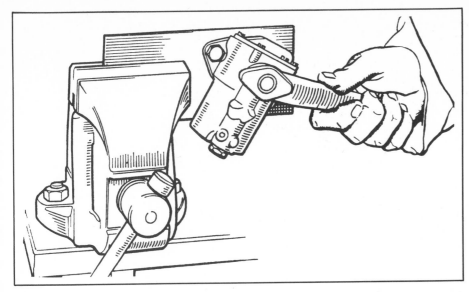

31 Testing a lever-type shock damper by bolting it to a plate held firmly in a vice. Just trying it in two hands is not good enough — you can miss rough spots in the action

tends to mask wear. The best time to check is before the suspension is taken off the car, because the weight of the car can be used to help find the wear points.

Some people try to test for wear by jacking the front of the car up under the centre of the front crossmember and rocking the wheels about. This, particularly with coil suspensions, is quite the wrong way to go about it. The compression in the coil springs holds the suspension arms apart and masks the wear in the bushes.

The proper way is to support the weight of the car by putting stands under the frame and jacking up the suspension with a jack under that part of the linkage which is directly attached to the stub axle, so that the suspension is working exactly as it would were the weight of the car on the wheel. Do not jack up under the hub. You need to jack up just enough to start the spring compressing and take the suspension off its bump stop, but not so much that the jack is supporting the weight of the car. This must remain firmly on the stands.

Now get a long crowbar and try to lever the suspension up and down and from side to side look for movement in the bushes. With bronze bushes you can often see the movement, but

with rubber bushes it is not so easy to spot. A fairly sure way is to get a helper to wield the crowbar while you put your hand over each bearing joint. It is surprising how small an amount of free play you can feel this way. On rubber-bushed suspensions do not be entirely satisfied, even if you can feel no movement. When rubber bushes get old they tend to squash out from their housing, and though movement may be hard to feel, the rubber will be too flexible and may let the suspension wander on the road. A small amount of belling out at the ends is nothing to worry about — many rubber bushes belled out slightly when they were put in — but if the end of the bush is swollen and has gone soggy or cracked it is time to renew it.

In the immediate post-war years, when designers were experimenting with independent front suspensions, there was a variety of designs, many of which were something of a compromise in that the designers kept a very similar king pin to the one they had on pre-war beam axles but linked this to an independent suspension layout. Study the suspension very closely before you start to take it apart. With some designs you can support the frame and let the suspension hang to take all the residual compression out of the springs. With others there is considerable residual compression even when the suspension is down on its rebound stops. This is the case with just about all designs of coil spring suspension, and could be the case with some designs of transverse leaf spring and torsion bars.

This residual compression, or torsion, has to be let down before any parts of the linkage are undone or the spring could take charge in a most dangerous way. With many coil spring layouts the plate at the top carries a hook, or an eye, which sticks down into the centre of the coil. The bottom plate has a hole in it, and the tool for taking the spring out consists of a long threaded rod with a hook at the top, a substantial circular plate to bear on the spring bottom plate, and a large nut. The compression of the spring is taken by hooking the tool in the top plate and screwing up the nut till the pressure plate on the tool is hard up against the bottom spring plate. Then the bolts are taken out of the bottom plate and the tool gradually undone to let the spring down.

On a few designs two of the bolts holding the spring bottom plate can be taken out and replaced with much longer bolts. Then the other bolts are removed and the spring let down by undoing the long ones a few turns each at a time. Some Austin, Morris and related suspensions can be dealt with in this way, but consult the manual, or check with the manufacturer's service department, to make sure you get long enough bolts. The pounds per inch (or kilograms per centimetre) of front suspension coil springs is high, and even ¼in (6 mm) compression will pack enough energy to take your fingers off if it flies free.

As a safety precaution it is an excellent plan to pass a chain, or a couple of turns of stout rope, through the coil of the spring and round the chassis or suspension member. Then, should you be unlucky enough to have a spring jump, it will stay with the car instead of flying off to injure anyone standing nearby.

I do not want to frighten you about front suspensions, but nasty accidents can often be avoided by taking simple safety precautions, and by thinking about what you are doing before you start undoing nuts.

When the coil spring suspended T series MG first appeared, the maker's recommended way of taking it down was to support the car on stands, put a jack under the coil spring and undo the top ball joint of the linkage. Then the

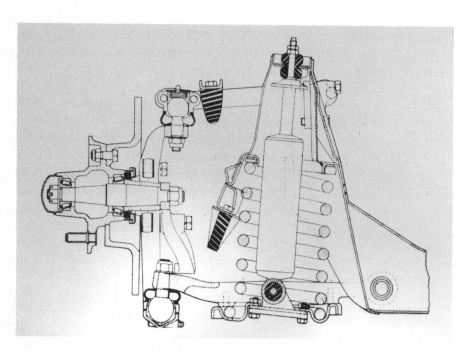

32   A typical front suspension layout, in this case a Jaguar, using wishbones and ball joints. Note how the whole thing would fly apart if either of the ball joints were undone without a spring compressor to hold the main spring. The compressor takes the place of the telescopic damper after its bottom plate is taken off

jack was slowly lowered to expand the spring.

With a good heavy trolley jack this is still a good method provided the engine is in the car. The little MGs are so light that if you try it without the weight of the engine to hold the car down you might find, as have some people to their cost, that when the top ball joint is undone the energy in the spring lifts the car body off the stands. In any case, I would not advise this method with a small bottle hydraulic jack, even less with most of today's rather flimsy screw scissors jacks. If you are going to use this method make sure the jack is heavy and not liable to topple over. Otherwise play it safe and use a spring compressor.

When the spring is out and you are taking the linkage apart be careful about any spacer washers or shims. Often these are used to set the camber and castor angles so they must go back in exactly the same places, at least for the initial reassembly. They might possibly need altering after rebushing, but that can be done later with a proper alignment jig.

The suspension may have bronze bushes, rubber bushes, threaded bushes, ball joints or a combination of any of these. In some cases the arms of the dampers form part of the linkage. Sometimes, but not very often, you may find bearings which are adjustable for wear. More often they seem to be adjustable

but are not. A case in point is the bottom ball joint on some Jaguar suspensions. The cap over the ball is shimmed, but this is only for adjusting the initial clearance on the ball joint to allow for manufacturing tolerances. You must never take out shims to compensate for wear on the ball or in the cup.

Most worn suspension bearings have to be replaced, and the same applies to worn king pins, bushes and thrust washers, either on independent or beam axle layouts. King pins are usually held in the axle by tapered cotters which can sometimes be almost impossible to shift. It is not advisable to apply too much heat to loosen them in case you upset the heat treatment of the axle. If the cotter absolutely refuses to be driven out, file the thread off flush, centre punch the end of it and drill through with a small pilot drill. Follow this with the largest diameter drill the cotter will take. This will leave just a shell which should punch out easily.

King pin bushes, and some bronze suspension bushes, have to be reamered in line after pressing in. You can do this with a set of parallel adjustable reamers and pilots, but this is not the sort of kit everyone has in the garage, so it is better to put the job out to someone. Some bushes have to be drilled for oilways after they are pressed in, so if you put the job out check that this has been done and try an oil gun on the nipple before you put the pin in to make sure all the oilways are free.

Provided you put all the shims back in the correct position you should be very close to the correct castor and camber angles on bronze or rubber bushed front suspensions. Threaded bushes are a different proposition. With these the castor, and sometimes the camber too,

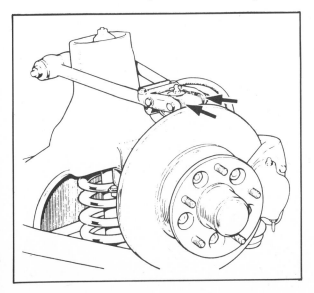

33   On some suspensions, the castor angle is adjusted by shims either side of the top wishbone mounting

is set by screwing the bush in or out of its threaded pin. The manual will give the approximate setting dimensions, but on all suspension rebuilds have the geometry checked on accurate alignment equipment as soon as possible. Wrong castor will give you terrible steering, and wrong camber will wear your tires out in no time at all.

On beam axles with leaf springs the camber is set by the machining of the stub axle and usually cannot be altered, but the castor depends on the set of the springs. The way to adjust the castor is by wedges between the spring and the axle pad. To increase the castor angle, tilt the bottom of the king pin forward so that the thick end of the wedge goes at the back on the more usual overslung spring. I cannot remember any post-war design, other than the Willys jeep, with springs underslung beneath the front axle, but if you find one the opposite applies.

With all rubber bushes, whether in the ends of leaf springs or on independent linkages, leave the final tightening of the bolts till the weight of the car is back on its wheels. That way you tighten the bush in a neutral position with the car standing level. If you tighten it with the suspension hanging loose the bush will be under torsion when the car is standing level and will have a short life.

34 Using a tapered guide funnel to press a rubber bush into a shock damper arm

35 A tapered guide pin is used to fit the connecting link once the bush is in the arm

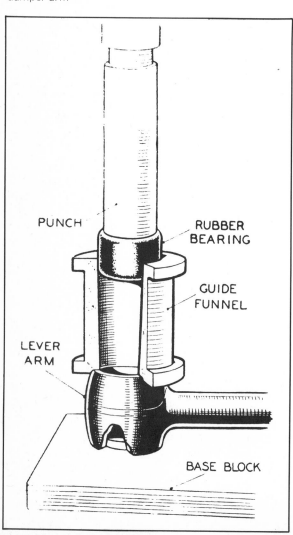

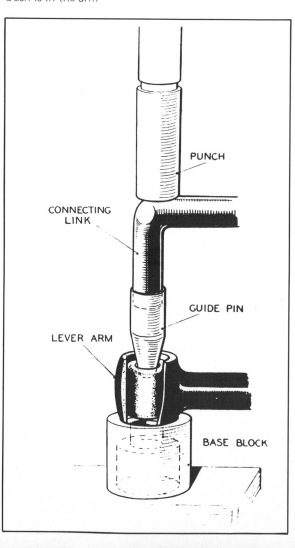

=9=
GOOD BRAKES

In the late forties and early fifties British cars were going through a transition period in brake design. Some makers kept their chassis design much the same as their 1939 models with mechanical brakes. Others (such as Morris) had used hydraulic brakes for years, and yet others used a combination of hydraulic and mechanical linkage.

Dealing first with full hydraulic brakes, start by draining out all the old fluid. It may come out looking in good condition, but more likely it will look like a brown soup. In either case it will almost certainly contain dissolved water because brake fluid readily absorbs water vapour from the atmosphere. This water can turn to steam with the heat of the brakes, and then the pedal can go right down to the floor in the condition known as vapour lock.

A word of warning here for those who didn't know already; brake fluid is an excellent paint stripper, so keep it well away from the bodywork and throw away any rags used for cleaning brake parts so that there is no chance of their being used later on bodywork.

To drain the system, open each bleed nipple in turn after putting a piece of rubber or plastic tube on it, and pump the pedal till no more will come out. This will get rid of most of the fluid, though there will still be some left

in the cylinders and pipes so watch your eyes if you have to lie under the car to take things off.

There are a number of designs of master cylinder, some with separate reservoirs and some with the reservoir incorporated in the cylinder. Either way the principle is the same, and the chances of getting new seals are good because they were almost all standard sizes. It may not be possible to get a repair kit for the master cylinder of your 1951 Grandmobile straight off the shelf, but the same size seals will have been used on other cars for which kits can be bought. Spares secretaries of one-make clubs are noted for their knowledge in cases such as this. In the USA replacement master cylinders and wheel cylinders, as well as repair kits for master cylinders and wheel cylinders, are available for all post-Second World War American cars from J.C. Whitney & Co., 1917-19 Archer Avenue, Box 8410, Chicago, Illinois 60680.

When you get the master cylinder off give the outside a good scrub off. Dirt is the big enemy of hydraulic systems, so the cleaner the cylinder is before the insides are exposed the better. Mineral oils, and that includes paraffin, attack the rubber seals in cylinders, so keep clear of them. I usually give the components a dry scrub with an old wire brush to get off as much dry dirt as possible, and then wash the outside off with methylated spirit or with the special cleaning fluid that Girling agents supply.

When dismantling the cylinder watch carefully the order in which all the seals, plungers and springs come out. One component in some cylinders which is likely to be put back the wrong way is a small dished washer. Make sure it goes back with the dish facing the same way it came out.

Wash all the parts off in cleaning fluid and look carefully at the seals. If they are firm and not sticky, and the lip of the seal is not damaged or furred, then (if the cylinder was working before it was stripped) the chances are they are fit for further service. But if the lip of the seal is rubbed, or if the rubber feels soft and sticky then, even if they were working, the seals should be renewed. Except in rare cases where new seals are unobtainable I always play it safe and fit new ones as a matter of course.

Similar remarks apply to the wheel cylinders of drum brakes — I will deal with discs in a moment — and here save carefully any spreader springs or star shaped washers you find. In a complete repair kit there may be new ones, but if you have to hunt around for the correct size of seals you are unlikely to find all new washers and springs.

The bores of the cylinders may look corroded. If they are indeed badly corroded you will have to look for better ones, either new or secondhand, but much of the apparent corrosion in brake cylinders will turn out to be old dried out and baked on brake fluid. This can be cleaned out by shaving it off with the blade of a pen knife or, much better, use a Flex-Hone. These are cylindrical brushes made from hard nylon bristle with a globule of abrasive at the end of each bristle. They are made in various sizes to fit almost everything from brake cylinders to engine bores. They fit in an ordinary electric drill, and to use them you push the end of the brush up against the mouth of the cylinder, start the drill going and run the brush up and down the bore of the cylinder for about 10 seconds. If it is pulled out while it is still rotating it gives a clean finish without scratches.

A lubricant must be used with Flex-Hones, and though for engine bores mineral oil is used, it should not be used on brake cylinders because even a trace of it left in the bore would attack the new rubber seals. Use brake fluid after cleaning the bores to make sure every trace of grit is cleaned out. Despite what you might hear about not honing brake cylinders, Flex-Hones are completely safe provided they are used for about 10 seconds only.

Before putting new rubber seals in the

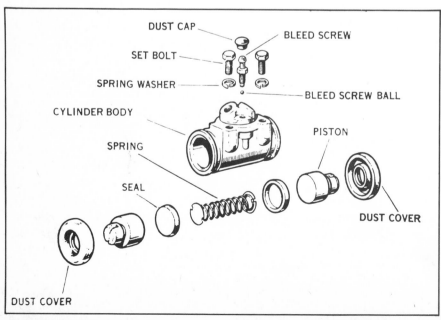

36   When cleaning a wheel cylinder make sure the pistons are free in the cylinder body. Aluminium ones often corrode after standing

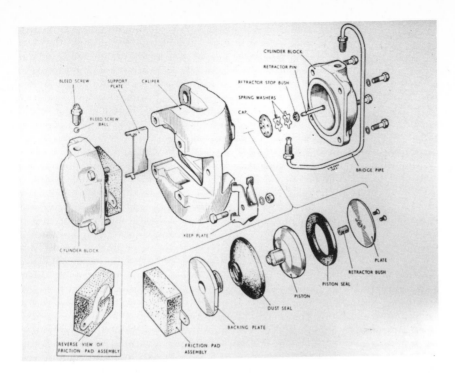

Labels in figure: BLEED SCREW · SUPPORT PLATE · CALIPER · CYLINDER BLOCK · RETRACTOR PIN · RETRACTOR STOP BUSH · SPRING WASHERS · CAP · BLEED SCREW BALL · BRIDGE PIPE · CYLINDER BLOCK · KEEP PLATE · PLATE · RETRACTOR BUSH · PISTON SEAL · PISTON · DUST SEAL · BACKING PLATE · REVERSE VIEW OF FRICTION PAD ASSEMBLY · FRICTION PAD ASSEMBLY

37　An exploded view of a disc brake, an early Dunlop design. In some cases you may find the plate retaining the piston seal is riveted to the piston instead of held by screws. In that case the seal has to be well soaked in brake fluid or special grease — NOT ordinary grease — and carefully stretched over the plate

cylinders, stand them in a tray of brake fluid to make sure they are thoroughly wet, smear a little brake fluid in the cylinder bore and push the seals in carefully so as not to damage the lips.

Disc brake hydraulic wheel cylinders work on a similar principle to those in drum brakes except that they are a much larger diameter and are self adjusting. The clearance between the pad and the disc is small, and the piston in the cylinder hardly moves to apply the brakes. It is more a case of the seal flexing than moving along the bore of the cylinder until the self adjuster moves.

For this reason, and because they are more exposed to the elements, disc brake wheel-cylinders are more prone to corrosion. If the protective rubber boots are damaged, or not properly in place, the part of the bore between the piston seal and the pad can become badly rusted. This sometimes leads to leaking cylinders for no apparent reason. The reason is that the adjuster moves the piston forwards till the seal meets a corroded part of the bore where it cannot make a good seal.

This part of the cylinder is also prone to becoming coated with baked-on deposits, not from brake fluid which has leaked, but from the grease which was used when the cylinder was assembled. This grease is a special one and is chemically the same as brake fluid, but thicker. Girling agents stock it, and it is the only grease that should be used anywhere near rubber seals.

Changing the seals on some disc wheel-cylinders can be tricky. The amount of seal protruding outside the diameter of the piston is small, and if you are not very careful you can nip the edge of the seal when putting the piston in the bore. It helps if the seal and bore are thoroughly wetted with brake fluid.

When pushing the piston and seal in, the chances are that the seal will slip in one side first. This is the danger point. To avoid damaging the last part of the seal as it goes in, ease it down with a smooth blunt edge while pressing on the piston. I have found the handle of an old spoon very useful for this job. Before you put the protective rubber boot on, smear the inside of the exposed cylinder with the special grease to protect it from corrosion.

On many designs of disc brakes it is possible to take the cylinders off without disturbing the calipers, but on others you have to take the whole assembly off. If this is the case, watch for any centralising shims put in to keep the mouth of the caliper central about the disc. They must go back in the same place.

Drums and discs which have seen long service become ridged. If they have been standing for years they rust, and if drums have been left for years with the handbrake on they sometimes go oval, all of which are reasons for having the surfaces skimmed on a lathe. Trust this skimming only to a company which knows what it is doing. It is possible for a lathe operator who does not realise what he is doing to take off so much metal that the drum or disc is weakened. If possible obtain from the manual, or the car maker, the maximum allowable inside drum diameter or the minimum disc thickness. If machining within these limits does not give a smooth surface the drum or disc needs replacing.

The shoes on drum brakes will probably need relining or the pads on disc brakes need renewing, this being the case if they are soaked in oil as well as if they are worn. Boiling linings in detergent to get rid of oil is seldom a success. If new pads or linings are available from the car's agents there is no difficulty, but you could be in trouble with older or rare cars. Unfortunately some parts shops offer pattern linings or pads which come from abroad, and which may be the correct dimension but may or may not be the correct friction material. The correct material will be hard or soft depending on the design of the brakes, and different materials should be used in cast and pressed steel drums.

If it is not possible to obtain genuine replacement linings or pads, write to the company which made the brakes for your car, or to any reputable brake lining manufacturer, quoting the make, year and chassis number of your car. If they cannot supply linings off the shelf they will be able to tell the correct type of friction material, and possibly suggest a current lining from their range which will fit or which can be modified to fit. I always tread unbranded linings with caution, particularly if they are considerably cheaper than nationally known brands.

Linings for drum brakes will be either riveted or bonded to the shoes. I prefer bonded linings because there is no danger of their wearing down to the rivets, which scores the drum. They should, however, be renewed when they wear to the point where a rivet would be exposed.

38   Before taking off the drums, the adjusters may have to be slackened off because of the ridge

There is nothing wrong with riveted linings, and many cars from the fifties and sixties have them as standard. Bonding cannot be done at home, but there is no reason why you should not rivet linings yourself. Chisel the old lining off and clean the shoes, and make sure the new linings bed down properly on the face of the shoe and that the rivet holes line up. Start riveting at the centre of the lining and work to each end. That way there is no danger of the centre of the lining standing proud and cracking when it is riveted down.

After riveting, heel and toe the linings, that is chamfer the leading and trailing edges, fit them to the backplate and try the drums on. The linings will need bedding in, and you can help this by spinning the drum, putting the brakes on and looking to see how much of the lining has been in contact with the drum. At first you will find it touches only in a few high spots, so ease these down with a file and carry on trying and filing till you get contact over most of the lining area. Half an hour's work can achieve what would take hundreds of brake applications on the road.

With mechanical brakes dismantle and clean the expander units inside the drums. Some designs of twin leading shoe mechanical brake were quite complicated, so before you take the linkage off take a photograph or make a sketch of it for future reference. On some Girling mechanical brakes the expander unit is free to float on the backplate. It may not appear to float because it has seized, but you can recognise the type because the holes in the backplate are elongated, the nuts will be either split-pinned or self locking and there will be double spring washers under them. The idea is that on a leading and trailing shoe brake the lining shoe wears faster, so the expander is free to move as the brakes are applied to keep the unevenly wearing shoes central in the drum.

It must not be so loose that it slides about. When the backplate and housing are clean,

and the expander is bolted on with a smear of high melting point grease, the nuts should be tightened so that the housing resists hand pressure but will move if given a light tap with a mallet. When this type of brake is assembled it should be applied hard several times during adjustment to make sure the shoes are centralised.

Mechanical brakes will be applied by either rod or cable. Cables should be taken off, washed out in paraffin and lubricated. Some have a nipple on the outer casing to take a grease gun. I prefer to use heavy gear oil in the gun, rather than grease, which tends to cake and make the cable stiff in cold weather. If there is no nipple, hang the cable up and make a cup of Plasticine over the top to make a reservoir of oil and let the oil run through till it comes out the other end. If the inner cable shows any sign of shredding the whole cable needs replacing. Do not be tempted to unwind one broken strand. The rest will soon follow.

Cable brakes are notoriously difficult to balance. When I worked in a garage we used to have a tool we called the 'spare man'. This was an adjustable length of steel tube which we put between the brake pedal and the seat frame and lengthened till the brakes just started to come on. Then we played with the adjusters at each wheel to get the same amount of drag, lengthened the 'spare man' to put the brakes on harder and repeated the process till the drums would no longer turn by hand. Even then we had to make final adjustments on the road test. Adjusting by road test alone can be misleading because you can get an apparently balanced brake system which is only balanced diagonally across the car. This can be dangerous in the wet, so try to get some form of 'spare man' even if it is a length of timber and some packing blocks.

Rod brakes are easier in that they have some form of compensating trees on the axle, sometimes called swivel trees or swingle trees. These

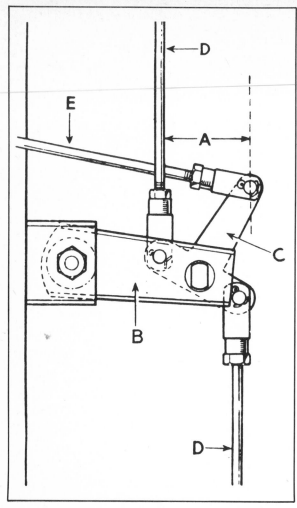

39   Setting up the swivel tree on rod brakes. B is the main arm of the tree, C the swivel arm, D the rods to the drums and E the rod along the chassis. Sometimes the setting is given as a dimension such as A, but if not, set the swivel arm to pull towards its point of maximum leverage

ments are not available it is quite easy to make new ones from mild steel plate of case-hardening quality or tool steel if you have it. After they are filed to size they should be hardened. In the case of mild steel heat it to a cherry red and roll it in case-hardening powder. If you have used tool steel harden and temper to a light blue.

When it comes to setting up the linkages on rod brakes, or on hybrid mechanical-hydraulic systems, there were some quite ingenious arrangements of links and bars in the fifties, but they all used the same principles. The first is that if the pull of a rod is going to be divided equally the arm or balance lever which divides the pull must be free to float on its bearing so it takes up its own position. The second is that all relay levers and arms must be arranged so that they are pulled towards their position of maximum leverage.

If you have a manual it will give measured setting dimensions for the various rods and levers. If not, start at the brake drums and work towards the pedal. Adjust the shoes so they are hard on, then set the lengths of the axle cross rods so that the two arms of the compensating tree are angled at about 15° to 20° towards the wheel to which they are connected. You will find that this brings the control arm about the same angle either backwards or forwards of the axle depending whether you are working on the back or front brakes. You will see that as the control rod pulls the compensating tree all the levers

are arranged so that each brake is applied against the reaction from the brake at the other end of the axle, so they should both exert the same braking force.

In time these compensating trees wear. Some can be rebushed, some cannot. The ones without bushes can sometimes be reconditioned by reamering out the hole about which the tree pivots and fitting a larger bolt, or by fitting bushes, but care must be taken to make sure the tree is not weakened.

All the yokes and clevis pins on the ends of the rods must be checked for wear. The pins will probably need renewing, but if the holes in the yokes are worn oval they can be filled with weld or braze and drilled out to size.

The ratchet, or both the ratchet and pawl, on the handbrake may be worn. If replace-

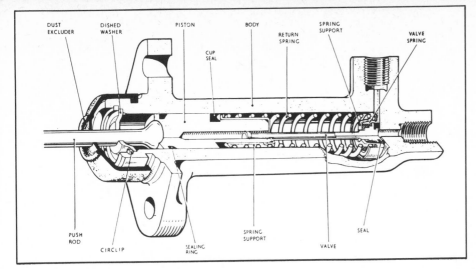

DUST EXCLUDER DISHED WASHER PISTON CUP SEAL BODY RETURN SPRING SPRING SUPPORT VALVE SPRING

PUSH ROD CIRCLIP SEALING RING SPRING SUPPORT VALVE SEAL

40 A cross section through a typical master cylinder (in this case by Girling) with a separate reservoir

move towards the point of maximum leverage.

Repeat the same idea of pulling towards the maximum leverage all the way through to the pedal. You may find that part of the linkage, often immediately behind the pedal, is a push tube instead of a pull rod. If this is the case the tube must be set up so that it has a slight clearance to stop the brakes binding. You will find a number of pull-off springs. The more complicated the linkage, the more springs, as a general rule. If any of these is broken you can fit new ones easily — most parts shops keep a box of assorted sizes — and as long as the pressure is similar it does not have to be exact. You may find, either near the base of the pedal or at one of the balance links, that the curved ends of two levers butt against one another, usually with curved ends to allow them to roll as the angle changes. Check the rounded ends for wear, and if you do not have the manufacturer's settings set them to have slight freedom with a minimum of clearance and coat them with grease.

Somewhere in a rod handbrake linkage will be a slotted link to allow the main brakes to be applied without putting on the handbrake rods. As a general rule, the link should be set so that the handbrake is fully on after four or five notches of the handbrake lever.

As I said earlier, some cars from the fifties have hybrid systems, partly hydraulic and partly mechanical, usually with the hydraulics to the front. In these systems the master cylinder often formed part of the mechanical linkage to the rear wheels. Should the hydraulics fail, the pedal went partly down till the master cylinder acted as a solid link to give mechanical braking to the rear wheels.

Setting up these systems is quite straightforward once you analyse what happens when the brake pedal is pushed down, and set the hydraulics before tackling the mechanical side. If the mechanical part is set first you might find, when the master cylinder is applying the front brakes, that the linkage to the rear is not set up to give a proper leverage.

Heavier cars usually have a servo in the system. Those on Rolls-Royce and Bentley are special to those cars, and service information is available from Rolls-Royce. Other cars use proprietary servos made by one of the brake manufacturers. Though they differ in design they all work on a similar principle. The master cylinder operated by the brake pedal feeds a second cylinder on the servo, and when pressure is applied it opens a valve in the servo. The main chamber of the servo contains a diaphragm or piston which is pulled in one direction by the chamber being connected, often via a reservoir, to the depression in the inlet manifold. Though they are commonly called vacuum servos there is nothing like a full vacuum in the chamber.

When the valve operated by the pedal master

cylinder opens, it allows air at atmospheric pressure in the chamber to exert pressure on the piston or diaphragm. This presses through a rod or linkage of some sort on the servo cylinder, so adding to the hydraulic pressure from the pedal cylinder and giving power assistance. Should the servo fail for any reason it fails safe, so that the hydraulic pressure from the pedal cylinder alone is available for braking.

The servo cylinder is overhauled in the same way as the pedal master cylinder, but the design of individual servos differs too much to give detailed overhaul instructions here. Check the servo cylinder, the non-return valve to the inlet manifold or reservoir, the reservoir for leaks, and the condition of any plastic or rubber pipes from the servo to the reservoir. Check also that the connection to the inlet manifold is not restricted with carbon, or even caked upper cylinder lubricant, which I once found.

If, after this, the servo still refuses to work properly try to get detailed overhaul instructions from a manual or find a replacement servo. Many are still available on an exchange basis.

It is most unlikely that the steel piping in a hydraulic system, or the flexible hoses, will still be in good condition. The steel pipes may look as if they have only surface rust but it will have bitten more deeply than you think, and the pipe could give way in an emergency. To be on the safe side renew all the piping and the flexibles.

The pipes can be replaced with new steel ones which are quite cheap, but they have two disadvantages. One is, as you have already found, that they corrode. The other is that steel pipe is not the easiest of materials to bend into the sometimes sharp contours needed without bending tools. It tends to kink, and once that happens the pipe is only good for scrap metal.

For a few pence more a foot a cupro-nickel pipe can be used which will not corrode in the car's lifetime, is easy to bend with your fingers and, unlike the copper pipes of pre-war days, does not work harden. Some manufacturers — Volvo is one — now fit it as standard. (The one I use is Kunifer 10, made by Yorkshire Imperial Metals.)

A flaring tool will also be needed to form the ends of the pipes, and a supply of new connections. (Any Girling agent can supply these.) If you are repiping just the one car you can get a cheap flaring tool like a pair of pliers which will last the job; but one of the professional flaring tools is more long lasting. They start at about £30 ($60), but they last a lifetime. (The one I use is made by Sykes Picavant.)

When the system is fully piped it has to be filled with fluid. A garage will do this with a machine which both fills and bleeds the system at the same time. Filling through the reservoir and pumping the air out takes longer, and is more expensive in wasted fluid, but it does the job just as well.

When you fill the reservoir with all the bleed nipples closed the reservoir will appear full but the pipes will still be full of air. It is a great help to enlist someone to help you pump this out. Ask your helper to sit in the car and pump up and down on the brake pedal. At first there will be no resistance at all, but gradually the air in the pipes will compress and the level of fluid in the reservoir will drop. Keep it topped up.

When your helper feels a resistance at the pedal, even though it is springy, connect a plastic tube to one of the bleed nipples at the wheels. Start with the one furthest from the master cylinder. Put a small quantity of brake fluid in a container, hold the free end of the plastic pipe under the fluid and slacken off the nipple. Now tell your helper to pump the pedal with long slow strokes if the reservoir is separate from the master cylinder; the type of master cylinder which has the reservoir incorporated in it responds better if the pedal is pumped in a sequence of one long stroke, three quick half strokes, one long stroke and so on.

At first there will be a steady stream of bubbles in the container as the air comes out, but after a few seconds the pipe will spit and squirt as a mixture of air and fluid comes out. At this point shout 'Hold!' to your helper. This means you want him to stop pumping, with the pedal held firmly down, while you tighten the bleed nipple.

Then transfer the plastic pipe and container to the next furthest nipple from the master cylinder and repeat the process. Do this till all four wheels have been done. By now your helper should be feeling a definite resistance at the pedal when the bleed nipples are closed.

Go back to the first nipple and this time ask your helper to pump away till he gets the pedal to hold up from the floor under pressure. It will feel spongy, but it will begin to feel like a brake. Ask your helper to hold the pressure while you slacken the nipple. The pedal will immediately fall to the floor, but must be held there while you retighten the nipple. Then get your helper to pump up pressure again. Do this several times until you are getting more fluid than air out the pipe, then go round all the wheels in turn.

After this circuit the brakes should begin to feel much better. Go round again, and again

if necessary, till you get a rock-hard brake at the pedal. Remember to keep topping up the reservoir or it will suck in air and you will have to start all over again.

The idea of pump — hold — pump — hold is to compress the air in the lines so that it comes out of the nipple in a rush. It is possible to bleed the system by just pumping away till no more air comes out the nipples, but it uses a great deal more fluid — which is far from cheap. Even though it is expensive, do not be tempted to re-use the fluid which comes out the nipples. It will be full of air, and even if it is left standing till all the air bubbles disappear it is likely to have attracted moisture. Brake fluid has a great affinity for water vapour and on hard braking this could turn to steam and cause vapour locks in the system, which are just as bad as having air.

Later cars with split hydraulic systems and two master cylinders, or one tandem cylinder are treated the same way except that one cylinder feeds the front brakes and the other the rear, so that there are two systems to deal with. Some cars have a G pressure regulating valve in the lines to prevent locking the rear wheels under heavy braking. With some of these layouts the handbrake has to be used during the pumping sequence, so refer to the manual. They are fairly recent and therefore manuals should be available.

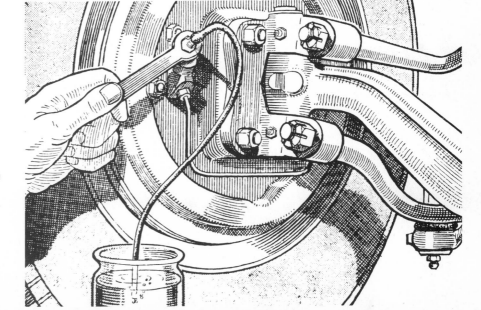

41 A vital last stage when dealing with hydraulic brakes is bleeding out the air. You need someone on the pedal while you bleed at the drums

=10=
HUBS AND WHEELS

The front bearings will be either ball or taper roller, both designed to take side thrust. To test the bearings, jack up the wheel and back off the brake adjuster so there is no chance of the brake binding. Then spin the wheel and listen. A growling or gritty sound from the hub indicates trouble. With ball bearings there should be no rocking at the edges of the wheel, but taper rollers need clearance so the wheel should rock slightly.

To take a ball bearing hub off you will need a puller. Remember that some cars have left-hand threads on one side. The puller usually bolts to the wheel studs, and its centre screw bears on the end of the stub axle. If you use the wheel nuts to hold the puller in place reverse the nuts so that the cones do not get damaged. If the nuts have double cones use plain nuts.

It is quite likely that the inner bearing and oil seal will pull out of the hub and stay on the stub axle. It is possible to pull the inner bearing off with a long-clawed puller, but if the bearing is worn there is a chance it will come apart and the inner track will stay on the axle. There is often no clearance to get a puller on this, so you have to resort to more brutal methods. Press a cold chisel down between the track and the shoulder of the stub axle, and give it a sharp blow with a fairly heavy hammer. There

is a slight chamfer on the edge of the track and this is enough to let the chisel act as a wedge and force the track off. Check afterwards for any burrs which the chisel has raised on the stub axle shoulder, and if there are any dress them down with a file so that the new bearing will seat properly.

If you are taking the hub off for some reason other than renewing the bearings (for example to renew the king pins), and the inner bearing and oil seal stay on the axle, you will still have to get them off. It is useless to put the hub back on and try to feed the bearing in. The bearing itself may oblige but the oil seal never will and you will have grease leaking on to the linings.

Bearings cannot be checked properly while there is oil and grease on them, so if there is any doubt about their condition wash them off in paraffin and spin them dry. If they still sound rough, or you can see marks or pitting in the tracks where the balls or rollers run, they need renewing.

Press the new bearings, together with any distance pieces, into the hub after filling each bearing — and the space between them — with grease. Fit a new seal, push the hub on the shaft and take the nut up tight for ball bearings. If it is fully tight and the hole for the split pin does not line up with one of the slots in the nut do not back the nut off to suit. Take the washer off and file it thinner.

With taper rollers do the nut up tight then back it off about 60°, or two flats of the nut, and split pin it securely. On some hubs you may find a screwed collar with holes in it instead of a split pin and nut. The same procedure applies: do it up tight, then back it off about 60° and lock it. If taper rollers in a hub are done up tight they will have a very short life.

On the back axle you will meet two different types of half shaft and two types of bearing arrangement. The easiest to deal with is the fully floating axle, which is rare if not unknown on American made cars of this period. This is the type where the hub bearings are carried on the outer casing of the axle. All the half shaft has to do is transmit the torque. This type of half shaft ends in a flat plate which is fixed to the hub with set-screws or studs and nuts. When taking it out watch for oil seals and gaskets and, if they are damaged, make new ones; if you do not, oil from the differential will work its way out along the shaft and on to the brake linings.

The hub is drawn off the axle with a puller after taking off the nut, and it usually comes off fairly readily though some are a little reluctant. Even more reluctant are hubs on semi-floating axles.

In this type of design the half shaft is a press fit in the hub, sometimes with splines and sometimes with a taper and key. If they have been undisturbed for years they can be really tight. Some are even pressed on to the shafts with an interference fit needing literally a few tons to separate them.

In these cases the easiest way to go about things is to strip out the brakes, undo the nuts and bolts holding the outer carrier of the bearing to the flange on the axle casing and pull out the hub and half shaft as a complete assembly. Then if you have no equipment for pressing the shaft out of the hub, take the whole thing along to a garage and ask them to do it. They can also renew any seals and bearings necessary and return it ready to put back on the car.

A variation of the semi-floating axle is found on early Morris Minors. The hub is splined to the end of the half shaft, and also locates on a split tapered collar which presses up against the inner track of the hub bearing. The hub will come off the splines with a puller, or a few blows with a hide mallet, after the bolts through to the flange on the axle casing have been removed. But the half shaft stays in position. There is a special tool for extracting it. This is a slide hammer with one end threaded to fit over the end of the half shaft. If this tool is not available, the half shaft can be drawn out complete with its bearings by making up a bar with a hole drilled through it to fit over the thread on the end of the half shaft. Hold this bar on with the hub nut and use two hammers, one at each side, to draw the shaft out.

Always examine carefully the splined ends of half shafts where they fit in the differential. If there is any sign of stepping or twist in the splines the shaft is on its way out.

Whenever you take a rear hub apart watch out carefully for any spacers or shims. Make sure they all go back in their correct order. On some designs the nip in the bearing is allowed for in the thickness of the gasket. Try to obtain the proper gaskets, but if you have to make them choose a gasket paper of the same thickness as the gasket you are replacing.

When the hubs are off check the condition of the wheel studs. If any are damaged get new ones. In almost all cases the studs are a pressed splined fit in the hubs. Many sports cars have Rudge Whitworth-type hubs with knock-off hub caps and the wheels splined to the hubs. These splines must be cleaned and examined carefully. If they are damaged, usually caused by a wheel running loose, the only remedy is to have them built up and remachined by a

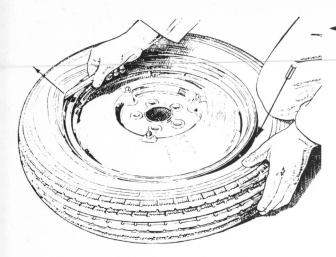

◄ 42   Much of the hard work of levering off a tyre disappears if you push it down into the well before starting to lever at the valve

43   To get the tire right off the wheel, lever down here and, if necessary, thump the bead over the edge of the rim with a mallet or hide-faced hammer ►

specialist. Never be tempted to pack a loose hub out with shims or, as I once found, with aluminium kitchen foil! It is asking for trouble. Similarly, if the thread on the end of the hub is damaged take it to a specialist for rectification.

Faults you may find on pressed steel wheels are cracking at the bolts holes and distortion on the flanges. If you find cracking at the holes it is probably cheaper to find some good secondhand wheels, but if this is impossible have the cracks cut out to a vee and welded. Local rim damage, usually caused by hitting a kerb, can be taken out with a shaped dolly and hammer. Mount the wheel on a front hub and spin it to check for wobble. If the wobble is serious (e.g. more than 1/8 in (3 mm) at the vertical part of the flange) the wheel is too buckled for comfort. It is hopeless trying to straighten a buckled steel wheel at home. Either find a replacement or take the wheel to a specialist.

Spoke wheels are a case in themselves. The first check is on the condition of the spokes. If you rescued the car from a field the spokes are likely to be badly corroded, even to the point where they could give way on hitting a bad bump. The whole wheel needs rebuilding with new spokes. There are a number of firms that will do this. It is not impossible to do it at home if you are used to the job, but without a jig to hold the hub and rim at their proper offset it can be difficult.

It is not difficult, however, to replace the odd damaged or loose spoke. The first job is to go round the wheel checking that none of the spokes is bent, and tapping each one with a screwdriver. This should produce a clear 'ting'. The 'tings' will not be all at the same musical pitch, but they should be clear. If any give a most unmusical 'tonk' then they need attention.

Take off the tire and the rim band and soak the ends of the nipples in penetrating oil or a freeing agent (such as WD 40). Then clean the thread of the spoke under the nipple with a wire brush. The nipples have squares on them to take a special spoke key. This is the best tool to use, but a thick-jawed spanner will serve if it is a good fit. Thin chrome-vanadium spanners are likely to slip round and ruin the nipple. The nipple should be screwed down the spoke till the spoke 'tings' like the rest.

If a spoke is bent, or the thread of a loose spoke is so corroded that it cannot be tightened, the spoke must be replaced. The easiest way to get it out is to cut it. The new spoke is threaded in and its nipple tightened till it 'tings'. The new spoke will be far too long, so it must be cut off flush with the head of the nipple. Then, because it is likely to settle down and stretch in service, the nipple should be undone and a further 1/8 in (3 mm) cut off the spoke. Then it can be adjusted to take up stretch without taking the tire off and with no danger of the end of the spoke poking through the head of the nipple to cause a puncture.

After all the spokes are adjusted wire brush

all round the well of the wheel rim, treat it with rust killer, paint it and fit a new rim

Before fitting the tire mount the wheel on a front hub and check the rim for run out wobble. Like a steel wheel it should run true to within 1/8 in (3 mm) at the rim. If it does not, mark the high spots with a piece of chalk and try the effect of slightly tightening or loosening any new spokes you have put in or any you have adjusted. You will find that tightening or loosening the spokes on one side of a wheel affects the run out diagonally opposite.

It is easier to learn the effects of adjusting spokes by trial and error than by reading about it. If adjusting a spoke does not have the effect you want put its tension back before going on to another. That way you will not get a number of spokes loose at the same time. The object is to get the wheel true with all the spokes under sufficient tension to 'ting' at about the same pitch. You will never finish with them all the same, but you should never end up with any producing a dull untensioned 'tonk'.

Some people struggle for hours taking off and refitting tires. Of course, the professional in the tire bay has an easy time of it with his tire-changing machine, but given three decent tire levers and a means of freeing the bead anyone should be able to tackle it without much fuss.

Freeing the bead is the first, and really the only hard part, of the whole business. Start by taking the valve core out to make sure there is no air left inside. Now you have to get both sides of the bead away from the edge of the rim and down into the well of the wheel. With luck, and if you are fairly heavy, you will be able to heel the tire down away from the edge of the rim, but it saves time, temper and ankles if you have a tool to do it.

You can buy these tools at tire shops where they are known as bead breakers; or you can make a very satisfactory one by getting a long piece of steel bar — an old half shaft is ideal — and grinding one end to a blunt chisel shape. Then pin and weld a substantial steel collar about eight inches from the chisel end and find a piece of heavy steel tube, like a piece of steel scaffolding, which fits over the bar.

To use the tool lay the wheel flat on the ground, or on a couple of baulks of timber if the centre of the wheel sticks out from the edge of the rim, put the chisel end against the bead close to the rim and use the tool as a slide hammer by thumping the tube down against the collar. After a few hefty blows the bead will fall into the well.

Free the bead on both sides of the tire and you are ready to lever it off. Here there is a golden rule — start and finish at the valve. It applies particularly to tubed tires, but it is a good rule with any tire. Tread the part of the tire opposite the valve well into the well, put two levers under the bead on either side of the valve about 6 in (15 cm) apart and, with a one-two action, lever the bead over the rim. Cross the free ends of the two levers so that they can be held down with one foot or knee, take the third lever and apply it about 6 in (15 cm) to one side of the first two. When this lever is pulled down the middle lever will come free, so you can take another bite and carry on till the whole side of the tire is free. Then the tube can be taken out.

This is as far as you need to go if you are

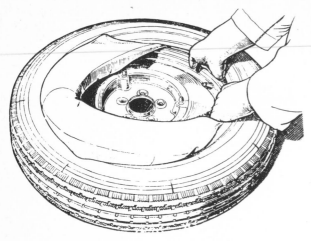

44   On a tubed tire
make sure the valve is
well seated in its hole
before feeding in the rest
of the tube

just mending a puncture in the tube. Here, I would say that the old method of mending punctures with plain patches and rubber solution is out. The best and permanent way of repairing punctures is to have them hot vulcanized. Next best is one of the home cold vulcanizing processes, but I feel safer with hot vulcanizing.

While we are on the subject of punctures, the idea of repairing a tubeless tire by pushing a plug through it is no longer looked on with favour, though it can be found in manuals even as late as 1970. It should be regarded at best as a get-you-home measure, and the tire should be properly vulcanized at the first opportunity.

If you want to take the tire completely off the wheel stand it upright and use one of the levers to pull the second bead of the tire over the same rim from which the first was levered. Push down on the lever to start the bead coming, then thump along the bead with a mallet or hide-faced hammer and the wheel will drop free.

To put a tire back on, stand the tire upright, hold the wheel in your other hand with the outside of the wheel facing the tire, and jam it down in the bead as far as it will go. Then lay the wheel down with the tire uppermost and bang the rest of the bead over the rim with the hide-faced hammer. It helps to coat the rim liberally with soap solution.

Next, if you are using a tube, put it in and make sure it is evenly distributed around the wheel with no twists, and that the valve is fully and squarely through the hole in the rim. Then, starting opposite the valve, tread the top bead of the tire down over the rim working round each side towards the valve. Stop every now and then to kick the part of the bead opposite the valve well down into the rim.

The hardest part to get on is the last 6 in (15 cm) or so, but you should not have to use levers. If you tread down on the tire about 2 in (5 cm) outside the bead, instead of trying to kick the bead itself, the wall of the tire will flex and the bead will come down over the rim.

Once the tire is on give it a few kicks and thumps — just to let it know who is the master — so that it sits concentrically round the rim. There are a series of rings moulded round the tire to help you. On some tires you will find a marking, often a series of white dots, to indicate the lightest point. Some tubes are also marked, often with black dots, to indicate their heaviest point. If the tube and tire are put on with the two sets of marks together the whole assembly will need fewer weights to bring it to balance. If you have a marked tire but an unmarked tube, fit it with the white dots next to the valve. I would always recommend having a wheel and tire balanced after the tire has been on and off again.

You will need a tourniquet round a tubeless tire to hold the beads to the rim while it is being inflated till there is enough pressure to seat the beads and make a firm seal. It is possible to use a rope and bar as a makeshift, and I have known people seat the beads by pushing the tire up against a wall while they use the airline, but for my money a proper tourniquet tool is the best way.

=11=

GOOD STEERING

No one, except perhaps a fanatical old-car enthusiast, will pretend that the steering on older cars is as good as that on more modern designs, but there is no reason why your classic should wander about the road, nor why you should have constantly to saw to and fro on the wheel to hold a straight line.

Assuming that the suspension and steering swivels have been put into good order, the next links along the steering chain are the ball joints on the steering arms and track rods. It is difficult to check these by holding the rods and trying to push the joints backwards and forwards; you do not reproduce the steering loads accurately. Go under the car with the wheels on the ground, clean all the dirt off the joints and hold your hand over each joint in turn while someone rocks the steering wheel back and forth to take up the play. You will be able to feel even slight wear in a joint which you might miss by just looking at it.

You should also test for up and down movement by grasping the rod and trying to lift it up and down along the line of the ball pin. If there is any sloppy free play the ball needs replacing. Do not confuse sloppiness with movement against a spring. Some ball joints are spring-loaded and the ball can be moved off its seat by levering the joint apart. So long as the spring tension is firm, and there is no sideways play, the joint is serviceable.

There are two ways of freeing the tapers of ball pins from their housings. One is to use a forked wedge which is driven under the ball to

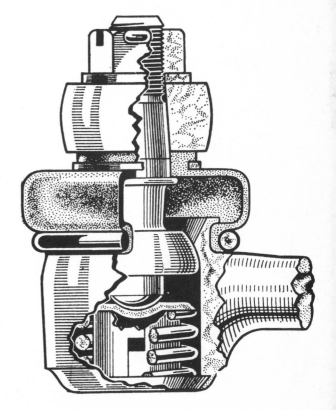

45 Section through a spring-loaded ball joint

force the taper apart. The other is to spring the taper by jarring both sides of the taper housing. Steering arms are resilient forgings, and jarring with two heavy hammers will not harm them. What you should never do is put a jack or block under the small end of the pin and hammer the arm down by hitting it direct. You are liable to nick or dent the edges of the forging and set up local points of high stress that could later lead to a fracture.

Provided you can get to both sides of the boss holding the taper pin, a fairly sharp blow from two heavy hammers simultaneously on both sides of the boss will jar it sufficiently to spring the taper out. This is the method I would recommend if you are taking apart the joint for some reason other than to renew the ball, because it does not damage the joint or the protective gaiter which keeps out road dirt and wet. Sometimes it is impossible to hit both sides of the boss. In this case, try putting a lever between the arm and the rod and at the same time hitting the end of the boss directly opposite the arm.

If all else fails, or if you are renewing the joint, a sure way of freeing the taper is to use a forked wedge. You can buy them in most larger car tool shops. To avoid possible damage to the arm the wedge should be driven between the ball and the boss, in line with the arm, to avoid a sideways shock load on it. As well as being on a taper the ball will be held in the boss by either a self locking nut or a castellated nut and split pin. If yours have split pins make sure the nut is absolutely tight when the holes line up. There should be a plain washer under the nut, so if the hole in the pin and the slots in the nut do not line up when the nut is tight, file the washer slightly till it does. Never back the nut off to line up the hole.

Other causes of play in the steering are wear in the steering box and, if fitted, in the idler box. Many independent front suspensions have an idler box sometimes called the steering relay box. It has a bell crank on the bottom which transmits the movement of the steering box to a cross tube and side steering tubes.

In time the bushes and sometimes the shaft of the idler box wear. If there is any side movement of the idler shaft as it turns it must be rebushed. In most cases the bushes are plain bronze and rebushing is quite straightforward provided you have a long reamer, preferably with a pilot, to make sure the top and bottom bushes are reamered in line.

As with other bronze bushes it may be possible to get them off the shelf or to get some turned up for you. If the shaft is worn and you cannot get a replacement, have it built up and turned down to original size. I would not recommend having the diameter reduced to take out wear, even if there appears to be enough diameter of taper spline left at the end to hold the bell crank. Renew the oil seal or felt ring when rebuilding the box. Most of them wear because the seal leaks and the box runs dry.

The main types of box are the cam and lever, cam and roller, worm and nut and rack and pinion. The cam and lever, often called the Bishop box, became popular in the thirties as a cheap mass-produced box for light cars. In its cheapest form it was not very positive nor long lasting compared with the massively engineered boxes of the vintage years. On a few cars these cheap cam and lever boxes were carried on after the war, but the introduction of independent front suspension made improvement necessary. In its later forms this type of box became much better and lasted adequately for years.

In time, however, as with all mechanisms, things begin to wear and the box needs overhauling. The basic Bishop box uses a bronze cam, cut like a very coarse thread, on the end of the steering column. Engaging with this cam is a peg on the end of a lever, and at the other end of the lever is a shaft carrying the drop arm. As the column is turned the peg runs up and down the cam to turn the shaft.

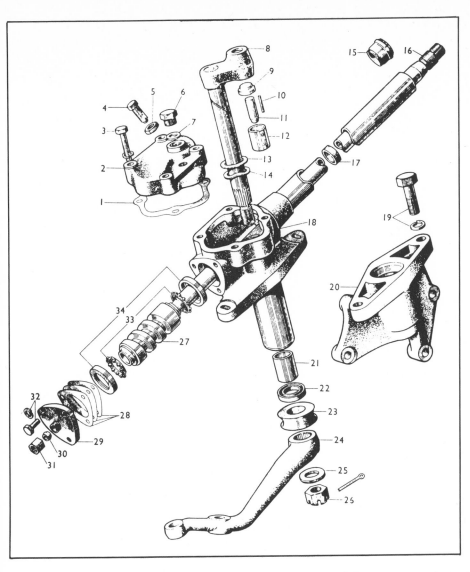

46 A typical Bishop cam steering box. The key is: 1, joint washer; 2, top cover; 3, top cover bolt; 4, adjusting peg; 5, locking nut for adjusting peg; 6, filler plug; 7, washer; 8, steering shaft; 9, thrust cap; 10, needle roller; 11, cam follower peg; 12, needle roller housing; 13, flat washer; 14, spring washer; 15, bearing for top of column; 16, steering wheel spline; 17, felt bush; 18, steering box body; 19, bracket fixing bolt; 20, holding bracket; 21, shaft bearing; 22, oil seal; 23, dust excluder; 24, steering lever (drop arm); 25, plain washer; 26, castellated nut; 27, cam and column; 28, adjusting shims; 29, end cover; 30, olive; 31, stator tube nut; 32, end cover bolt and washer; 33, ball races; 34, ball race tracks

There are four main areas of wear. The cam itself wears, though fairly slowly, the peg wears and, with earlier designs of fixed peg, develops flats, the ball races carrying the cam wear and so do the shaft bushes. Parts are available for many of these boxes, and overhaul is not difficult.

The cam is usually held to the column by splines, and the bottom end of the column is splayed out into a recess at the bottom of the cam to hold it on. You may be offered a cam and column as an exchange unit, or you may be able to get only the cam. There is only one satisfactory way to get a cam off the column at home. Thread a heavy piece of iron pipe over the column, use a blow torch to heat the bottom end of the column and cam to a bright red and thump the cam off with the pipe. The end of the column which has been spread will close in again to let the cam come off. If it is left to cool naturally it will stay soft so that it can be spread again in the new cam. Be careful when driving the new cam on to get it the right way round, and peen the end of the column into the recess with a ball pein hammer. This can be done when it is cold.

The ball races on which the column turns are caged, but the tracks are separate. There are two tracks, one at the top and one at the bottom. The other sides of the races bear on the cam. Assemble the column and races in the box dry and adjust the end float by the shims under the end cover. The column should turn freely but without any end float at all.

On the older and cheaper boxes the peg was a drive fit in the lever and developed flats on two sides. On the better type of cam and lever boxes the peg is carried in needle rollers or ball bearings. These pegs last longer than the fixed type because they rotate and wear more evenly. Because the wear is even the peg can be put deeper into mesh to compensate, but it must never go so deep that its end bottoms on the base of the cam thread.

The depth of engagement of the peg is governed by shims under the top cover on the cheaper boxes and by an adjusting screw and lock nut on the better ones. The adjusting screw is directly over the centre of the drop arm shaft, and cheaper boxes can be modified in many cases by drilling a hole in the top cover and welding a ½ in (12.7 mm) nut over the hole.

The depth of peg engagement should be such that there is a minimum of free play at the steering wheel before the drop arm shaft turns, but the box must not go stiff on full lock. The bushes for the drop arm shaft are plain ones and can be renewed in the usual way. If the shaft is worn and a new one unobtainable, it can be built up and machined down in the same way as the idler shaft. Adjustments should be made in the first case with the box dry. Renew the felt seal or oil seal at the drop arm shaft. At the steering wheel end of the column, if there is no ball race, the column is supported by a hard felt bush which can be renewed. Soak the new bush in oil before pressing it in.

The Marles cam and roller box has an hourglass shaped cam, and the rocker shaft carries either a single or double roller. End float of the column is governed, as in the cam and lever box, by shimming the end cover. Depth of engagement of the roller with the cam is adjusted either by a thrust screw or button, or sometimes by an eccentric. It is most important to check this design of box for freedom on the extremes of lock after adjustment has been carried out in the central position. Otherwise, overhaul of the box is similar to a cam and lever.

With worm and nut boxes the worm is usually steel and may be splined to the end of the column or it may be cut directly on the end of the column. The bronze nut which runs up and down it has either a hole in it to engage with a ball on the end of a rocker shaft or there is a roller between the two or, in some cases, sector teeth. Replacement worms and nuts almost always have to be lapped in with fine abrasive till the nut runs freely but without backlash.

Make sure every trace of abrasive is removed by scrubbing out the inside of the worm with an old toothbrush and paraffin; if any is left behind it will wear both the worm and nut in a very short time. Adjustment of the end float of the column and engagement of the rocker shaft with the nut are much the same as with cam boxes.

A variation on the worm and nut, and much superior to a plain worm and nut, is the type which has ball bearings between the two, usually called a recirculating ball box. With these designs there are either passages in the box body, or conduit tubes, so that the box contains a greater number of balls than are actually between the worm and nut. The method of feeding in the balls varies, so it is best to consult a manual, but generally as many as possible are inserted then the nut is moved up and down the worm to distribute them. More balls are fed in and distributed till the total number is accommodated.

Some makers supply balls in oversizes to

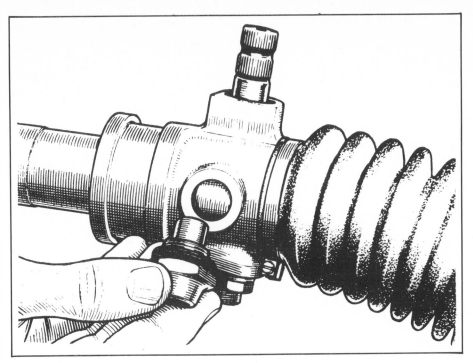

47 Some steering racks have dampers which are to stop rattle, not to take up wear

compensate for wear, but these must be fitted as a set. Mixing ball sizes could damage or even jam the box solid.

Overhaul of a rack and pinion is straightforward, but often there is no adjustment for wear. If there is roughness, or chipping of the teeth, or if the pinion has worn a trough in the rack, both must be replaced as a pair. With some designs the pinion runs in renewable bearings, and on others it bears direct in the housing. If this is worn the only cure is replacement.

It is usual to allow a slight end float of between 0.002 in (0.05 mm) and 0.005 in (0.13 mm) on the pinion. Some racks have one, or two, dampers in the form of thrust buttons to stop the rack rattling. These are shimmed but are not intended as adjustment for wear. To fit the dampers assemble the rack with the pinion, and screw in the dampers without their shims and without their springs till the rattle is taken from the rack, but

while it is still free enough to be pushed back and forth so that the pinion rotates. Then measure with feelers the gap between the head of the damper and the machined boss on the rack housing. Select shims so that their total thickness is 0.002 in (0.05 mm) to 0.005 in (0.13 mm) greater than the gap.

There is an adjustable ball at one end of the rack, sometimes at both ends. These should move freely without play. When the assembly is fitted back on the car, leave the mounting clamps slightly loose till the top of the column is fixed to the body, otherwise there is a danger of putting a twisting stress on the rack.

Independent front suspensions have a variety of layouts for the rods between the box and the wheels. Some tubes are adjustable for length and some are fixed. Unless there are instructions in the manual to the contrary set the box in mid position, set the wheels straight ahead and assemble the tubes so that the drop arm on the box and the lever on the idler are

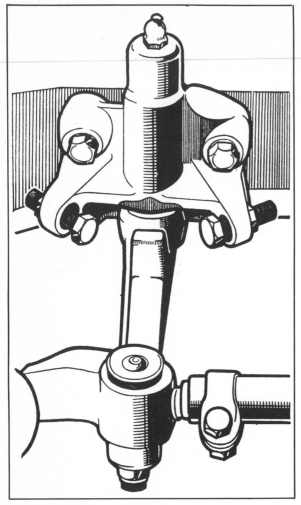

48   Somewhere in the
system will be a pair of
lock stops. They must
engage before the steering
box reaches the end of
its travel

It is important that the angle between the tube and lever should not be so acute that it folds like a jack-knife, nor so wide that they are nearly in line. Either situation could lead to a dangerous stiffness or even jamming on lock.

All steering systems have stops somewhere so that the movement of the wheels is stopped positively before the steering box comes to the end of its travel. The stops may be fixed or adjustable. If they are adjustable, screw them fully in and, with the car jacked up, turn the steering wheel till the end of travel in the steering box is reached. Then turn back half a turn of the wheel and screw out the stop to make contact. Do this on both locks.

The correct setting of the toe-in of the front wheels is so important for good tire life as well as steering quality that I would advise against trying to set it at home. Set it as near as you can and take the car straight to a garage for them to set it accurately. They will have accurate and expensive instruments for this, and the charge for the service is so small compared with the damage a wrong setting can do to your tires that it is foolish not to use it.

either parallel or at the same angle to the centre line of the car. Then turn the wheels on each lock and watch the angle each rod makes with its lever or arm. On full lock the angles at each side should be near enough the same.

=12=
OVERHAULING
THE ENGINE

Assuming you are doing a complete engine overhaul, the first thing to do is to drain the oil. It sounds elementary, but I have known people forget this and take the sump off or turn the engine upside-down with the old oil still in. The language was quite educational! When the old oil is out I usually put the sump plug back in, pour in a pint or so of paraffin and leave it there for about half an hour to help get the sludge out of the sump. I would not do this on a normal oil change because I do not like the idea of having parafin in the oil, but all the old engines I have taken apart have been liberally coated in thick sludge, and when they are being stripped down the

paraffin makes cleaning the sump so much easier.

While the paraffin is doing its job take off all the engine accessories. The carburetters are best left on the manifold at this stage, and often the inlet and exhaust manifolds come off together. Make a note, or take photos, of how the throttle and choke linkages go together. It may be a long time before you sort them out again.

Take off the dynamo, starter, water pump, oil filter, petrol pump (if it is on the engine), and any water manifolds or branches. Put all these, and the dipstick, safely away in cardboard boxes.

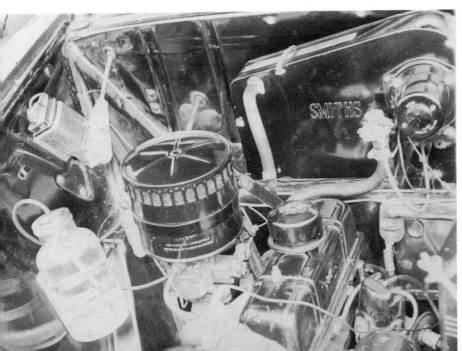

49   Not perfect — note the chipped paint in places — but a most presentable engine compartment on a Standard Super 10

Next, take the head off. When I worked in a garage many years ago the Guv'nor used to be fond of saying: "Just whip the head off and we'll have a look inside". It sounds easy put like that, but some heads can be really difficult to shift if they have been undisturbed for decades.

If the head is held on, American fashion, by long set bolts, things couldn't be easier. Once the bolts are out a sharp blow with a mallet will shift it, despite previous owners' attempts to glue it on with gasket cement. On most British engines, however, the head is held on by long studs and nuts. These studs can be a real nuisance, even on cast iron heads. If the head does not lift absolutely straight it cross binds on some of the studs and there is a good chance of bending them.

With a long, heavy, overhead valve head it helps to get someone to give you a hand. With one person at each end it is easier to get a straight lift. If you are by yourself you will find it easier to stand inside the engine compartment straddling the engine, if there is room. Once the head is free you can balance it on the top of the studs while you get down. Be careful not to dislodge it, though, while climbing down.

This supposes that you have managed to break the head-to-block seal. Resist the temptation, except as a last resort, to hammer a screwdriver in the joint face to force it apart. Try first tapping all the way round the joint with a mallet or copper faced hammer. If all else fails, and you have to use an implement in the joint, choose something nice and wide like a chopper or axe head and use one each side. If you have only one, work all round the joint a little at a time. Try to split the old copper-asbestos gasket rather than get the tool up against the metal faces.

Aluminium heads held by studs can be terrible things to get off. Many people tackling Standard or Triumph aluminium side valve engines have found these impossible to tackle by normal methods. The head seizes solid on the studs and no amount of banging will shift it; the only way is to buy a special cutter to fit over the studs. These are in the form of a tube with teeth cut at one end, and should have walls only about 1/64 in (0.4 mm) thick. I have seen some with walls nearer 1/16 in (1.6 mm) which, in my opinion, is far too thick; there is a danger of weakening the wall between the stud hole and the water jacket.

When taking the head off a side valve engine all that is taken off is the head. On overhead valve engines the rocker gear has to be taken off first. This is not strictly true of some overhead camshaft engines where the shaft, or shafts, can be taken off with the head, and this is where a manual comes in so useful. I am not too keen on taking camshafts off with the head unless all I am doing is changing a head gasket. For one thing there is a danger of forgetting a nut that is masked by the camshaft and (more of a potential danger) some of the valves will be open when the head is lifted off. If you forget, and stand the head down on its face, or if it topples over while you are taking the camshaft out, the valves that are open will undoubtedly be bent. I prefer to take the camshaft off while the head is still on the block.

Watch out for any shims under camshaft bearings or under rocker pedestals. If you find any take them out and put them in numbered envelopes so that you know exactly where they go back. The same goes for any shims used to adjust valve clearances. You will save a great deal of time on reassembly if you start with the shim packs as they were before you took things apart. Watch out too for any external oil feed pipes to camshafts or rocker shafts, and make sure you know how they go back.

On push rod ohv engines take the rocker shaft off and leave it as an assembly for the moment. Some people like to keep the push rods in order when they take them out. There is a great deal to be said for keeping working parts together, but with push rods I must admit I do not usually bother. Nor do I bother about saving valve springs unless I am working on a rare engine. I prefer to fit new valve springs.

Valves I do keep in order. The easiest way to do this is to take a strip of wood and drill a series of holes along it to take the valve stems. Mark one end of the wood 'Front' and then you cannot go wrong.

The accumulation of carbon in the combustion chambers and ports can be softened with proprietary compounds, but I usually just attack it with a selection of scrapers, old screwdrivers, and wire brushes in an electric drill. Do not be brutal with an aluminium head because they are quite easily damaged. Clean the valve guides with the special tool that can be bought to go in the drill, and use plenty of paraffin as a lubricant.

Some years ago there was a fetish among enthusiasts for polishing the ports in the head and the manifolds to improve the gas flow. Unless you are going in for racing and looking for the last ounce of power I do not think it is worth the bother. It is certainly not worth it on a touring car. It is worth profiling the manifold gasket, but I will deal with that when we come to reassembly.

Check the head face for flatness with a long steel straight edge, and if you can see more

than a few thousandths of an inch (or a few hundredths of a millimetre) of daylight under the straight edge, send the head for refacing. Tell the machine shop to take only the absolute minimum off the face of the head. The manual might say how much it is safe to take off, but someone might have had a go before, so beware. Rely more on a quoted minimum dimension from the face surface to a machined surface on the top of the head rather than on anyone's say-so that it is safe to take off such and such a fraction.

There is less likely to be distortion on the block face, but check it all the same. Check also for signs of metal being pulled up round the studs or bolt holes. This can sometimes stop the gasket from seating properly, so if there is any have the studs out by using a stud box or two nuts locked together and run a countersink bit over the holes.

The best way to clean valves is to clamp an electric drill firmly in a bench stand, put the valve in the chuck and run it at a fairly slow speed. Hold an old (but strong) knife against the valve to clean off the carbon, and finish off with fine emery cloth. If the stems are stepped where they have been working in the guides, you will want new ones if they are available. You will also want new exhaust valves if the edges of the heads are worn paper thin from successive facings and grindings. The edge of the head should be at least 1/16 in (1.6 mm) thick. Exhaust valves with thin heads are liable to distort and burn. Inlet valve head thicknesses are not so critical.

In the days when side valve engines were the most popular, the standard valve spring compressor looked like a large pair of pliers but worked the other way round. When the

50   Even if you find a cracked block do not despair. Either you can have it welded or, as here repaired by a cold process (such as Metalok)

handles were pushed together the jaws opened, with a ratchet to hold them open. I always found this type of compressor fiddly and awkward to use. I prefer the G-cramp type of compressor for both overhead and side valves. On a few ohv engines with very wide heads it may be difficult finding a G-cramp compressor with a wide enough throat. This is the case on Jaguar XK engines. Here the best bet is to make up a rounded block of wood to fit in the combustion chamber, stand the head on it, and lever the springs down from the top or press them down with a bar with a hole drilled in it to take the valve stem.

On side valve engines it pays to block off the holes from the tappet chest to the sump with pieces of rag. If you forget you are bound to drop at least one valve cotter and it will, of course, go through one of the holes. If the sump is going to come off it is less of a nuisance, but if you are only doing a decoke it can be most annoying.

On most side valve engines the tappet blocks come off and, if you are doing a complete overhaul, dealing with the valve springs will be easier if you take the blocks off. Mark them so they go back in the same places.

British Ford side valve engines, and American Ford and Lincoln side valve engines before the late forties, used valves of a design all their own. The bottom of the stem finished in a head like a flattened lollipop. On these there is no tappet adjustment for valve clearance, the correct clearance being obtained by grinding the end of the stem if the clearance is too small and grinding the valve further into its seat if it is too large.

Because of this large end on the stems the valve will not pass up through the normal guide, so the guides are split and pushed into place with a taper, from inside the tappet chest. There is a special Ford drift to knock them out, which has a hollow half sphere to fit over the valve head. If you cannot get this tool the guides can be knocked down by using a slim drift down the side of the valve head, but it is tricky. Be careful not to bend the valve. Make sure to keep the halves of the guides in pairs and the pairs in order. Once again, holes in a piece of wood come in handy to take the wired-together pairs.

Ford used to sell a valve grinding tool which took the place of a guide while the valve was gound into its seat. It looked like a tapered cylinder with ball bearings in it. Some people get on fine with it, but I find it awkward and prefer to use the guides themselves when grinding the valves in.

Before starting to grind in the valves on any engine examine all the valve seats carefully, especially the exhausts. Many engines have replaceable valve seat inserts, so that if the seat is cracked or badly pocketed a new seat can be put in. On aluminium heads there will be renewable seats for both inlet and exhaust, but on cast iron heads, if renewable seats are fitted, they will be on the exhausts only. Inlet seats seldom give trouble.

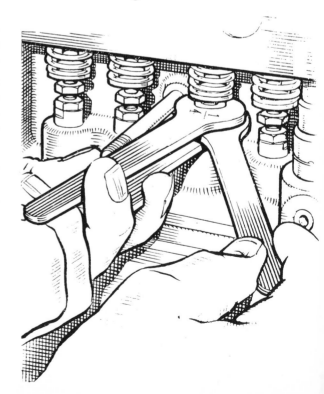

51   Using three spanners to set side valve tappets

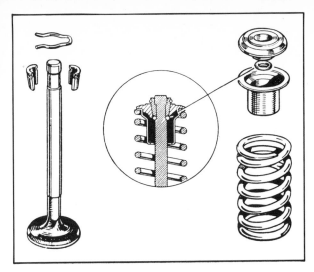

On engines without renewable seats you might find that repeated grinding and refacing has left the seat sunk so far down that the valve head shrouds the opening and restricts the gas flow. There are two ways to get round this. If the pocketing is not too deep the edges can be cut back to a shallower angle than the seats. The other method is to have the head or block machined out to take an insert. Before doing this check with the service department of the manufacturer or, if he has gone out of business, with the one-make club, that there is enough metal round the seat to take the machining. On one or two engines the water jacket comes too close to the valve ports for comfort. If you cannot find out do not chance it. Chamfer the edge of the seating and let it go at that. The performance will not suffer all that much.

If you are having new inserts the easiest way is to take the head or block to a garage and let them do the job. At the same time they can fit new guides and face the inserts. If, however, you are keen to do everything yourself, check on the interference fit of the new seat inserts. Some are so tight they have to be put in solid carbon dioxide to pre-shrink them. This is not a job to try at home.

Many inserts however can be dealt with at home. First the old insert has to be got out. There are special puller tools for this; or it can be broken up. Take care if you adopt this method; the inserts are hard and brittle and fly with a frightening velocity when they break. Cover the old insert, and the end of the chisel, with a stout cloth and wear heavy gloves. Wear eye protection too to be on the safe side.

Choose a chisel with a sharp but fairly broad-angled edge. Hit the insert squarely in two places to crack it, then put the edge of the chisel under the lip at the bottom of the insert, lay it over and bang down on the other end to lever the cracked insert out. Be careful not to damage the seating into which the insert fits.

The new insert can be pulled in with a nut, bolt and heavy washer. If you are going to renew the valve guides, knock these out first so that you can use a heavier bolt. If you are not going to renew the guides, make up a short distance piece to fit over them so that the washer bears on the distance piece and not on the guide. Guides fit less tightly than inserts, and if the washer touches them you will find you are pulling them out instead of pulling the insert in.

Check to see if the guides are worn. It is difficult to lay down an acceptable amount of wear. If new guides are readily available do not put up with any slop between the guide and valve stem. This is more important on inlet guides which, if they are worn, will allow oil to be sucked in. On ohv engines worn guides probably account more for high oil consumption than worn bores.

The old guides can be knocked out either with a stepped drift or by putting a bolt in them and using a plain drift on the head of the bolt. Some guides are stepped so there is no danger of pressing the new ones in to the wrong depth. Others are parallel, so before driving the old guide out cut a piece of tubing to the exact height the guide protrudes from the top of the head, and use this as a distance gauge when you put the new guides in.

Guides on ohv engines can be pressed or driven in from the top again using a stepped drift or a plain drift and a bolt to protect the end of the guide. On side valve engines it may be possible to drive them in from the top, but you may have to draw them in from underneath with a long bolt, a nut and a couple of heavy washers. After the guides are in place check the ends to make sure you have not raised any burrs. If there are any burrs, take them off with a smooth round file.

Refacing the valve seats should be carried out after the new guides are in place. It pays, on a complete overhaul, to reface all the valve seats, even if only lightly. They must be refaced after the new guides are in because they may not go in exactly concentric with the old seatings. You can buy cutters to reface seats at home, but for a small charge most larger garages will do it for you. They have power tools which will do the job quickly and accurately.

New valves and newly refaced seats are not ground in on assembly lines, but I prefer to give them at least a light touch. I only ever use fine grinding paste. If a valve needs coarse grinding paste it probably needs refacing, and so does the seat. Make sure you get rid of every trace of grinding paste.

Before leaving the head, take off any plates covering the water jacket and clean out the water jacket. I like to do this with core plugs as well, not only to clean but to make sure there are no leaks from old weeping core plugs. Before you take them out make sure you can get new ones the right size. With the normal domed welch plug there is usually no difficulty because they come in standard sizes, but obtaining new screwed plugs could be difficult. If they come out easily the old ones can be reused, but if they do not want to come out with reasonable force, leave well alone.

To get domed welch plugs out hit them dead centre with a sharp centre punch. The punch will go right through the plug, and it will lift out skewered like a piece of kebab. Clean round the housing with a screwdriver, smear a little jointing compound in the recess and place the new plug in position. Hit it firmly once with a fairly heavy hammer and it will spread into the housing to give a water-tight seal.

Any plates taken off the head or block will have gaskets, and even on fairly recent engines these can be difficult to get new, so this part of the book seems a good place to go through the general process for making gaskets.

First clean and, if necessary, face up the mating surfaces with a file. Always use files which are in good condition, and fit handles over the tangs. Do not rub the file backwards and forwards over the work; that is the clumsy way. Treat it for what it is: a cutting tool. It cuts on the forward stroke and should be lifted off the work on the backward stroke. For cast iron and mild steel a medium grade bastard cut file is best, but for aluminium a fine grade single cut file is needed. Hold the file slightly at an angle to the direction of cut so that it slices rather than cuts straight, and tap the edge on the bench (or wire brush the teeth from time to time) to clear the swarf. On aluminium the teeth will clog less, and it will give a smoother finish, if you rub a little French chalk on the file.

Now get the piece of gasket material. I usually use Hallite for water jackets, Oaken-strong paper in various thicknesses for things such as mechanical fuel pumps, and cork sheet for sumps and timing covers. There are two types of cork sheet: plain and laminated. The laminated sheet has two layers of cork with a sheet of cotton or nylon in between. It is more expensive, but nicer to use as it does not break easily.

There are two ways to mark out the shape. With thin gaskets lay the gasket over the face of the metal and rub round with your finger to leave an impression. With thicker gaskets mark the surface of the metal with engineers blue, or even thinned down paint, lay the gasket material on top and tap all over lightly with a hammer to get a print.

Punch all the holes in the gasket before you cut the outline. The only satisfactory way to make holes is with a hollow punch. You can buy them, or make them up by sharpening the ends of pieces of steel tube of varying diameters. There is no need to harden your homemade punches. Ordinary mild steel tube will cut quite a few holes without resharpening if you have a plank of soft wood under the gasket.

Some people love using gasket cement. I try to avoid it if I can. The only time I use it, and then reluctantly, is if the metal is corroded and there is not enough metal left to reface the joint. In all other cases I smear the gasket with water pump grease, and I seldom get any leaks. The only exception is with a thin mild steel head gasket. These have to go on dry. The holes in manifold gaskets should be checked to see they match the manifold and engine. If they protrude they will upset the gas flow.

To get back to our engine, the next job on an ohv engine is the rocker gear. Strip it off its shaft, keeping the parts in order by threading them on a stout piece of wire, and dump them all in the paraffin bath to clean.

If the shaft is badly worn you will never get quiet tappets, so it pays to renew it and fit new rocker bushes. Some rocker bushes are plain bronze and can be reamered. Others are thin-wall wrapped bearings and must not be. If the bushes have a hole to feed oil to the push rod, make sure it lines up with the hole in the rocker when the bush is pushed in. On some bushes the feed hole or holes are provided, and on others they have to be drilled after the bush is in place. Some have the main feed hole drilled, but not the smaller hole to feed the push rod end. Just because one hole is provided it does not necessarily mean there is only one. If you press in a wrapped bush with the hole out of line never try to press it out again; it will be ruined. Leave it where it is and drill a new hole.

The pads on the end of the rockers which bear on the valve stems are bound to be worn. The tappets can never be set properly with indentations in the pads, so they should be stoned out. This can be done with a carpenter's

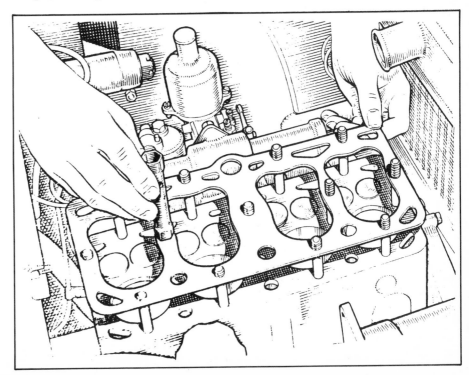

53   Use a box spanner or a piece of tube to ease the cylinder head gasket down over the studs

oil stone, or a small grinding wheel — if you take care to keep the proper profile of the pad. Alternatively, some garages will put the rocker in a jig and regrind the profile for you. If the indentations are very deep they may have gone through the hardening at the end of the pad. If they have, get the garage to build up the end of the pad with stellite or manganese hard facing and grind it down. This should be done before the new bushes go in as the heat of refacing may melt the bearing material in some lead-indium wrapped bushes. Re-profiling should be done after the new bushes are in.

The heads of the tappet screws on side valve engines will also have indentations. These can be dealt with at home quite easily. Grind the ends flat and, if the dent was deep, reharden the ends by heating to cherry red and rolling the head of the screw in case hardening powder.

With the valve gear reconditioned you can turn your attention to the pistons and bores. If the bores are worn enough to warrant reboring or resleeving there is nothing to do to the old pistons except throw them away, but if they are only slightly worn you will probably get away with re-ringing and special oil control rings — at least for a few thousand miles. It is unlikely that the old rings will be much good, so it does not matter if you break them getting them off. Indeed, an old broken ring makes a very good tool with which to clean the oil deposit and carbon from the ring grooves on the piston.

On a complete rebuild the pistons should be absolutely clean. I have always had mixed feelings about the old practice of leaving a ring of carbon round the edge of the piston head to stop excessive oil consumption. It may be true if you are just doing a top overhaul of an old worn engine, but if the pistons need carbon to stop burning oil it is time they were changed.

With some special oil control rings it is necessary to send the pistons for machining,

but others fit straight into the grooves. All other rings have to be gapped before they are fitted to the pistons. The correct gap will be given in the manual, but if you do not have one work on the rule-of-thumb figure of 0.0025 in to 0.003 in (0.06 mm to 0.08 mm) gap for each inch (2.5cm) of bore diameter. To measure the gap, put a ring in the bore and push it about halfway down with a piston to make sure it is square in the bore, then measure the gap with feeler gauges. If it is too small, the end of the ring can be taken down with a fine file. Support the ring in the vice close to the end while filing because they are very brittle.

If you are not reboring the engine there is bound to be a ridge at the top of the bore. There are tools made for taking this ridge off, but a much easier way of dealing with it is to fit 'ridge-dodger' top rings. These have a small shoulder cut in the top edge to miss the ridge. If they are not used the engine will sound terribly clattery as the new rings hit the ridge, and the top groove in the piston will soon wear.

The bores will have a very hard shiny finish. This must be taken off or the new rings will take thousands of miles to bed in and will give high oil consumption. Go over the bores with wet and dry rubbing-down paper well lubricated with paraffin till the high shine has been reduced to a smooth matt finish. Don't be afraid of taking too much off. You would have to rub a long time with wet and dry paper to take off any measurable amount. Alternatively the bores can be de-glazed with Flex-Hones which I mentioned in the chapter on brakes.

Fitting new rings on a piston can be tricky if you have not done it before. There are tools to do the job, and some people recommend using thin strips of metal like feeler gauges to ease the rings down. I find these methods fiddling, and have always used my fingers. Stand the piston on the bench and, starting

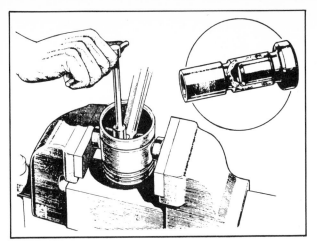

54 Use either these special buttons, or two small bolts, to hold the gudgeon pin on fixed little ends while you undo the fixing bolt

with the bottom ring, put your fingers round it so that your thumbs are on the ends at the gap and your middle fingers are cupped round the ring to control and support it. Ease your thumbs out gently to expand the ring just enough to lower it over the top of the piston and into the groove. Practice with old rings and you will soon get the knack.

On engines with little end bushes — or wrist pin bushes, as some manuals call them — check the bush on the gudgeon pin, or wrist pin, and if there is any slap, renew the bush. If you are going to the expense of fitting new pistons, fit new little end bushes as a matter of course. Check that the oil feed to the little ends is clear.

Some gudgeon pins are clamped to the ends of the connecting rod, and I always prefer to use new bolts. The old ones may have stretched, and if one gives way to let the pin drift out it can ruin the engine. To undo the clamp bolt to take the piston off, put a small bolt in each end of the gudgeon pin, and clamp it in a vice to hold it steady. Always fit new locking tabs.

Thin-wall shell main and big end bearings should always be replaced, but with the older cast-in-place white metal bearings you will have to decide whether or not to renew them. To my mind it is worth having them done on a complete overhaul, and probably having the crank ground as well; then they can be fitted and forgotten. If, however, they look in good condition and they were nice and quiet when

the engine was running, with good oil pressure, you may get thousands of miles more out of them. It is one of those things you have to decide on each individual engine.

With cast white metal bearings the crankshaft will have to be ground only enough to take out the score marks, but with thin-wall shell bearings it will have to be ground down to the next undersize. If the shaft has already been ground to its minimum diameter it can be metal sprayed and ground back to standard. Always make sure you can obtain the shell bearings in the size you want before having the shaft ground. A number of undersizes may be listed in the manual, but only some of them may be obtainable now.

Timing gears on an engine seldom give a lot of trouble except where there is a fibre or plastic one running against a steel or iron one. These are very quiet when new, but if they are worn there is no cure except replacement. It is easy to say that, but sometimes not so easy to do. You might be lucky through the spares secretary of a one-make club, but if not, and if the gears are bad, you may have to have a set cut.

Possibly the best place to go for this is a local engineering shop. There may well be other parts you need making, and if you can get the shop interested in your restoration they might well undertake some small jobs which might otherwise be uneconomic. But make sure the shop is equipped to do what you want. I have come across back-street shops proclaiming themselves to be precision engineers when their idea of precision is better suited to farm implements than cars. This applies particularly to gear cutting. If new gears, either timing gears or for the gearbox, are not cut accurately, they will whine for evermore. Make sure the workshop is able to recognise the tooth form. Some gears are cut with special profile teeth for quiet running. If the shop does not realise this you might end up with basic mangle-shape teeth which will never run quietly.

The shop will want the old gears as a pattern and will also want to know the pitch centres. That is the distance between the centres of the gears when they are mounted on the engine. It is not good enough to measure this with a steel rule. If you do not have access to precision measuring equipment, take the block along to the shop for them to measure it. Then if the gears do not mate properly the shop can with justification be blamed.

The other method of timing on most cars is by chain. The toothed belt for timing overhead camshafts did not come in till quite recently. I always make it a practice to renew the timing chain on a rebuild even if it looks in good condition. There should be little trouble getting a chain. It may not be available from the car's agents but it is unlikely to be anything other than a standard pitch, and any good engineering supply house will be able to order it by the foot complete with connecting links. What will be missing are any timing marks, such as polished links, which were on the original chain.

There are three ways of overcoming this lack: one is to keep the old chain and mark the new one with dabs of paint using the old chain as a pattern; the second is to mark the timing gear wheels before you dismantle the engine. Turn the engine till it is at some recognizable and repeatable position — say, top dead centre, number one piston, compression stroke, that is with both valves closed. Then lay a straight edge across the wheels in line with their centres and scribe a line right across them. The point about choosing a repeatable position is that the camshaft will not be 180° out of phase when the thing is put

together again. When reassembling the engine, set the crankshaft with number one piston at top dead centre, set the camshaft with both valves to number one cylinder closed and line up your scribed marks. You may find with a new chain that the lines do not match exactly because the old chain will have stretched, but they will not be out by as far as one chain pitch. If there is any doubt, try turning the camshaft wheel one tooth. The correct setting will be obvious. The third method is to work from the timing diagram in the manual. This will give the number of degrees before top dead centre on the crankshaft at which the inlet valve opens. Transfer this number of degrees into inches or centimetres round the flywheel rim, using a full scale drawing if necessary, and mark the rim of the flywheel using the top dead centre mark as a datum. Turn the flywheel back from top dead centre to your valve opening mark, set the camshaft till the valve is just about to open and connect the chain. Read the manual carefully; sometimes the valve timing is given with a different tappet clearance from the running clearance.

If the previous owner had run the engine till the timing chain nearly fell apart you might find that the teeth of the gears are hooked; there will be a definite undercut in the tooth shape where the chain has worn it. It is not a common fault, because timing chains run in a good supply of oil, but it is a point worth checking. The teeth have to be pretty bad to be useless, but if they are hooked they will wear a new chain quickly. You will have to decide whether it is worth trying to get new wheels, or ones in better condition, or resign yourself to replacing chains more frequently. It is a matter of availability and cost.

Camshafts do not often wear to any great extent, though some engines seem to have an appetite for them. If you are unlucky, and a replacement shaft is not to be had, there are specialist firms who will build up the worn cams and regrind them. If the camshaft bearings are white-metalled the shop that did your mains and big ends can remetal and line-bore them. If they are plain bronze most engineering shops can turn new ones. The difficulty arises when they are thin-wall wrapped bearings and new ones are not available. It is possible, if you are lucky, that they are a standard bearing from the bearing maker's catalogue, and still made for some other application. If not, the bearing company might make a set for you, but they will be very expensive. Try the spares secretary of the one-make club. He might know of another easily obtainable bearing that can be modified or, if not, the club may have had a batch made up.

It is always worth while checking the oil pump thoroughly. Post-war oil pumps will be either the eccentric rotor or gear type, with possibly a few piston types about. If a piston pump is worn the only thing to do is try to find one in better condition or trust an engineering shop to make new parts, or else to build up and machine the old parts. There is little you can do in a home workshop, and new piston pumps are scarce.

Rotor or gear type pumps are easy to check. You will be unlucky if the rotors or gears are badly worn, or if they are sloppy on their spindles. Again, if they are, try to find a pump in better condition.

You check for wear with feeler gauges. Correct clearances will be given in the manual. If a manual is not available, average working clearances for a double gear type pump are: radial clearance between the edges of the teeth and the pump body, 0.005 in to 0.007 in (0.13 mm to 0.15 mm); end float on the pump gears, 0.003 in to 0.004 in (0.08 mm to 0.1 mm). On an eccentric rotor pump typical clearance figures are: clearance between inner and outer rotors, 0.005 in to 0.007 in (0.13 mm to 0.15 mm); clearance between outer rotor and pump body, 0.01 in (0.25 mm). These are representative figures. Most pumps will work quite satisfactorily with them, but try to obtain the maker's figures for checking.

If the side clearances are much too large the best thing is to try to get another pump. Both types of pump will work with clearances well above these figures, but the pressure will be lower than it should be. End float, if it is too great, can sometimes be adjusted by shims on the drive shaft, but if this is impossible try lapping the face of the pump body. It is unlikely to be too small because wear increases the end float.

Check the bottom cover for scoring where the gears or rotor may have worn it. Wear here can be lapped out with fine emery cloth on a flat surface. A few gear pumps (some MGs for example) have the drive held on the bottom end of the shaft by a circlip, and there is a counterbore in the end cover to accommodate the end of the shaft. If you lap the end cover make sure there is still clearance for the end of the shaft.

The oil pressure will be controlled by a relief valve. Sometimes this is in the pump, and sometimes it is in the oil gallery on the block. In either case, check the spring and the seating as well as the ball or plunger. If the plunger is a cone type it can be lapped into its housing with valve grinding paste till you get a bright clean ring round the cone. Take care

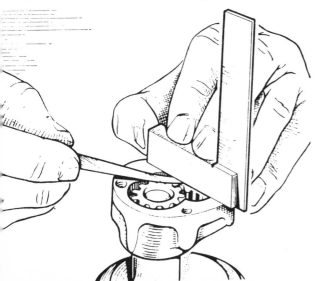

55 Use a straight edge and feeler gauges to check for wear on the oil pump gears

107

to get rid of all the abrasive afterwards. If the valve uses a ball and this shows signs of corrosion — as they often do — use a new one. Set it into its seat by putting it in position and using a drift and hammer to give it just one sharp tap onto its seating. Use only one blow. A double blow is likely to give a double seating which will not hold pressure properly. The spring is checked by measuring its free length, and the only check is to obtain the correct figure from the manual.

When finally cleaning the oil pump clean it only with a brush. With any sort of rag there is a danger of leaving shreds behind. If you discover this after you start the engine it is too late. Always use plenty of oil on the parts when putting them together, and prime the pump well through the inlet port after it is assembled.

When putting all the parts of the engine together again, check all the mating faces of everything which fits together to see that they are clean and making good contact. Pressed steel covers and oil sumps often pull up round the bolt holes, so dress the faces down with a block and hammer and finish off with a file. Give a liberal coating of oil to everything as you assemble it, and check the freedom of all moving parts as you fit them.

The starter ring gear on the flywheel will show wear in definite places where the engine has come to rest on a compression stroke. Unless the wear is light it is best to renew the gear if you can get one. It is not an easy thing to do at home because the new ring has to be heated to an even red to expand it before it is put on the flywheel. To do this without a proper forge hearth is tricky, so get a garage to do it. If the teeth are badly worn and you are unable to get either a new ring or a flywheel in better condition, it is sometimes possible to bring unworn portions of the ring into use by turning the flywheel through 90° on the end of the crankshaft. You may have to drill a new hole for the dowel, and it

should be regarded only as a last resort. The timing marks on the flywheel will be 90° out, and useless. On some high performance cars the flywheel and crankshaft may have been balanced as an assembly, and turning the wheel will upset this; so will fitting a secondhand flywheel. Ideally in this case you should have the crankshaft and flywheel rebalanced together, or use the crankshaft that went with the secondhand flywheel.

On some designs the starter ring teeth are machined in the edge of the flywheel. If they are worn the only remedy is replacement. Try to find this out if possible before buying the car and, if the teeth are worn, as indicated by unusual noises when the starter turns the engine, allow quite a lot of money to put it right.

Apart from changing the flywheel because of the wear in the ring gear, you might also consider it if the part which engages with the clutch centre plate is badly scored. There are bound to be some marks where the plate has been rubbing, but light marking does no harm. If the scoring is deep because someone ran a centre plate down past the rivet heads, the flywheel will soon wear a new plate. In this case the face of the flywheel can be skimmed. It should not be necessary to take off much metal. Indeed, it is imperative not to take off so much that the strength of the flywheel is affected. It is impossible to give any limits for the amount which can be safely machined off. It will differ from car to car. Refer to the manual or to the car maker. If the maker is no longer in business, and you are unable to obtain authentic safe machining limits, it is better not to chance things. Try to find a flywheel in better condition. Never trust the machining of a flywheel to someone who works by guesswork or by 'that'll be safe enough' methods. It is just possible he could weaken it, and a flywheel which flies apart at high revs can do an incredible amount of damage, and possibly injury.

=13=

THE CLUTCH, GEAR BOX AND REAR AXLE

If the car was a runner when you bought it you will have some idea of the clutch condition. Even if it seemed all right, examine it carefully while it is dismantled.

Assuming it is a dry clutch, as most postwar clutches are, check the centre plate (the one with the linings) to see that there is still a reasonable amount of lining above the rivets. If any of the rivets are worn bright from rubbing it is time to renew or reline the plate. Most British cars use a standard size Borg and Beck clutch, and the chance of getting a new plate is good. If this proves impossible it might be possible to get new linings. The old rivets must be drilled out, not punched out, or there is a danger of distorting the plate. After riveting, the plate should be mounted on a mandrel to check the run-out — the amount by which the lining faces are out of true when the plate revolves. As a general figure the maximum run-out at the rim of a 8 in (20.32 mm) clutch should be less than 0.015 in (0.38 mm).

Two causes of rejecting a centre plate for relining are that the splines have worn, so that it rocks badly on the first motion shaft of the gearbox, or that the ring of torque reaction springs round the plate has worn loose. If possible it is much safer to get a new plate.

Even though the linings may not be worn they will still look polished. This is as it should be, but polish should not be confused with the glaze that comes from oil leaking onto the plate. The heat of the clutch burns the oil either to a highly-glazed carbon or partly to a resin-like deposit.

Provided the linings are only polished and the grain of the friction material is visible through the polish, a small amount of oil will not affect the performance of the clutch to any extent, and you have caught it in time. But if the surface is completely black, and no grain can be seen, it is likely to slip under load and judder as it takes up the drive. If there is any sign of oil on the plate make sure to find out where it came from and stop the leak.

Most clutches on restorable cars are the coil spring type, though some later cars with diaphragm spring clutches are now also becoming restorable — as distinct from repairable. If the pressure plate is scored the chances are that the whole assembly needs overhauling. An exchange unit, if available, is best, but it is possible to overhaul clutches at home if the new parts are available and the pressure plate does not have to be changed. If the plate is changed the whole assembly needs rebalancing. This really needs special equipment to do properly. The most likely parts to need replacing are the eye bolts and pins, possibly the

109

56 Without a special
clutch compressing tool
a clutch can be taken
apart by using a press
and blocks of wood

knife edges and release levers, and all the springs.

Mark the cover plate, the release levers and the pressure plate before they are taken apart, so that they are put back in the same relative positions to preserve the balance. If the flywheel is off the car, stand the clutch on it but do not bolt it down. If the flywheel is on the car and you do not want to take it off, cut two blocks of wood so that when the clutch assembly is stood on them they support the pressure plate but allow the cover to move down. Put the assembly under a drill press or a hand press, rest another block of wood across the cover and compress it down while undoing the three nuts over the release levers. Considerable force will be needed to undo them because they are staked into slots on the bolts. When the nuts are off release the press gradually to avoid the parts flying all over the workshop.

Lay the parts out round the clutch plate as a reminder to put the levers back in the same places. Replace the worn parts and the springs with a smear of high melting point grease on all the working faces. Put the assembly under the press again and guide the bolts through the cover as you apply pressure. Put the nuts on and release the press.

The next job is to set the release levers. On a clutch setting jig there are gauges to do this, but they will have to be set either from the

figure in the manual or from measurements made before the clutch was taken to pieces.

Put the centre plate in position on the flywheel, bolt the clutch in place and set the levers by adjusting the nuts till the measurement is correct. It is important that all three levers are set to the same height within close limits. Borg and Beck's tolerance is 0.005 in (0.13 mm). After the first setting, unbolt the flywheel, turn the centre plate half a turn, bolt the cover down again and recheck the settings. If all is well stake the nuts into the slots in the eye bolts with a small punch to lock them. Then fit the pressure pad against which the carbon block pushes to disengage the clutch, together with its anti-rattle springs.

This method of putting a clutch together and setting the levers is not so accurate as using a special jig, so resort to it only if a replacement clutch is impossible to find. If you have any doubts, get a specialist firm to rebuild it.

When the assembly is finally put back on the engine you will need something to line up the centre plate accurately while tightening the clutch holding bolts, or else you will never get the gearbox back again. Most manuals recommend using a special tool or a spare first motion shaft. This is fine if you have the special tool, or a spare gearbox to take to pieces to get a spare first motion shaft, but few of us have, so you will have to make up a tool.

If you have a woodworking lathe, or a power drill with a lathe attachment, you can make up a tool from hardwood that will serve 99% as well as a spare first motion shaft. I have turned up several from pieces of broomstick. All that is needed on the tool are two fairly accurate diameters, one to fit in the end of the crankshaft, or inside the crankshaft bush if one is fitted, and one to fit the splined hole in the clutch plate. There is no need to cut the splines.

If there is a bronze bush in the end of the crankshaft it should be a reasonably tight fit. If the bush looks oval or if it falls out of the shaft, renew it. It fits in a blind hole, so it cannot be driven out in the normal way. Use the time-honoured method for dealing with blind bushes. Find a piece of steel or round wood that is a sliding fit in the bush, fill the bush with oil, put the rod in it and hit it hard with a hammer. The oil will find its way behind the bush and the hydraulic pressure will force it out.

The thrust release bearing will probably be a carbon disc, though one or two cars carried on after the war with thrust bearings. The carbon disc is carried in a cast iron housing and for most cars replacements are available. In cases where they are not you may be able to get the carbon by itself. The carbon disc chips easily, so treat it with care. It is pressed in while the housing is red hot and then the assembly is quenched in oil. It is possible to do this at home if you have a small firebrick hearth and a blowtorch, but if not there are specialist firms that will do it, and probably supply the carbon block as well.

Next in the transmission line is the gearbox. Here there are so many different designs that it is impossible to go through the detailed points of dismantling and repairing them. If you are not familiar with the box a manual is almost essential. There are, however, a few pointers I can give which apply to most gearboxes.

The most common reasons for wanting to strip down a gearbox are that gear selection is difficult, the box is noisy or it jumps out of gear on the over-run. Difficult gear selection may be due to worn or burred selectors, and a noisy gearbox can often be quietened by fitting new bearings. In many cases this can be done without special tools, but jumping out of gear usually indicates worn synchromesh clusters, which are not so easy to tackle without special tools.

On a three or four speed manual box where the change lever operates in the top of the box it is not uncommon to find the selector forks bent or with burrs on them. Put the gear lever in neutral before taking it out, and watch the position of any anti-rattle springs above or below the ball, either in the housing or in the cover. Take the top cover off the box gently, because on some designs the springs and balls which engage in detents on the selector shafts are held down by the top cover, and will fly out if allowed to.

The selector forks will be locked to the shafts, often with square-headed bolts, and these will be locked with wire. When the bolts are slackened the shafts can be withdrawn, either forwards or backwards depending on the design, after the appropriate end cover has been taken off. You may have to take out the speedometer drive gear before taking the rear cover off. If you are dismantling the whole box it is easy to forget the speedometer drive, so take it out now otherwise it may get damaged when you come to take out the mainshaft.

As you withdraw the selector shafts, leaving the forks in place for the moment, watch for any balls, pins and springs mounted horizontally between the shafts. It is notoriously easy

57   A mandrel to align the clutch plate is essential when bolting it back on the flywheel

for them to drop down in the box, and if you miss their fall they can have a merry if short life chewing up the gear teeth.

Make a sketch of where each selector fits and take a little time to study them to make sure you know in which order they come out and go back. You can have quite a game trying to refit them if you forget. The layshaft spindle, and the spindle holding the reverse gear, are usually held in by dowel bolts from outside the casing. The standard method of taking things apart is to take out the layshaft spindle dowel and drift out the spindle so that the layshaft cluster drops to the bottom of the box. Then, depending on the design of the box, the first motion shaft and its bearing come out from the front using an extractor, or the whole mainshaft assembly is tapped forwards with a brass drift to drive the first motion shaft out.

Then the mainshaft is tapped back again till its bearing comes out of the casing. The bearing is taken off with a puller, complete with any bearing plates. After this the mainshaft cluster can be manoeuvred out through the top of the box, the layshaft cluster lifted out and the reverse gear taken out.

Make a careful note of the order in which everything came out, even the smallest ball or pin, so that when putting it together you do not forget anything. It is most annoying to

have to take a box apart twice just because you have forgotten to put some small part in.

Dismantling and reassembling synchromesh clusters varies. In many cases they can be taken apart after depressing various plungers, but to put them together often requires special tools, such as slave dogs or rings, to get all the locating balls and springs back. In most cases, too, you need a press, and sometimes special mandrels to take some of the gears off the shafts. Unless you are experienced with gearboxes a manual is essential.

When putting it all back oil everything liberally as it is assembled. Remember to lock, either with tab washers or wire, everything you unlocked, and renew all oil seals, felts and gaskets.

If you are unlucky enough to find broken teeth in the box, and an exchange box is unobtainable, look for a good secondhand one. You may have to put new bearings in it, but the teeth will have bedded in together. If you try to marry partly worn teeth from two different boxes you will get noisy operation and probably notchy gear changing as well.

Difficulty in gear changing with steering column mounted shifts is often due to worn pins and bushes in the linkage, a stretched cable if one is used, or a burred selector plate inside the box. Some column changes, though, never did work nicely and many restorers fit

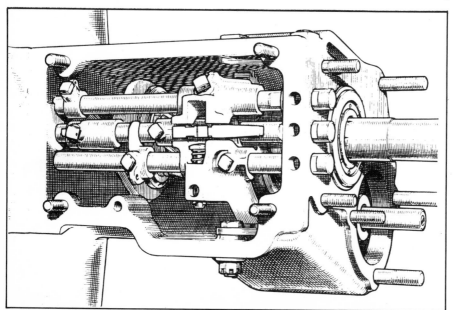

58   When taking the top cover off the gearbox watch out for springs and balls in the holes at the ends of the selector shafts. The square headed bolts must be locked in pairs with locking wire

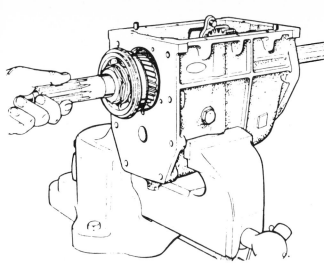

a floor mounted change if one was offered as an option when the car was new. A breaker's yard will probably yield one complete with the box.

If you want to stay with the column linkage, or if a floor change was never offered, things can often be improved. If you find you can adjust the linkage to get first gear but not second, it is almost certain to be because there are worn bushes, or that the gearbox mountings are sagging. The only cure for worn bushes is to renew them, and the same goes for a cable that is stretched to its limit. Packing washers may get you out of trouble for a time but they are never a lasting cure.

On Standard Vanguards there is a small gearbox in the change linkage with a baulk plate to stop anyone going from first to third without going through neutral. Sometimes this baulk plate is bent or burred, which makes finding neutral difficult.

On other column change boxes (early Austins are an example) part of the linkage swings a selector plate just inside the box. A badly adjusted linkage and a heavy hand on the lever can distort this plate, so make sure it is flat, and take off any burrs with a file. It can be got at when the side cover is taken off. Get someone to operate the shift while you watch the plate. Any difficulty in selection is easy to spot and remedy. Apart from the selectors

being at the side instead of the top of the box, a column shift box overhaul is the same as a floor shift box.

Overdrives usually bolt on to the back of the main gearbox and can be taken off as a unit. Most have planetary gearing and operate hydraulically with electric solenoid control. It is unwise to take them apart without a manual. If you want to take one apart to see how it works operate the overdrive selection at least a dozen times to make absolutely sure there is no hydraulic pressure left, otherwise there could be a nasty accident. The only home maintenance I would recommend is draining and refilling the oil, cleaning the oil filter (which is usually under the drain plug), and — if necessary — replacing the solenoid unit.

Much the same advice goes for automatic gearboxes. Apart from making certain that the selection and throttle linkages are adjusted correctly — once again refer to the manual — all I would advise is changing the oil and filters. Even if you have a manual, reassembly of an automatic sometimes needs pumps, rigs and gauges to set the box up. Without them it is a hopeless task.

Any automatic box which has seen long service benefits from a change of oil and filters. This is recommended in service schedules after every 25,000 miles (40,000 km). It should be done after a run, or after the engine has been idling with the handbrake on and the selector in the L position till the box comes up to full working temperature.

Be careful. The temperature of the hydraulic fluid is enough to give nasty scalds. Keep your hands and face out of the way.

First drain the main transmission casing, then turn the converter round till you can get at its drain plug through the hole in the bell housing. When this plug is out take out the pressure-take-off plug to allow the converter to vent. On Borg-Warner boxes this plug is at the bottom of the casing on the left hand side.

The filter is inside the box above the oil pan which is held by a large number of set-screws. The filter itself is held by a screw and a clip. There will be dust from the bands in the filter, and possibly some metal dust; this does not mean the box is wearing out. A small amount of dust from the discs and thrust washers is normal. Brush the filter in clean transmission fluid and leave it to drain. Do not use rags of any description in case they leave lint or fluff behind; absolute cleanliness is essential if the box is to work properly. Use new gaskets when the pan is put back, and never take jointing compound anywhere near an automatic box. Put all the gaskets on dry.

The quantity of fluid needed for refilling will be around a pint or so less than the capacity given in the handbook, because you never get it all out. Put about three quarters of this in the box, then start the engine and let it idle for a minute or two with the selector in the L position to transfer the fluid to the converter. Then switch off and top up to the Full mark.

If you are restoring a Daimler, Lanchester or Armstrong Siddeley there will be a pre-selector box with a fluid flywheel. Many people fight shy of these boxes, but they seldom give much trouble and the bands are self adjusting. When they reach the limit of self adjustment they can be set up again quite simply. If the car is a non-runner when bought and you are towing it home, take the prop shaft off because the box gets its lubrication from the engine side of neutral.

If the bands slip select each gear in turn and pump the change pedal — the one in the position of the normal clutch pedal — ten times. If this does not cure the slipping it means the toggle action inside the box needs

setting up again. After taking the top cover off you can see the adjusters for each band. Adjustment takes place automatically each time a gear is disengaged, when the heel of the adjuster ring strikes a pin and the wrapping action of a spring turns a nut. If you operate the selector and pedal with the top off the action is easy to understand.

The amount of automatic adjustment is governed by the setting of adjuster stop screws on the brake bands. If the adjustment is near its limit it can reduce the toggle action and allow slipping.

Select the gear which is slipping and mark the adjuster nut with a pencil. Then pump the pedal till you are sure the nut has stopped moving. Watch carefully because it moves only very little each time the pedal is pumped.

To cure slipping, select and engage another gear and unscrew the adjuster nut one turn. There is a special tool for doing this but it can be done easily with a 5/16 in BSF bolt and locknut. Now unlock the adjuster stop screw, take it in half a turn and lock it. Then select and engage the gear being adjusted, hook the spring back round the adjuster nut and pump the pedal till the nut stops turning. If adjusting first or reverse, select second, third or top. Do not select neutral as this partially engages both first and reverse.

If the opposite of slipping occurs — harsh gear engagement — it means the toggle action is too fierce. Go through the same procedure, but this time unscrew the adjuster stop screw half a turn.

If the car has been standing for years the fluid flywheel may be leaking. There is a synthetic rubber seal in the centre of the flywheel cover, where the drive shaft to the box goes through. It is held by a distance piece and a plate which has a gasket and three set-screws. It is not too easy to get out, and you may have to take the rear cover off the flywheel. Mark the cover and the flywheel before taking them apart so that they will go back in correct balance, and be careful with the thin gasket between the two. If the box needs a complete overhaul, including relining the bands, there are specialist firms who will undertake it. Daimler, now part of Jaguar, does not keep stocks of spares any more.

Next in the transmission line comes the prop shaft. Nowadays many cars have prop shafts with peened-in universals, but fortunately all those likely to be found on restorable cars have universals that can be replaced.

Most British post-war cars have Hardy Spicer universal joints of standard sizes. Replacement kits come with a cross tree, new needle rollers and housings. The sliding joint of the shaft will pull apart when a knurled ring is undone. On some there is an arrow or a master spline to help line the shaft up again in its proper balance and relationship of the universals. If neither is evident, mark the shaft before taking it apart.

The needle bearing housings are held in by circlips. After these are taken out the housings can usually be jerked up sufficiently to grip them in a vice or a Mole wrench by hitting the yoke with a hide faced hammer. If they

are really seized in you may have to use a thin drift and hammer to shift them. They will break, but that does not matter as you are renewing them.

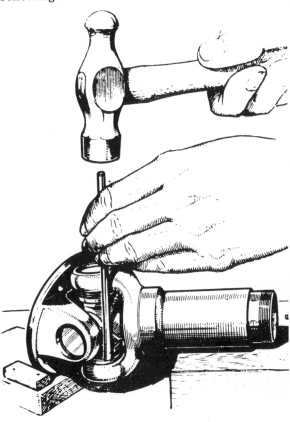

▲
61   If jarring fails to shift the needle roller housings it will have to be knocked out with a slim punch

◀60   Often a universal joint needle housing can be jarred out by hitting the yoke with a hide-faced hammer

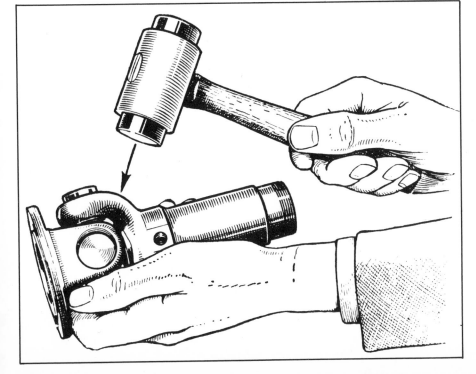

115

Replacing them is a simple matter of feeding the cross tree in the yoke, packing the needles with grease to stop them falling out and pressing the housings in. Treat the cork seals with care and press them on the cross tree with a tube to save breaking them. Make sure the circlips are properly seated in their grooves.

If you forgot to mark the shaft before taking it apart make sure the cross trees at each end of the shaft are in line. If they are not you will get transmission vibration.

When it comes to overhauling rear axles the biggest job is meshing the crown wheel and pinion. All post-war manuals specify setting gauges, but with care the mesh can be set by blueing the teeth and watching the engagement pattern. This was the standard method when I first started in a garage. Even so, a manual is a great help.

Before you can get the differential out the half shafts have to be taken out. If the axle is a fully floating design — that is, if the hubs and their bearings fit on the outer casing of the axle — the half shafts will pull out after their holding bolts are taken out. In other cases the hub will be pressed on to the end of the half shaft, and it may be a very tight interference fit. In these cases it is better to undo the back plates and pull the hub and shaft out as a complete unit. If the bearings and seals need renewing they can be taken off the shafts with a press.

With the half shafts out the differential unit can be unbolted and taken out of the casing on most axles. On a few the two halves of the axle casing may have to be taken apart. Unless it is necessary to strip the differential assembly because of broken teeth or worn bearings I would advise washing it out and leaving it alone. The ends of broken half shafts can usually be driven out without taking the whole thing to pieces.

If it is to be taken to pieces watch carefully for any adjustment shims, and mark any screwed collars which are adjustable so that it can be put together with a reasonable chance of being near the correct mesh. Most pinions have the bearings pre-loaded; that is, the holding nuts for the bearings are done up tight, then taken up further to a pre-determined torque figure. Sometimes the pre-load is by shims. On some axles the crown wheel bearings are also pre-loaded. The proper settings are essential for a long lasting and quiet axle.

Crown wheels and pinions are lapped together during manufacture and must always be installed as a matched pair. Because of manufacturing tolerances the settings for one pair will be slightly different from the next. This is usually indicated on the end face of the pinion where there is a number such as +3 or -2. This indicates that the pinion is set 0.003 in further away or 0.002 in nearer the centre line of the crown wheel than the standard setting using the manufacturer's figures and gauges. On continental cars the figures will indicate hundredths of a millimetre.

If you do not have setting gauges, press the new bearings on the pinion shaft and set it in the casing using the same distance pieces or screwed collar settings as the pinion you took out. Now you have to pre-load the bearings to allow for expansion of the casing when it gets hot.

The pre-load may be specified in two ways. It may be given as a setting dimension, say 0.002 in (0.051 mm), or it may be given as a torque drag figure when the pinion is turned. The proper way to adjust the pre-load as a setting dimension is to add shims till there is a small amount of end float. This end float is measured with a dial gauge mounted on the casing. More shims are added to this dimension to make up the end float plus the setting load. For example, if the end float is 0.005 in (0.127 mm) and the pre-load is 0.002 in (0.051 mm), shims to a total of 0.007 in (0.178 mm) have to be added.

It is possible, though not so accurate, to adjust the shims till the end float is zero, judged by feel, and then add the pre-load shims. I have known it done with success, but it is not so sure a method as using a dial gauge.

If the pre-load is given as a torque drag figure it will be quoted with or without the oil seal in position. An example could be, say, 10 to 14 pounds-inches (1.8 to 2.5 kg-cm) torque. This is checked either with a torque rod which is bolted to the pinion flange and which has a sliding weight on it, or with an arm bolted to the flange and a spring balance. Bearing spacers and shims are adjusted till the weight on the rod is opposite its correct reading when the flange just turns, or till the torque which just moves the flange is measured with the arm and balance to be within the quoted limits.

The crown wheel will be either bolted or riveted to the differential carrier. When installing a bolted one, make sure the mating faces of the wheel and carrier are clean and dry, then tighten the bolts opposite each other in pairs to pull the wheel evenly down on to its seating. When replacing a riveted one, drill the heads off the old rivets on the crown wheel side so as to avoid any damage to the carrier. Put the new wheel on and bolt it down with four evenly-spaced bolts. Rivet the empty holes before taking the bolts out. Riveting is carried out cold with the rivet heads peened on the crown wheel side, once again to avoid damaging the carrier.

After fitting a crown wheel it should, strictly speaking, be checked for run-out by mounting it on vee blocks and using a dial gauge. The maximum allowable run-out is in the order of 0.003 in (0.076 mm) at the rim. If, however, it has been mounted clean and dry, and bolted or riveted evenly, it should be safely within run-out limits.

On many axles the crown wheel bearings are also pre-loaded. Once again the load may be given as shim thickness after all the free play is taken up. When all the shims are in position you will have to drive the assembly into the housing with a hide faced hammer because the extra pre-load shims will make it a slight interference fit. If the adjustment is by screwed collars, the setting will be the number of holes or notches in the collar by which it is screwed in after all the end float has been taken up. In this case, reassemble to the previous marks, then back off one collar and retighten it till the bearing just starts to turn with it. This is the point where all the end float is taken up. Now tighten it to the setting given beyond this point, an average figure being two or so notches plus any further amount needed to bring one of the notches level with the locking screw.

With the pre-loads taken care of you can mesh the crown wheel and pinion. Most manuals give a backlash setting which can be used only if the pinion has been set in the housing with a depth gauge. If it has not, you have to use tooth markings. Paint the crown wheel teeth with engineer's blue, or a mixture of red lead or yellow ochre and oil. Then load the crown wheel by holding your hand on it and turn the pinion till the crown wheel has made one complete turn. Then turn the pinion back the other way till it is back where it started. There will be markings on the crown wheel teeth where the pressure of the pinion teeth has squashed out the marking mixture.

The ideal contact pattern, as shown in the illustration, should be halfway up the crown-wheel tooth, about 60% of the length of the tooth and biased towards the toe, the inner

62   Ideal tooth contact on a crown wheel when tested with engineer's blue

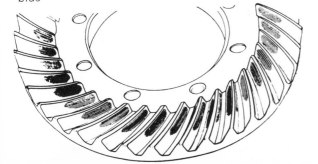

	TOOTH CONTACT (DRIVE GEAR)	CONDITION	REMEDY
A	HEEL (outer end) / Coast / TOE (inner end) / Drive	IDEAL TOOTH CONTACT Evenly spread over profile, nearer toe than heel.	o ——— o
B	HEEL (outer end) / Coast / TOE (inner end) / Drive	HIGH TOOTH CONTACT Heavy on the top of the drive gear tooth profile.	Move the DRIVE PINION DEEPER INTO MESH. i.e., REDUCE the pinion cone setting.
C	HEEL (outer end) / Coast / TOE (inner end) / Drive	LOW TOOTH CONTACT Heavy in the root of the drive gear tooth profile.	Move the DRIVE PINION OUT OF MESH. i.e., INCREASE the pinion cone setting.
D	HEEL (outer end) / Coast / TOE (inner end) / Drive	TOE CONTACT Hard on the small end of the drive gear tooth.	Move the DRIVE GEAR OUT OF MESH. i.e., INCREASE backlash.
E	HEEL (outer end) / Coast / TOE (inner end) / Drive	HEEL CONTACT Hard on the large end of the drive gear tooth.	Move the DRIVE GEAR INTO MESH. i.e., DECREASE backlash but maintain minimum backlash as given in "Data"

63 The different markings on a crown wheel, what they mean and how to adjust the mesh to obtain ideal contact

smaller end of the tooth. When the axle is running under load it will spread slightly towards the heel, or larger end of the tooth.

If it is in the correct position along the tooth but too high, the pinion needs to be moved deeper into mesh towards the centre line of the crown wheel. If it is in the correct position along the tooth but too low, the pinion needs to be moved out of mesh. Make sure you do not alter the pre-load when you do this.

If the marking is in the correct position up and down the tooth but too near the toe, the crown wheel needs to be moved out of mesh. If it is correct up and down but too near the heel, the crown wheel needs to be moved closer into mesh.

If the crown wheel pinions are shimmed for pre-load, adjusting the mesh is a matter of taking shims from one side and putting them in the other. If it is by screwed collars, the collars must be moved an equal amount on each side to retain the correct pre-load.

This method of meshing a crown wheel and pinion has been superseded in garages by manufacturer's setting jigs and gauges mainly because they are more certain and quicker. With care, however, the mesh can be set just as accurately.

118

=14=
SORTING OUT THE ELECTRICS

Part 1.
The Wiring

The electrical system is the Achilles heel of almost all older cars because they were wired with rubber covered cable. Unlike modern PVC covered cable which lasts almost indefinitely, rubber insulation hardens to the point where if you bend the cable the rubber cracks off. I know of nothing more likely to cause that sick feeling in the stomach of an old car enthusiast than the smell of burning rubber. It brings visions of the whole car going up in flames — a vision which, unfortunately, can be only too real.

If the car has old rubber-covered wiring, and the rubber has age-hardened, then for safety's sake — as well as the convenience of having all the electrics working — make rewiring a high priority job on the restoration list. On a complete rebuild it is almost essential.

There are three ways to go about it. The job can be put out to a professional, which will free you from all the work and cost a tidy sum of money. Or you can rewire it yourself using one of two methods: the first is to buy the wiring looms already made up, which is the most convenient, provided they are obtainable; the second is to buy the cable and rewire each circuit separately making up looms as you go along.

Try as hard as you can to get hold of a wiring diagram because it makes sorting out the circuits so much easier, even though most wiring diagrams are schematic rather than a true picture of how the cables run. But if you have a rare model, and a wiring diagram is unobtainable, do not lose heart. I will go through a method of building up a wiring diagram to suit any car, starting completely from scratch.

The first circuit to sort out is the charging circuit. I will go through the circuits for compensated voltage control systems using the Lucus RF and RB series control boxes, two of

64   Sometimes when rewiring you can buy a complete new loom. It looks a nightmare tangle, but with the wiring diagram and colour coding it is not such a puzzle as it seems

the most popular on British cars of the forties and fifties. If your car uses a different make or model of control box use these circuits as a guide to principles. If you cannot get a wiring diagram for your car get one for any car using the same dynamo and control box. The rest of the wiring will be different from yours but the charging circuit will be the same.

On the Lucas RF series control box there are nine terminals labelled F, D, E, A, A1, A2, A3 and two A4. Usually the system uses a Lucas PLC rotary combined lighting and ignition switch.

From the diagram you will see that everything except the starter motor is fed from one main cable running via the ammeter to terminal A on the control box. If your car is not fitted with an ammeter, and you want to fit one, this is where it goes in the circuit so it will tell you what is happening to the whole system. If you do not want an ammeter, run the main feed cable direct to terminal A.

I have drawn this feed cable starting from the solenoid switch of the starter, but it could come from the battery itself, and did on many models.

From terminal A1 on the control box a cable runs to terminal A on the ignition-lighting switch to feed the lights and the circuits controlled by the ignition. Terminals F and D on the control box are connected to terminals F and D on the dynamo. Also from D on the control box a cable goes to the ignition warning lamp and from there to terminal IGN on

the switch. Terminal E on the box goes to chassis earth.

Terminal A2 on the box feeds the auxiliaries not controlled by the ignition switch. It draws its current, via a fuse, from terminal A1.

Terminals A4 feed the auxiliaries controlled by the ignition switch. They draw their current, again via a fuse, from terminal A3 which is in turn fed from terminal IGN on the switch. Also, from terminal IGN on the switch, or from a separate terminal on the switch if it has a key start, a cable goes to the starter push and from there to energise the starter solenoid.

And that, basically, is that. All the rest of the masses of lines on the wiring diagram show how the cables feed the lights and the rest of the auxiliaries.

The circuit for the later Lucas RB series control boxes is very similar except that the fuses are carried in a separate holder instead of being in the control box itself. The box has five terminals, F, D, E, A and A1. The fuse holder has terminals labelled A1, A2, A3 and A4. Sometimes there are two A4 terminals linked together to avoid having to feed too many cables into one terminal.

As with the RF boxes the main feed goes via the ammeter to terminal A on the box, D and F on the box go to D and F on the dynamo, another cable from D on the box goes to the ignition warning lamp and from there to IGN on the switch. A1 on the box feeds A on the switch, and E on the box goes to earth.

Terminal A1 on the fuse holder is fed from A1 on the control box and A3 is fed from IGN on the switch. A variation of this is when A2 on the fuse holder feeds only the horn relay for a pair of Windtone horns, or

Combined ignition & lighting switch
Coil, oil warning etc
Fused auxiliaries not controlled by ignition switch
Side tail & panel
Head
Ignition warning lamp
Chassis earth
Starter push
Ammeter
Main feed
Dynamo
Starter
Solenoid switch
Battery
Fused auxiliaries not controlled by ignition switch
Lucas RF 91 regulator
Fuse
Fuse

65   The basic charging circuit for the popular Lucas RF 91 control box. Other Lucas R series boxes are similar

sometimes the horns and the interior light. In this case, the *A1* terminal on the fuse holder is fed direct from the main feed cable and the current for the horns and any auxiliaries fed from *A2* does not record on the ammeter. (An example of this layout is the 1953 Series 1 Morris Oxford.)

Early post-war Ford Anglias and the Popular introduced in 1953, being Fords, have a system all their own with a cut-out, only one cable from the dynamo, and no fuses. Wiring diagrams for these cars are readily available from Ford, so when rewiring one stick strictly to the diagram.

Another exception is on the earlier post-war Rolls-Royce and Bentley. Being Rolls-Royce they ignore convention on their CVC circuit and take the main feed first through a fuse, then to the switchbox on the fascia — itself exclusive to these cars — then to the ammeter and finally back to *A1* on the control box. Terminal *A* on the control box is treated with fine contempt and left severely alone.

Rolls-Royce had other little ideas of their own like ignoring colour-coded wiring and using black cable with marker sleeves for everything. They also have beautifully made multi-fused distribution boards and junction boxes so that the body can be lifted off the chassis with the minimum of disconnection. When rewiring a Rolls-Royce or Bentley get hold of the diagram — once again available from the company — and follow it exactly.

To get back to the majority of cars, I have drawn auxiliary and lighting circuits in schematic form to suit any car. These circuits look nothing like the way the cables run on the car, but this is the easiest way to follow the connections. All three circuits follow the same pattern of a main trunk feed and branches for the feeds to individual components.

Look first at the scheme for auxiliaries not controlled by the ignition switch. Theoretically it makes no difference which auxiliaries you choose to be controlled by the ignition switch and which you choose not to be. In practice the ones not controlled by the ignition are the ones likely to be wanted when the ignition is off, and the ones which take a heavy current and might overload the ignition switch contacts.

I have followed convention and chosen the usual ones of interior light, horn, headlamp flash, cigar lighter, boot or underbonnet light and clock. Others can be added, such as a radio, though on later cars this, and a few other

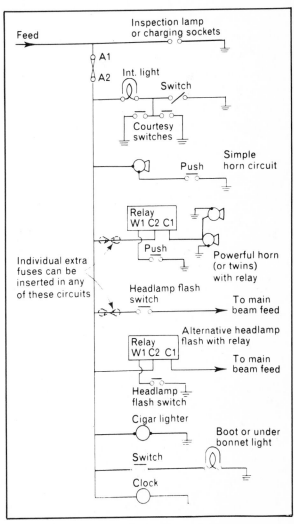

66 You can draw up a schematic for the auxiliaries not controlled by the ignition switch

auxiliaries, are controlled by a separate first position on the ignition switch key so you do not forget and leave them on. If you are drawing your own diagram work out how many of the auxiliaries are likely to be on at the same time so you do not overload the *A1-A2* fuse. If necessary fit another fuse and feed it also from *A1* on the control box.

The current load can be calculated from the simple formula: volts multiplied by amps equals watts. Transposing this, add together all the watts taken by your components, divide by the voltage and you get the current in amps.

Most *A1* fuses are 35 amps which, on a 12 volts system, means they can theoretically take an applied load of 420 watts. In practice there is a surge current around twice the normal steady running current when a component is switched on, so this cuts the load to 210 watts. Give yourself a 100% fuse safety tolerance so it blows only for a dead short, and call the maximum load 100 watts.

I have shown alternative circuits for the horn and headlamp flasher using relays. The purpose of the relay, which is only a heavy duty electrically operated switch, is to reduce the current load to the horn push or flash switch to avoid arcing and burning the contacts. All that these contacts have to carry is the current to operate the relay, which is much less than the current needed to operate the component. In the fuse calculations the wattage of the relay should be included as well as that of the components.

I have marked the terminals of the relays *W1, C2* and *C1*. These are the markings on a popular modern relay. If your relay has extra terminals or the markings are different, consult any wiring diagram using your model relay — or ask an auto electrician — to find out which are the input, output and control switch terminals. If you have no relays, and want to use them, put a modern relay in the position I have shown.

You will notice that the switches on the horn and interior light circuits are in the earth line, after the component. In the case of the interior light this is so that one can have courtesy light switches in the doors with only one cable going to them. In the case of the horn it saves taking two wires up the steering column because the other side of the horn push can be wired to earth on the column itself. If you have a split column with a universal joint in it make sure the top part is a good earth by running a bonding wire from it to the chassis or body.

On the scheme showing auxiliaries controlled by the ignition switch there are two trunks. One is fed through the *A3-A4* fuse and one is not fused at all. This is the usual practice for production cars, but if you want to put an extra fuse in the second trunk there is no reason why not. Some rally cars have a separate fuse in each branch from the trunk so that a short on one component does not stop any others from working.

I have drawn the heated rear window branch as a simple circuit of feed, switch, and component with the warning lamp in parallel. This arrangement is quite adequate for older heated rear windows of the fifties but modern ones, including the stick-on type, are more powerful and take a much higher current. Check the wattage. If it is 36 watts or more use a relay in the way I have shown for the horns and headlamp flash.

The direction indicator flasher circuit is quite straightforward. If you want to fit repeater flashers on the sides of the car just add another bulb in the left and right hand branches. You may have to use a heavier-duty flasher unit to avoid flashing too slowly, though if the repeater is only a 6 watt bulb

67   The schematic for auxiliaries controlled by the ignition switch. Note that some are taken before the A3-A4 fuse

most modern flasher units will cope.

If you want to keep your old semaphore direction indicators just delete the flasher unit and substitute a semaphore for each pair of flasher lamps. In this case the indicator warning lamp is usually incorporated in the switch but some semaphore circuits use two warning lamps, one for each side. In this case there is an extra pair of contacts in each semaphore arm which are closed when the arm is raised. The indicator lamp is fed each side as a branch from the trunk, and from the other side of each lamp a cable runs to one side of

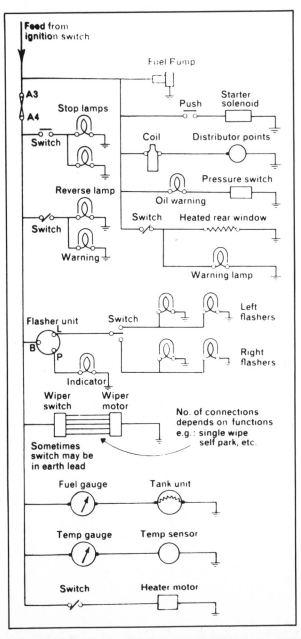

the contacts in the appropriate semaphore arm. The other side of each contact is earthed.

The last tree is for the lights. For schematic purposes I have drawn the ignition switch separate from the lighting switch, but many British cars have a combined switch as I drew in the charging circuit. Though the switches are combined, they can be treated as two switches with a common feed. An example of a car with a separate ignition switch is the Jaguar. In this there is a fog lamp switch incorporated in the lights switch. This sort of variation affects the practical wiring, but does not alter the diagram principle.

I have shown a position for extra fuses in the main and dipped beam light circuits. It is not usual production practice to fit them — indeed many cars do not have fuses in the headlight circuits — but I like them because if a short should develop in either the main or dipped beam wiring you are not left completely without headlights.

The schemes I have drawn will cover the majority of cars even though they may not be exactly the same as the production circuits. When rewiring without a wiring diagram draw up your own schemes to suit the components on the car. If you want to add extra components to any of the trunks just draw in another branch, but keep the fuse ratings in mind.

Now the schemes have to be converted into practical wiring diagrams. In the illustrations I have converted the scheme for the auxiliaries not controlled by the ignition. The others follow the same principle.

Get a large sheet of paper for each one and lay out the components in roughly the same position as they are on the car. Then run the trunk feed, as I have, round the components trying to avoid more than two cables at any one component terminal. This is not always possible, but you can spend a pleasant evening trying different routes for the cable. Try to keep the wiring short by linking the feed trunk to components near each other on the car. By drawing a practical diagram for each trunk you will avoid the masses of lines on the average circuit diagram and they will be easier to follow when putting in the cables.

Cables for car wiring are coded by a series of numbers divided by a stroke. This code indicates the number of wire strands and the wire size. All the new cable you buy, at least in Britain, will be metric. For example, a cable with a code of 14/0.30 will have 14 strands, each one 0.30 mm diameter. The older Imperial code, which was used on most cars till quite recently, was similar except that the wire diameter was in inches. The equivalent of the metric 14/0.30 would be 14/012, which denotes 14 strands, each one 0.012 inch diameter.

Auto electricians often make a distinction between the metric and Imperial codes in the way they say the numbers. They often call 14/0.30 'fourteen-thirty', and 14/012 'fourteen-O-one-two'.

The size of the cable governs the current it will take. Specifications vary slightly from one car maker to another, but for a 12 volt system you will be safe using 14/0.30 for the coil, sidelights, tail lights, interior lights, panel lights and similar general body wiring. Use 28/0.30 for headlights, spot lights and fog-lights, 65/0.30 for the ammeter, dynamo and control box feed circuits, and 97/0.30 for the main feed from the battery to the control box.

For a 6 volt system you will need heavier cable because the same power in watts needs twice the current for 6 volts compared with 12 volts. You are still safe with 14/0.30 for the coil, sidelights and so on, but you should go up to 84/0.30 for the ammeter, dynamo and control box feed circuits, and either 120/0.30 or 80/0.40 for the main feed from the battery to the control box.

When putting in new cables from the battery to the starter motor you will probably be offered cable in your accessory shop as 'suitable for 12 volt' or 'suitable for 6 volt'. I would

69   This is a practical wiring diagram constructed from the schematic for the auxiliaries not controlled by the ignition switch. Note how the cable is taken round the components to avoid too many junctions at one terminal

◀ 68   Constructing a schematic diagram for the lighting circuit

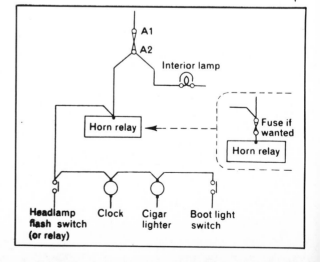

not rely too much on this broad classification. These suitabilities are often based on the minimum size cable when the battery is under the bonnet and the cable runs are short.

On longer runs they will carry the current all right, but if the battery is under the seat or even right back in the boot you will want a good heavy cable to avoid a severe voltage drop at the starter.

For twelve volt systems the usual specification when the battery is under the bonnet is 37/0.75. If the battery is way back I would advise 37/0.90. For 6 volt batteries under the front seat of a small car 61/0.90 is suitable, but with a large American classic with a 6 volt system, and the battery a long way from the starter, I would go as high as 61/1.13. All the cables I have quoted are standard production sizes, and any large auto-electrical supply house should stock them.

For the battery earthing cable go for the type usually described as 'heavy duty'. This is usually 16 bunches, each of 32 strands of 0.30 mm wire. The so-called 'standard' earthing strap is usually 16 bunches each of 16 strands of 0.30 mm wire. A really heavy battery earth is a great comfort on a cold morning when the starter is taking maximum current and the battery is down a little on voltage because of the temperature.

Earthing straps can be bought in various lengths complete with the battery terminal at one end and a lug for attaching to the chassis frame at the other. Remember to specify negative or positive earth so that you get the right size battery terminal.

The longer cable from the battery to the starter or starter solenoid, and the shorter one from the solenoid to the starter motor, do not usually come complete with terminals; the cable is bought by length. You can buy heavy duty terminals which fix to the cable with screws, but I do not like them. They often form a high resistance joint and starve the starter.

Nor do I care much for trying to solder heavy duty terminals on the cable. The terminal has to be so hot to make the solder flow properly that the heat spreads along the cable and melts the insulation. Many large garages, and most large auto-electric supply firms, have equipment for crimping the terminals firmly and cleanly to the ends of the cable, and will do it for you if you specify the length and whether you want positive or negative earth. It saves a good deal of time and trouble and you are assured of a good connection.

The rest of the wiring will either fit into a hole on the component and be held by a screw, be held in a housing by a split taper plug, or have a ring or spade terminal to fit on the component with a nut and washer. Whichever is the case, provide the end of the cable with the appropriate terminal connector. Winding the wire round and twisting it, even with a nut and washer, is extremely sloppy.

As to how much cable you will need, this, like the length of a piece of string, depends. As a rough guide for a medium-sized 12-volt car, work on 30 metres of 14/0.30, 8 metres of 28/0.30, or 16 metres if you are wiring fog and spot lights, 4 metres of 65/0.30 and 2 metres of 97/0.30.

The old wiring on the car will be colour coded to help trace the cables through the looms. Unless you are wiring with a pre-formed commerical loom I do not think it is worth while going to the trouble of using different colour codes. You will end up buying dozens of different lengths of different colour cable with different colour tracers on them. My practice is to wire all in one colour. Where there is a danger of cables being confused I put on marker sleeves made from short lengths of PVC tube roughened with emery cloth so that they can be marked with indelible ink.

With regard to tools, get a good pair of side cutters, and keep them for electrical work, a pair of crimping pliers for fixing terminal connectors to the cables and a proper insulation stripping tool. (By 'proper' I mean the adjustable sort which looks like a pair of pliers, not the 'bit-of-metal-with-a-hole-in-it' sort often found in the handle of give-away screwdrivers.)

There are far too many possibilities in wiring layout for me to give much guidance about how and where to run the cables, but there are a few points which apply to all cars. Try to keep the cable runs clear of road dirt and salt spray. This is not always easy, but take a leaf from the book of current car designers and run all the wiring to the back of the car inside the body instead of clipping it to the chassis frame.

When you get to the boot of the car it is often handy to use a junction box, either the closed type or one of the long strips of junction blocks sold in most household electrical shops. You can also buy snap tubular connectors at most component shops, and tools to fit the ends of the cable inside the connector which save the ends of the fingers when you have a large number to connect. The nipples on the end of the cable are either soldered or crimped. If you solder here, or anywhere in the car's electrical system, use non-corrosive resin-cored solder from a radio shop.

When wires need to go under the wings to reach lamps they will be subjected to constant grit blasting from the tires, so run them either through plastic sleeving or, if the cables show as they do on some sports cars, you can buy vintage-style armoured conduit which looks very smart. Always use grommets where cables pass through holes in sheet metal panels. If you have a detachable instrument panel it makes life a deal easier if you can unplug all the cables to it so that it can be taken right out for servicing the instruments and switches. On some high-priced luxury cars of the fifties the cables to the instrument panel went through one or two multi-pin connectors so that the panel could be unplugged. This is a feature which has come back on many modern cars with printed circuit instrument panels, so you can buy the multi-pin connectors from many dealers.

Some cars have cables for the horn and direction indicators, and sometimes the dip switch as well, running up a stator tube inside the steering column. You can buy special multi-cored cable for this, but watch the cable sizes if the dip switch cables are included. The two for this should be heavier than the rest. Take a piece of the old cable along to compare.

As each cable is wired into the car cross it off the practical wiring diagram. I usually make a tracing or photo-copy of the diagram for use in the garage and cross off each cable in coloured pencil as I wire it in place. Run all the cables neatly as though they were in a loom, and where the cables run together hold them with a twist of wire so they sit neatly in place. Neatness in wiring is half the battle to getting it right first time. If you wire like a ravaged bird's nest you will never know where you are. When all the cables are in place they can be formed into looms with plastic insulating tape. Finish off the job by clipping the looms with proper cable clips to the body or chassis.

70   Good quality junction boxes are made for commerical vehicles (this is on a Ford D series truck) and are most suitable for wiring open-chassis cars. The cables here are carried in plastic tubing

=15=
SORTING OUT THE ELECTRICS

Part 2.
The Components

Many of the electrical components on the car, lamps and so on, are straightforward things to recondition. Of all the others, the control box seems to cause the most head scratching among home restorers, so I will go through it in some detail. The trouble with electricity is that you cannot see it. If the control box is suspected of giving trouble many people prod the parts hopefully, perhaps run a piece of emery cloth through the points, and hope for the best.

There is no need to prod uninformed provided you have a decent quality moving coil voltmeter and ammeter. Unless they are mechanically damaged or burnt out the popular Lucas two-bobbin control boxes are quite easy to set up.

Provided the dynamo is in good order and all the cable connections are tight, the control box is number one suspect in cases of low charge or no charge. The box may be burned out if you are unlucky, and this may not always show when the cover is taken off. If you take the box off the bulkhead and look underneath you will see a number of connecting straps and resistors. If any of these are burnt, or even badly blackened, there is little that can be done except get another box. If they are all sound you can move on to cleaning and resetting the points.

If the points are only lightly pitted they will clean satisfactorily, but if they are really blackened and burnt it means one of the resistors under the box is useless, even though it looks all right.

Assuming the points are not too bad, the first part to tackle is the voltage control regulator. This is the bobbin with the fewer number of turns round it. It operates on a very simple principle. A small part of the dynamo output energises the bobbin to make it into an electro magnet. When the voltage reaches around 16 volts the magnetism is powerful enough to pull down a rocking arm known as the armature. This opens a pair of contacts, stops the dynamo charging, and the magnetism collapses. This allows a spring to pull the armature up again, the contacts close and the cycle is repeated. At normal engine speeds the points open and close very rapidly — too rapidly to see — but if the arm is rocked slowly, with the battery disconnected to be on the safe side, the action can be seen quite clearly.

You will find that the regulator is one of two types. Either the contact points, one of which is adjustable and held by a locknut, are at the end of the bobbin facing you when the cover is off, or they are mounted above the coil of the bobbin between it and the frame.

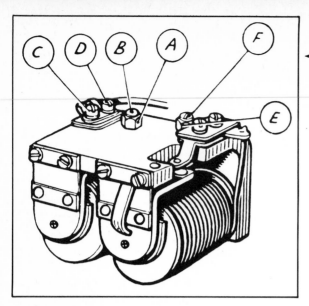

◀ 71   A typical regulator and cut-out assembly. A and B are the lock nut and adjusting screw for the voltage regulator setting; C and D are the screws holding the plate carrying the fixed contact, E and F are the lock nuts and screws for the cut-out adjustment

72   On this type of ▶ regulator, 1 and 2 are the locknut and voltage adjustment screw; 3 is the armature tension spring; 4 the armature fixing screws; 5 the fixed contact adjustment screw; 6 the armature; 7 the bobbin; 8 the setting gap which varies from model to model. 0.02 in (0.51 mm) is a good all-round setting

Dealing first with the type which has the adjustable contacts at the end of the bobbin, the armature is held by two vertical screws just above the adjustable contact. The voltage regulating screw is vertically on top of the frame just in front of the plastic body.

To get at the points to clean them you can either take the armature out, or just take off the adjustable point for refacing on a fine oilstone and clean the point on the top of the armature with an emery strip. After cleaning the points you will have to reset the armature.

Slacken off the adjustable point, and the voltage regulating screw, and loosen the armature fixing screws. Then put a feeler between the end of the bobbin and the underside of the armature. On some Lucas boxes the thickness of the feeler should be 0.015 in (0.38 mm), and on others 0.021 in (0.53 mm). I have found they all work satisfactorily at a setting of 0.02 in (0.51 mm) which is the nearest there is to 0.021 (0.53 mm) on a set of feelers.

With the feeler in position, hold the armature flat down on top of the bobbin and tighten the armature fixing screws. Now, with the feeler still in position, screw down the adjustable contact till it just meets the contact on top of the armature. It must meet it true and square. If it does not, you have sloped the face of the points when they were cleaned.

If all is well, lock the adjustable point and take the feeler away.

With the second type, where the points are mounted above the coil of the bobbin, the armature has to be taken out to clean them. In this case the armature fixing screws are the two on the end of the frame facing you when the cover is off. One of the points is on the armature itself, the other is held by two screws to the frame. There will be either a small packing piece, or a pack of shims, between the arm of this point and the frame.

When putting the armature back, slacken the voltage regulating screw (the one beside the two screws holding the fixed contact) put a 0.02 in (0.51 mm) feeler between the horizontal part of the armature and the regulator frame, and push the armature up against it, and down against the end of the bobbin, while you tighten the fixing screws.

When the feeler gauge is taken out, the gap between the end of the armature and the end face of the bobbin should be between 0.012 in (0.3 mm) and 0.02 in (0.5 mm). If it is outside these limits adjust it by moving the fixed point, the one held by two screws to the frame. If it has shims these form the adjustment. If it has only a packing piece make the adjustment by carefully bending the arm of the contact. Never try to bend the armature.

With the gap between the armature and the end of the bobbin between 0.012 in (0.3 mm)

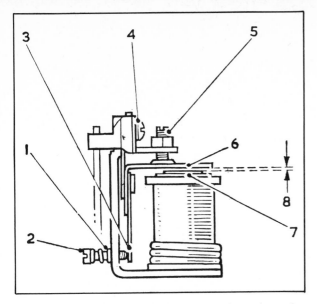

dynamo is not charging, the points, which are slightly domed in this case, are open. When the dynamo output reaches about 13 volts the magnet becomes strong enough to pull the armature down and close the points. This puts the dynamo in circuit with the rest of the system.

The cut-out points can be cleaned in position by drawing a strip of fine emery cloth through them. To set the points, unlock and slacken off the cut-out adjusting screw. This is alongside the screw holding the insulated fixed point. Loosen the two screws holding the armature, push the armature squarely in against the end of the bobbin, and retighten the screws.

When the armature is pressed in to the bobbin there should be a gap of between 0.025 in (0.6 mm) and 0.04 in (0.1 mm) between the top face of the armature and the curved stop plate above it. You adjust this gap by gently bending the stop arm. When you let the armature go, and the points open, the gap between the points should be set to 0.018 in (0.45 mm) by gently bending the arm of the fixed, insulated, point.

When the armature is pressed into the bobbin after this there should be between 0.01 in (0.25 and 0.02 in (0.5 mm) of follow through after the points make contact. That is, the point on the armature should push the fixed

and 0.02 in (0.5 mm), the gap between the points when the armature is held down to the bobbin should be between 0.006 in (0.15 mm) and 0.017 in (0.4 mm).

I will go through setting the voltage regulating screw after I have dealt with cleaning the cut-out. This is the other bobbin, the one with more turns of wire.

The purpose of the cut out is to put the dynamo out of circuit when its output, at low engine speed, is less than the battery voltage. If it did not put it out of circuit, the battery would try to turn the dynamo. The cut-out has an electro-magnetic bobbin, similar to the one on the voltage regulator. When the

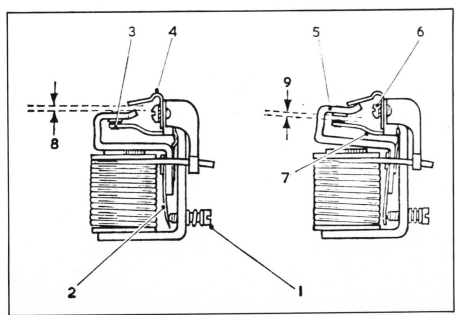

73 Setting the cut-out. 1 is the cut-out adjusting screw; 2 the armature tension spring; 3 the points which must follow through 0.01 to 0.02 in (0.25 mm to 0.5 mm); 4 the adjustable stop arm; 5 the armature holding the moving contact; 6 the armature fixing screws; 7 the fixed contact blade. Gap 8 should be 0.03 in (0.76 mm), and gap 9 should be 0.01 in to 0.02 in (0.25 mm to 0.5 mm).

129

insulated point between 0.010 in (0.25 mm) and 0.020 in (0.5 mm) after it makes contact. This follow through gives a wiping action to the points and helps to keep them clean.

With both the regulator and cut-out points cleaned the next things to adjust are the voltage settings. Start with the voltage regulator. As you have not yet set the cut-out points adjustment, you will have to close the cut-out points manually while adjusting the regulator. Disconnect the two cables from the terminals marked A and A1 on the control box, join them together with a clip and keep them well out of the way while you make the adjustment. Remember whether you have positive or negative earth so that the voltmeter is connected the right way round, and connect it across terminals marked D and E. Start the engine, and as you rev it close the cut-out points so that the voltmeter registers a charge. With the engine running at about half throttle adjust the voltage regulating screw so that the voltmeter reads 16 volts. This adjustment should be made within 30 seconds of starting the engine because by joining the cables from A and A1 the dynamo is put on open circuit and the shunt winding in the control box will heat up and give a false voltmeter reading. Remember to open the cut-out points again if they do not open by themselves when the engine is stopped. Lock the voltage adjusting screw and reconnect the cables to A and A1.

To adjust the cut-out setting, leave the voltmeter in position between terminals D and E. Start the engine and screw in the cut-out adjustment screw so that as the engine is gently revved up from tick-over the cut-out points click shut when the voltage is at 13 volts. They should open again as voltage falls to between 10 and 8.5 volts. Lock the adjusting screw, unclip the voltmeter and replace the cables.

I said earlier that the control box should be suspected in cases of lack of charge pro-

vided the dynamo is in good order. There is a simple spot check you can make to find out if a dynamo is putting out a charge.

Disconnect the two cables from terminals F and D from the dynamo. Mark them to make sure they go back correctly — if they are reversed you will undoubtedly burn out the regulator in the control box. With the cables disconnected and held out of the way, bridge the two terminals on the dynamo with a bare piece of wire. Now connect an inspection lamp fitted with a headlamp bulb between the bridged terminals and chassis earth. Start the engine and rev it *very gently*. Do not run the engine fast or you will blow the bulb, because the dynamo is running virtually off-load and all its output is going through the bulb filament. As the engine speed is gradually increased the lamp should glow with increasing brightness. No light, or a dull glow, means either that the fan belt is slipping or that the dynamo needs to be stripped for attention.

A voltmeter can be used instead of the test lamp. Do not let the voltage rise above 20 volts for a 12-volt dynamo, or above 10 volts on a 6-volt dynamo. Constant flickering of the voltmeter, or a low reading, means the dynamo needs attention.

Most dynamos, at least most Lucas ones, have a plain bronze bearing at the commutator end and a ball bearing at the drive end. Some continental ones, like those fitted to Volkswagen, have ball bearings at both ends, and when taking these apart be careful to keep the springs and washers in order. Some dynamos have windows in the yoke — the main part of the body — over the brushes, but some have not. If yours has, the cover ring can be taken off and the brushes inspected without taking the dynamo to pieces. You will find it easier to lift the bushes out if you hold the springs back with a piece of hooked wire.

The dynamo will come apart after taking the nuts and washers from the field terminal (the smaller one) and taking out the long

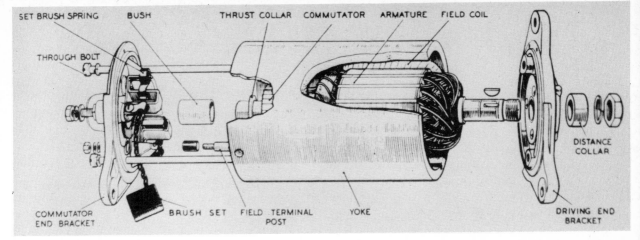

SET BRUSH SPRING   BUSH   THRUST COLLAR   COMMUTATOR   ARMATURE   FIELD COIL

THROUGH BOLT

DISTANCE COLLAR

COMMUTATOR END BRACKET   BRUSH SET   FIELD TERMINAL POST   YOKE   DRIVING END BRACKET

74   The component parts of a typical dynamo

through bolts. The commutator and end plate will lift off with the brushes, and the armature will come out complete with the driving end plate.

If the ball bearing in this is in good condition there is no need to disturb it. If it is sloppy or gritty it needs replacing. The bearing is covered by a plate on the inside of the bracket which is riveted to the end plate. Punch the rivets out to remove it and push out the bearing. Under it is usually a corrugated washer, felt washer and an oil retaining washer. Put them back in the right order before pressing in a new bearing. Pack the bearing with high melting-point grease and use new rivets with their heads on the inside to put the plate back.

The commutator will probably be blackened. It can be cleaned with a petrol moistened rag or a strip of fine glass paper. This is better than emery paper because the fine particles of emery or carburundum bed into the separators of the segments and could cause shorting. If the commutator is pitted or burnt, or if the brushes have worn a groove in it, a light skim on the lathe will restore it. This can be done without taking the drive end bracket off the armature.

75   Undercutting the segments on a dynamo commutator

The insulators between the segments should be undercut about 1/32 in (0.8 mm) deep with a hacksaw blade ground down to the insulator thickness. Try to cut them square and not to a vee shape.

Short circuits on the turns of the armature which are not obvious cannot be checked without using an instrument known as a 'growler' (which is seldom found outside a dynamo overhaul shop), but the fault is comparatively rare. It need be suspected only if

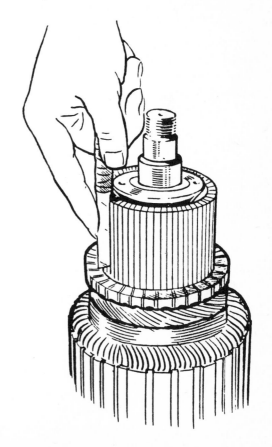

the windings look blackened or the insulation is charred. If two adjacent segments on the commutator are blackened and burnt, sometimes with a flattened look, this is a pretty sure sign of an open circuit somewhere in the armature winding. In either case the armature needs to be replaced.

The inside of the yoke will most likely be full of dust from worn brushes, so remove the dust as it is a good conductor and can cause shorts. To test the field coils, measure with an ohm-meter the resistance between the field terminal and a clean part of the yoke. It should be about 6.2 ohms. If an ohm-meter is not available, carry out the test with a 12 volt battery and an ammeter. Connect one side of the battery to the field terminal and the other side through the ammeter to a clean part of the yoke. The ammeter should read approximately 2 amps. No reading on the ammeter, or an infinite reading on the ohm-meter, indicates a break somewhere in the field winding. If the ammeter reads much more than 2 amps, or if the ohm-meter reads much below 6.2 ohms, it indicates that the insulation on one or both of the field coils has broken down.

Before leaving the yoke and field coils, check the insulating piece which prevents the junction of the coils from shorting on the yoke. Sometimes carbon dust from the worn brushes can collect on this and short across.

Replacing field coils is definitely a job for a service agent. The screws which hold the pole pieces in place are put in with a large wheel screwdriver to a torque that could never be matched with a hand screwdriver, and to fit new coils an expander is needed to hold the pole pieces in place while the screws are done up again.

The brushes should be checked for freedom in their housing and if necessary eased with a fine file. Worn brushes should be replaced. If the bronze bearing in the commutator end plate is worn enough to allow the end of the

armature to wobble, a new one is needed. As it is usually in a blind housing it cannot be driven out. The easy way to pull it out is to screw in a tap — 5/8 in (15 mm) on most Lucas dynamos — that is large enough to get a grip. The new bush should be soaked in light engine oil for 24 hours. If you are in a hurry, stand a tin of oil in boiling water and soak the bush for two hours. Under the bush is a washer, or washers, and a felt lubricating pad. The new bush can be pressed in, using a short shouldered mandrel in a vice or hand press.

When putting the dynamo together it helps to put the brushes in their holders so that they are clear of the armature by wedging the spring against the side of the brush. If there are no windows in the yoke you have to lift the springs in position with a wire hook as soon as the brushes come over the commutator.

A rebuilt dynamo, whether you do it yourself or get an exchange or new one, has to be polarized to match your car. New and exchange dynamos are suitable for either negative or positive earth systems and could be polarized for either when you get them.

Polarizing a dynamo is very simple. Mount it on the engine so that the yoke is earthed, connect a battery to the car and take a lead from the live, non-earthed, side of the battery. Hold the other end of this lead against the field terminal (the smaller one) of the dynamo for two or three seconds. When taking it off a fluffy blue flash should occur, and the dynamo is polarized to suit the car. It can be done off the car with a battery and two leads, but I prefer to leave it as the last thing before connecting the dynamo leads to the car. That way you are sure to get the polarity right, and you do not forget to do it.

Overhauling a starter is very similar to overhauling a dynamo except that there are four brushes. Two are on the commutator end plate and two are attached to the field windings. There is also a drive engagement mechanism to overhaul, and usually two bronze bushes instead of one bronze and one ball bearing.

The drive mechanism which engages with the flywheel may be one of several types. It may be held on the armature shaft by a castellated nut and split pin — and the nut may be left hand thread. Alternatively it may be held by a ring and circlip. If this is the case you will need a spring compressor to take the pressure off the ring before taking the circlip off.

Make a careful note of the order in which all the pieces of the drive lift off the end of the shaft. Wash them off in paraffin and inspect them for burrs. Any found must be taken off with a file. Many people will say that the drive must be assembled dry. Certainly, old sticky oil can stop the pinion moving on the helical splines. Lucas, however, recommends that the helix should be lubricated with Moly-kiron SAE 5 oil, and the straight splines with Shell SB 2628 grease. Do not overdo the grease or it may work its way up on to the helix.

The bearings, commutator and brushes are dealt with in the same way as those on the dynamo except that the segments on the commutator of a starter must *not* be under-cut. If the brushes need to be replaced, the two on the end plate are straightforward, but the braids of those on the field coils will be soldered or spot welded in place. They go to a common junction on a series wound starter, and to the ends of the field coils on a series-parallel starter.

If they are soldered there is no difficulty, but if they are spot welded you will never undo the weld satisfactorily. In this case cut the old braids about 1 in (2.5 cm) from the spot weld and solder the braids of the new bushes to them.

Checking the field coil continuity and insulation is different from doing it on a dynamo. On series wound starters test for continuity by connecting a 12 volt test lamp between the starter terminal and the junction of the field coils where the brushes are fixed. Then check the insulation between the starter terminal and the yoke. A 12 volt test lamp is not sufficiently powerful to do this properly. On load the starter can take up to 300 amps, which could leak across faulty insulation that a 12 volt test would not find. The check should be made with a mains test lamp of at least 100 volts. Please be careful what you are doing. Put the starter on a dry rubber mat to insulate it from the ground or bench, and connect to the starter terminal and the yoke with crocodile clips before switching on. Holding bare mains leads to them is a good way of electrocuting yourself. If the lamp lights, check for any obvious shorts at the junction of the field coils. If nothing obvious is wrong the yoke and coils need replacing. As with a dynamo, special equipment is needed to change the field coils.

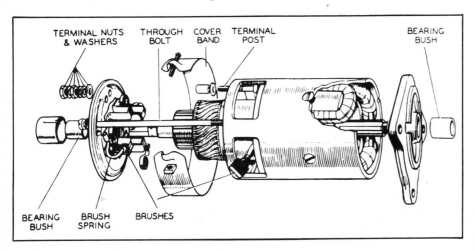

TERMINAL NUTS & WASHERS THROUGH BOLT COVER BAND TERMINAL POST BEARING BUSH

BEARING BUSH BRUSH SPRING BRUSHES

76 A starter motor is similar to a dynamo but often has a plain bearing bush at the drive end. The drive engagement gear is not shown

16

SORTING OUT
THE ELECTRICS

Part 3.
Ignition, Horns and Wipers

Ignition troubles, according to the Automobile Association, account for the majority of breakdowns on the road. Most of these troubles come from the plugs, plug leads or distributor points. These represent a very small proportion of the cost of restoring a car, so replace the lot. Of plugs, little needs to be said except to make sure you get the right sort for the car. The charts in the accessory shops may not go back far enough to cover your model, and the type

in the handbook may no longer be made. If this is so, write to the plug makers; they will know the correct modern type to use. This is safer than taking the word of the man in the shop. He might know, but then again he might be guessing.

The plug leads may look in good order, but old plugs leads invariably leak. Most present day cars are fitted with suppressor leads, some with carbon filaments instead of wire down the middle. Perhaps I am old fashioned, but I much prefer to fit the type of lead with a copper wire in it and use separate suppressors.

If the connectors at the chimney of the coil, and at the distributor cap, are the screw-in plastic type with split washers under them, inspect the screw connector for chips and cracks, and either clean the washers with emery or fit new ones. Many cars of the fifties had the leads running through either a metal or compressed cardboard tube for neatness. Metal ones can be cleaned, but the cardboard ones are almost always warped and twisted. A good replacement can be made from a piece of hard plastic piping of the type used for household water pipes.

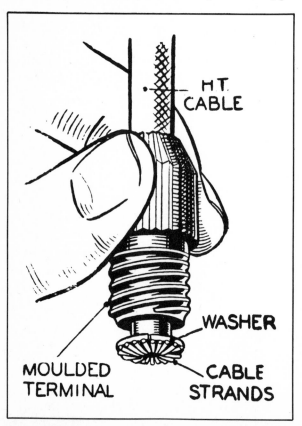

HT.
CABLE

WASHER

MOULDED
TERMINAL

CABLE
STRANDS

77   The correct way to assemble an HT plug lead with a separate wire down the centre

Coils do not often give trouble, though they are often suspected, mainly because one cannot see if they are in good order or not. They are easy to check. Take the high tension lead from the coil out of the distributor cap, and take the low tension lead from the coil off the side of the distributor, or take it off the coil and put a spare lead in its place. Switch on the ignition, hold the free end of the high tension lead about 3/16 in (5 mm) away from a clean part of the engine — not near the carburetters because there is going to be a spark — then take the free end of the low tension lead and touch it several times to another clean part of the engine. Each time it is taken away a spark should jump from the end of the high tension lead. If it does not, check that the engine is earthed to the chassis. If there is still no spark the coil is highly suspect.

If you have one of the more modern Lucas coils the low tension terminals will be marked + and −. The same coil can be used for either positive or negative earth systems provided the polarity is observed. On a negative earth system the negative terminal on the coil goes to the distributor; on a positive earth system the plus terminal goes to the distributor.

Some cars have ballasted coils. In this case the cable which goes from the coil to the ignition switch is either a resistance lead or has a ballast resistor somewhere along it. There is a second cable going from the same terminal on the coil to a terminal on the starter solenoid. The coil is designed to operate at a lower voltage than the battery voltage. But when starting, the drain on the battery results in a reduced voltage so the ballast resistor is by-passed by the cable from the solenoid. During starting the coil is actually being over-run to give a good spark but it is for so short a time that it does the coil no harm.

The distributor will have one, or possibly two, methods of automatic advance to advance the ignition as the engine speed rises, or as the load on the engine changes.

In the first type of automatic advance the distributor cam is moved relative to the distributor drive spindle by two weights, which move outwards to turn the cam and advance the ignition as the engine speed increases. They are controlled by two springs. These springs may be equal, or they may be unequal, in which case the manual will call it a differential spring assembly. With this type one of the springs is under slight tension when the distributor is at rest, and the other is slightly loose. This loose spring often has an elongated loop at its end. As the speed of the distributor increases the weights move out to advance the ignition controlled by only the first, tighter, spring. At a certain speed the second spring, often a stronger one, comes into action to change the rate of advance. This suits the engine requirements better than two springs of equal tension.

78   A typical Lucas distributor

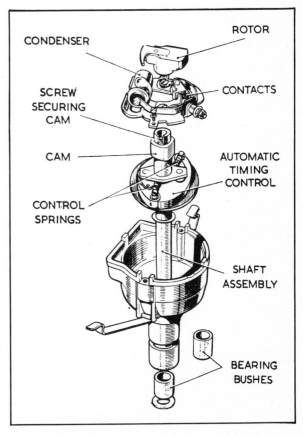

CONDENSER
ROTOR
SCREW SECURING CAM
CONTACTS
CAM
AUTOMATIC TIMING CONTROL
CONTROL SPRINGS
SHAFT ASSEMBLY
BEARING BUSHES

The action of the weights must be free, and the springs must be undamaged. They should be cleaned, the pivots inspected and lubricated with light engine oil.

The second type of automatic advance is a vacuum unit connected by a thin pipe to the engine inlet manifold. The diaphragm unit is connected to the contact-breaker plate inside the distributor. As the depression in the inlet manifold increases, at light throttle openings, the diaphragm flexes and pulls the contact-breaker plate round the cam. Things to check are that the thin pipe is not obstructed, the connection at the manifold is not clogged with carbon (as sometimes happens), and that the diaphragm is not punctured. This can be checked by taking the unit off and blowing through the vacuum connection. If you can blow right through, the diaphragm is punctured.

Another possible fault is a corroded spring at the diaphragm. This can be tested when the unit is off the distributor by pushing in the plunger which connects to the contact-breaker plate. It should feel firm and easy in action, not harsh or gritty.

If you have to change the vacuum unit make sure to get the correct replacement. It is not enough to go by the distributor model number. The same distributor may be fitted to a number of different cars, but each car manufacturer will have specified his own vacuum advance characteristics.

On Lucas units these are given a code number which is on the casing. An example of this coding is 3/24/12. The first figure shows the amount of depression in inches of mercury at which the unit starts to work. The second shows the depression, again in inches of mercury, at which it reaches maximum travel. The third is the maximum advance in degrees. Some vacuum units have a micrometer adjustment for fine setting of the static ignition timing. If you dismantle this take care not to loose the ratchet and spring.

If the distributor drive shaft is slack in its bearings you will never be able to set the points gap properly. It will also vary as the engine is running. On distributors for smaller cars the shaft is carried either in two bronze bearings or one long one. On some distributors for high performance cars the top bearing is a ball bearing.

To renew the bearings take off the driving member at the bottom of the shaft by punching out the pin. On some cars the driving member is a dog with offset segments to locate with similar segments on the shaft driven by the camshaft. On other cars the bottom of the distributor shaft carries a skew gear which engages directly with the camshaft. In the case of the driving dog note the position of the offset before you drive out the pin. When putting the rotor arm on (and looking from the drive end of the distributor) the offset dog will be pointing in the same direction as the rotor electrode but will be offset to the left of the centreline.

The old bearings can be pressed out and new ones pressed in with a shouldered mandrel. Soak the bearings in light engine oil for 24 hours before pressing them in. It is important in the case of two bronze bearings that they are pressed in exactly in line with each other. They should not be reamered afterwards as this spoils their oil retention properties.

When reassembled the distributor shaft should have approximately 0.002 in (0.05 mm) end float. On some models this end float is governed by the thickness of a fibre washer under the driving dog or gear. On others there is a brass washer. If you have a worn brass washer and renew it, the new one will have three small pips raised on one surface. The driving dog should rest on these pips when it is being pinned to the shaft. After pinning, the dog should be given a smart blow in with a mallet. This will squash the pips and give the correct end float.

Returning to the top of the distributor, fit a new set of points as a matter of course. I always fit a new condenser, or capacitor as they are often called nowadays. The only satisfactory way to check a condenser is by substitution, so you might just as well leave the new one in place. On older distributors you may have difficulty in finding the right size condenser to fit inside. In this case you can fit one outside with the lead of the condenser fitted to the low tension lead from the coil and the body earthed.

With age and use the insulation of rotor arms often becomes weak. To test this with the distributor on the engine and in working order take the cap off, take out the high tension lead which comes from the coil and hold it about 3/16 in (5 mm) from the rotor arm electrode. Switch on the ignition and flick the distributor points open a few times. If there is a spark from the high tension lead to the rotor arm the insulation has broken down and the arm is useless.

Clean the distributor cap in petrol and check for any burnt lines etched inside between the brass studs. If there are any they will cause tracking of the spark in damp weather, so the cap needs renewing. It should also be renewed if the studs are badly burnt. It is best when replacing the cap to replace the rotor as well. The electrode of the rotor may have a pip on the end where metal has been transferred from the studs. If you fit a new cap the air gap between the studs and the rotor electrode may be too small.

Before refitting the distributor to the engine set the points gap to the manufacturer's recommended figure, usually 0.012 in to 0.014 in (0.31 mm to 0.36 mm). When refitting it the ignition will have to be retimed, so follow the golden rule — set the engine, set the distributor and couple the two.

The manual will give the firing timing as so many degrees before top dead centre (tdc), usually on number one cylinder. Remember on inline engines that some makers number their engines from the back, the opposite way round from usual. This applies to Standards and Jaguars, who used to fit Standard engines and stayed with the convention. Most manufacturers, however, call the front cylinder number one. With vee engines, or flat fours, make sure which is the manufacturer's number one.

In most cases there will be a timing mark either on the rim of the flywheel or on the rim of the crankshaft pulley. Remember that on a four-stroke engine the mark will come opposite its pointer twice, once at the end of the exhaust stroke and once at the end of the compression stroke. Look for the one at the end of the compression stroke. Find this by putting your thumb over the plug hole while someone turns the engine. As the piston comes up on compression stroke the air will hiss out past your thumb. Make a double check as the mark comes near the pointer by checking that both valves on number one cylinder are closed. If there are no timing marks, and you have no manual, set the ignition to fire just a shade before tdc. This will get the engine started and you can make finer adjustments when it is running.

Now set the distributor by turning the shaft till the electrode on the rotor arm is pointing towards the stud in the cap for number one cylinder. Set it with the points just about to open. Then feed the distributor into the engine. If you have an offset dog drive it should go straight in, but if you have a skew gear the distributor shaft will turn as you feed it in. Note how much it turned, then lift it out, set it again and then turn the shaft backwards by this amount. Now when you feed it back it will turn forward to its correct position. Check again by twisting the distributor slightly so that the points are just about to open and lock it in place.

This timing will be sufficiently accurate for the engine to start, when final adjustments can be made. If you have timing marks this is best done with a strobe lamp. Connect it according

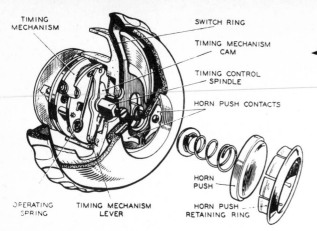

TIMING MECHANISM

SWITCH RING

TIMING MECHANISM CAM

TIMING CONTROL SPINDLE

HORN PUSH CONTACTS

OPERATING SPRING

TIMING MECHANISM LEVER

HORN PUSH

HORN PUSH RETAINING RING

◄ 79   Sometimes under the horn push (this is on a MG Y model) you will find a time switch for the turn indicators

80   Make sure to identify the terminals on a combined switch such as this. If necessary check them out with a lamp and battery while you operate the controls   ►

to the instructions and shine the light on the timing marks while the engine is ticking over. Because the lamp flashes every time number one cylinder fires, the mark will appear to stand still. The distributor can be rotated till it is exactly opposite the pointer. You can also check with a strobe lamp whether the automatic advance is working. If you speed the engine up slowly, with a small throttle opening, and the timing mark appears to move relative to the pointer, the centrifugal weights are doing their job. If you snap the throttle open to change the depression in the inlet manifold, and the mark appears to move, the vacuum unit is working.

Correct timing, and indeed correct running, can be achieved only if the distributor points gap is correct. The normal way of setting the gap with a feeler gauge depends very much on the accuracy of the feel of the person doing it. A more accurate method is to use a dwell meter. This measures the dwell angle, the number of degrees of rotation during which the points are closed. It is during this period that the coil builds up its charge to provide a spark. If the dwell meter is connected the angle can be read off and checked against the manufacturer's figure. If it is not correct, adjust the points gap till it is. This method has the advantage that one is measuring the average points gap on all the lobes of the cam.

Moving on now to the horn, this will be either a high frequency beep-beep type or a Windtone type with a cast coiled trumpet.

Both give long service, and generally all that is needed is adjustment and possibly cleaning the points on Windtones.

On the Lucas high frequency horn the adjustment screw has a click action. To set it, turn the screw anti-clockwise till the horn just stops sounding. Then screw it in six clicks. The best tone, which should be clear, will be within two clicks either way of this setting. Do not alter the two coil securing screws.

Windtone horns are marked H or L inside the flare of the trumpet to denote high or low pitch. The two pitches are a musical major third apart, and if you have two horns one should be high and the other low. Under the domed cover is an adjustable set of points which can be cleaned if necessary with an emery strip. Altering the points gap will not affect the tone but will affect the clarity. To adjust them, slacken off the locknut and turn the adjustable point till the points just open, indicated by the horn failing to sound. Then turn the adjustable point in the opposite direction half a turn and lock it.

If either type of horn is badly out of adjustment it will take excessive current. When it is in good adjustment a high frequency horn should not take more than 4 amps, and a Windtone not more than 8.5 amps. No horn will sound properly if its mounting bolts are not tight. If it is being tested off the car clamp the mounting plate firmly in the vice while you make adjustments.

Most post-war cars are fitted with twin windscreen wipers operated by a rack and driven by a geared motor. The motors vary in layout but dismantling for inspection is usually simple. If there is a cover plate it will

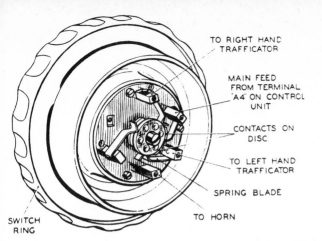

TO RIGHT HAND
TRAFFICATOR

MAIN FEED
FROM TERMINAL
'A4' ON CONTROL
UNIT

CONTACTS ON
DISC

TO LEFT HAND
TRAFFICATOR

SPRING BLADE

SWITCH
RING

TO HORN

unbolt, and if there is a canister this will either unclip or unscrew. On some canister motors the armature has to be locked by wedging the gears before the canister will unscrew.

The most likely fault is worn gears. When replacing a main gear, either new or second-hand, check it is the right one for the car. There will probably be a number on it which indicates the sweep of the wiper blades in degrees. Replacement carbon brushes which are crimped in their holders come as complete assemblies, and spares for Lucas motors are generally easy to get. Spares for some other makes are not quite so easy, and if you are really stuck you may have to get the nearest there is and adapt them to fit your motor. It is a fiddling business, but with a fine file and patience it can be done. The commutator can be cleaned with a petrol-moistened rag or with fine glass paper.

When reassembling make sure the armature can spin freely. On permanent magnet motors make sure the yoke goes back the same way as it came off or the motor will run backwards. This will not stop the blades from wiping but the parking position will be most peculiar. On most motors there is an adjustment for the position at which the striker operates the parking switch, either by moving the switch or the striker. If the limit switch is broken you will have to get a new one.

81   A popular Lucas
wiper motor

With the rack disconnected the motor should operate quietly and easily. If will get warm, but if it gets too hot it indicates there is something dragging in the armature. It could be that the gears have not been assembled properly, or their bearings are worn, or that the end float of the armature is wrong. It should be fairly close; about 0.005 in (0.13 mm) is about right.

With some AC-Delco motors there could be another cause. These motors have spherical self-aligning bearings on the main shaft. If the motor appears sluggish, or gets too hot, try tapping the body lightly with a mallet while it is running. If the self-aligning bearing is stuck out of alignment this will probably free it and allow it to come into line.

Some installations use mechanical cranks to connect the motor to the arms, others use a rack and wheel boxes. A frequent cause of worn racks is someone bolting it crooked. If the rack or its tube is bent there is little that can be done to straighten it, but if it is worn its life can sometimes be extended by taking it out, turning it through 180°, together with the gears on the wheel boxes, and replacing it. Both the motor gearbox and the rack should be well packed with grease, preferably high melting point grease in the motor box.

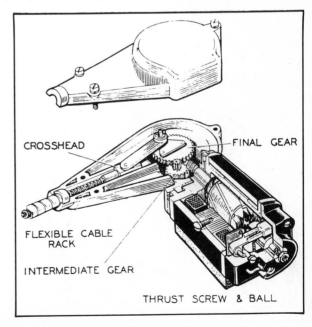

CROSSHEAD

FINAL GEAR

FLEXIBLE CABLE
RACK

INTERMEDIATE GEAR

THRUST SCREW & BALL

17

THE FUEL SYSTEM

The fuel tank and fuel pipes present little difficulty for a restorer. If the tank leaks but the metal is sound take it to a specialised tank repairer. Even though the tank may not have held petrol for some time the vapour can stay there for months — even years. If you take a flame to it to braze or weld it there could be a very nasty explosion. Even soft soldering is not safe without proper precautions. The specialist will steam the tank out before he starts work. If the tank is rusted right through, and it is a rare one, the repairer may be able to weld in new sections, but it may be cheaper to find a sound tank.

Many post-war cars have steel fuel pipes, and even if these are not badly rusted on the outside they often gather rust inside when they have been standing dry. For the sake of a

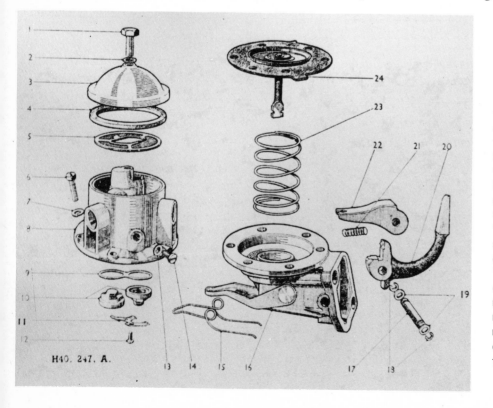

H40. 247. A.

82   On this AC mechanical fuel pump, 1 and 2 are the top cover screw and washer; 3 and 4 the top cover and washer; 5 the filter; 6 and 7 the screws holding the upper part of the body, 8; 9 the joint washer for the valves, 10, held by plate, 11, and screw, 12; 13 and 14 the drain plug and washer; 15 the priming lever spring; 16 the lower part of the body; 17, 18 and 19 the rocker pin with its clips and washers; 20 the rocker arm; 21 the anti-rattle spring for the rocker link, 22; 23 the diaphragm spring and 24 the diaphragm

pound or two renew them either in copper or in the Kunifer 10 tubing used for the brakes. This can be obtained in a number of sizes.

The petrol pump will be either mechanical, driven from the camshaft, or an SU electric. Fortunately spares for both these, and often exchange pumps, are fairly easy to find.

A repair kit for a mechanical pump includes a new diaphragm and spring, the small plastic valves and springs and the necessary joint washers. Mark both parts of the pump body before you take it apart. The diaphragm unlocks with a bayonet action from the operating lever, and often has a small pip on the outside as a guide for reassembly. Note where the pip is on the old one before taking it out. Almost all the troubles with these pumps come from blockages, valves not seating or a damaged or overstretched diaphragm. A thorough clean and a repair kit usually solves

the problems. Do not overtighten the bolt holding the domed cover; the body of the pump is a die casting and the thread strips easily.

When SU electric pumps fail the trouble is likely to be dirty, sticking or worn points and toggle. Once again there are repair kits including a diaphragm. Over the years SU pumps have varied in constructional details, mainly in the layout of the valves, but they all work on the same principles, and overhauling them is very similar. There are, however, differences in settings, so if you cannot obtain a manual for your car try to have a look at one for a car which uses the same model pump, or an SU leaflet. The leaflet should be included in the repair kit.

If the car has been out of use for some years there may be a nasty stale smelling varnish inside the pump. Some old manuals advise getting rid of this by boiling the pump parts in caustic soda solution followed by a dip in strong nitric acid and a rinse in boiling water. This method works, but both of these

83   A sectioned view of an SU electric fuel pump

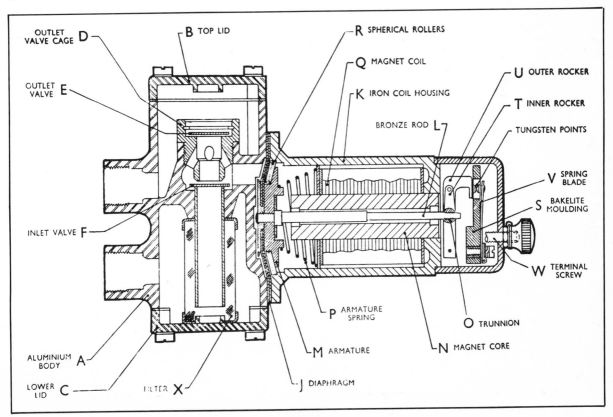

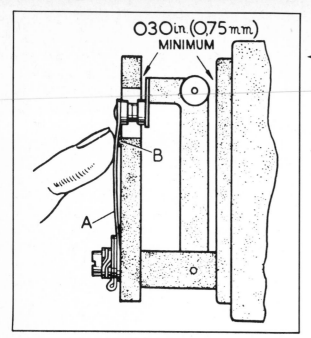

030in.(0,75mm)
MINIMUM

B

A

◄ 84 With the spring of the contact blade up against the ledge at B on an SU pump the gap shown must be equal either side

85 Setting the arma- ture to give the correct throw-over of the points on an SU pump ►

solutions are nasty things to handle, and the method is a hang-over from the older days when SU pumps had brass bodies. If one of the later aluminium bodied pumps goes anywhere near boiling caustic soda it will be ruined in a mass of frothing, spitting bubbles.

Nowadays there are gum and varnish removing compounds which are easier and safer to use. If the deposit is light it might be removed by scrubbing in methylated spirit, but this is not so good as a proper varnish remover for getting in the valve ports.

Start dismantling by taking out the filter and valves, then mark the two main parts of the pump before undoing the screws holding them together. Then the whole diaphragm assembly can be unscrewed. Take care not to loose the brass rollers fitted behind the diaphragm. Under the cover at the contact breaker end of the pump is a screw which forms a stop for the cover. Under this screw should be a lead washer which the nut squashes down to ensure a good electrical contact. The old washer has to be cut off with a knife before the terminal can be pushed down far enough to free the tag on the end of the coil. Take off the contact blade, and the two long screws holding the plastic pedestal, and the contact

breaker assembly can be lifted out. Be careful not to break the tag off the coil when pulling the assembly over the terminal screw.

The hardened rocker hinge pin is only a push fit, and new contacts are supplied as an assembly. Never try to take the core out of the magnet. There is no need to, and it can be replaced only with special tools.

When you come to reassemble the contact breaker make sure the spring under the contact blade sits flat against the plastic pedestal under the small ledge. The points should make contact when the rocker is in its midway position. To check this, push the contact blade up against the ledge on the pedestal. Then measure the gap between the rocker and the pedestal, and between the white roller and the body of the pump. They should be the same, and be a minimum of 0.030 in (0.75mm). If necessary, set the tip of the blade to get the figures even.

One of the pedestal screws acts as an earth terminal, and it is important that the spring washer goes between the electrical tag and the pedestal. The spring washer is not a reliable conductor, and the terminal must go directly under the head of the screw.

All the connectors — at the ends of the earthing tag, and the two ends of the coil — must be soldered. If anyone has had the pump apart and just wrapped the wire round the terminal find some proper connectors and solder them in place. When the armature is refitted the return spring goes with its large end against the coil and its small end towards the armature. Swing the contact blade to one side before you fit the armature.

When you screw the armature in it has to be set to give the correct throw-over of the

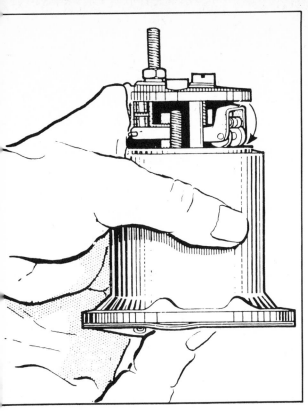

points rocker. Put the rollers in position under the diaphragm and screw the armature in till the throw-over action stops operating. Then unscrew it gradually till the throw-over just operates. You have to push the armature in to make the throw-over operate, and with a new diaphragm it takes quite considerable pressure. It must be a steady pressure, not a sudden jerk.

After the point of just throwing-over is reached, the diaphragm has to be unscrewed a further set amount. This is where you need the setting instructions for your model pump. As a guide, the earlier pumps on small and medium cars have the armature unscrewed a further two-thirds of a turn — that is four of the six holes — and pumps for larger cars either one turn or one and one-sixth — seven holes. If you cannot find setting instructions for your pump check the diaphragm when taking the pump apart by marking the diaphragm with a pencil and checking the amount it has to be screwed in till the throw-over action just stops working.

Be vary careful when screwing the two halves of the pump together that none of the diaphragm rollers drops out of position. If one falls inside it will cut a hole in the diaphragm.

Before tightening the six screws the diaphragm has to be stretched to its fullest throw. SU agents have a setting gauge for this, but it can be done with a matchstick. Put the matchstick behind one of the white rollers on the contact breaker assembly to hold the points in contact. Then connect the pump to the battery and the magnet will be energised and pull the diaphragm forward. While it is forward, tighten the screws.

Most assembly faults come from forgetting three things, so remember: swing the contact blade to one side when setting the armature for throw-over; find the throw-over point by pressing steadily on the diaphragm, not jerking it; and stretch the diaphragm to its full stroke before tightening the screws holding the body parts.

To go through the detailed overhaul of all the types of carburetter you are likely to meet would need a chapter for each one, so I will go through the general points to be watched on all carburetters, and deal in a little more detail with the main makes you will come across: the SU, Solex, Zenith and Stromberg.

The first point about overhauling any carburetter is to make careful notes, with photographs if possible, of the linkage. This is particularly relevant on twin installations, but even on a seemingly simple layout the various rods and levers can often go back in several ways. Unless you enjoy Chinese puzzles make sure you know how they are supposed to go.

Unless you are lucky enough to have a car with miniature ball joints at the ends of all the rods, you will see that the rods are linked by bending the ends over and pushing them through holes in the levers with a split pin to hold them. This rather crude method works well enough when everything is new, but after twenty or thirty years it can be excused for showing sloppiness. If you want the nice taut feel that the controls of a well restored car should have it pays to do something about it. Probably the easiest way is to make up new control rods from larger diameter mild steel rod and drill the holes in the levers to suit. Quite a nice touch is to braze a washer on the rod so that when it is fitted the lever butts up against the washer, and use one or more washers on the other side of the lever so there is very little sideways play.

Be careful on some linkages about taking out all the sideways play because the geometry of the linkage may be a compromise to save money, and the cunning designer relied on sideways play to accomodate a slight twist as the rod moves. Better still, of course, fit small ball joints at the end of each rod. You can sometimes find suitable ball joints in model engineering shops, or at diesel fuel injection specialists where precise control of the fuel pump linkage is important.

The carburetter will most likely be filthy, and if the car has been standing there may be the same varnish deposits that there were in the petrol pump. If gum remover does not shift it have a friendly word with an electro-plater. His chemical cleaning bath will shift almost anything, but make sure the chemical he uses will not harm the zinc or aluminium body of the carburetter. Bead blasting will clean the body of the carburetter beautifully, but will not get the internal drillings clean.

If you want to do the job at home, and gum remover does not do the trick, you can try paint stripper, or as a last resort a hot solution of a powerful floor cleaner (such as Flash). This will clean most things, but wash off afterwards with plenty of really hot water. Many of these powerful cleaners contain soda which will dry out as a white powdery deposit and slowly eat its way into the metal.

If you want your carburetter to be a dazzling concours finish have it bead blasted — not grit blasted — before buffing it. (You will probably find a firm to do it in the yellow pages of the telephone directory under 'Metal Finishers'.)

The two big wear points on any carburetter, or rather a wear and distortion point, are the throttle spindle and the flange where the carburetter bolts on to the inlet manifold. Some carburetters have the ends of the throttle spindle sealed with plastic washers to stop air leaks, but on the majority the spindle just runs in plain holes bored in the casting. The spindle wears, and the holes go oval, so that air leaks in and spoils the carburation.

Sometimes it is possible to obtain oversize spindles and reamer out the holes to suit, but great care must be taken to get the holes exactly on the original centrelines or the throttle disc will not close properly. Alternatively, a new standard sized spindle can be used and the holes bushed, but the same remarks apply. If the holes are not badly worn, but the spindle is and a new one cannot be found, it is possible to coat the worn parts of the spindle with soft solder and rub them down to size with emery cloth. It may not be a precision engineer's idea of a first class repair, but it will last a surprisingly long time.

To get the throttle spindle out the screws holding the throttle disc have to be taken out. Mark the disc so that it is put back the right way up and its chamfered edges meet the body of the carburetter properly. The screws are split and opened slightly to lock them. Lock them when putting the disc back or there is a danger they will come loose and be sucked in the engine.

The flange where the carburetter bolts to the manifold must be absolutely flat to avoid air leaks. I have yet to find an old carburetter where this flange was not bowed. Bring it back flat by rubbing it on emery cloth on a flat surface such as a piece of plate glass. Hold the body of the carburetter firmly to avoid rocking it and use slow, long strokes.

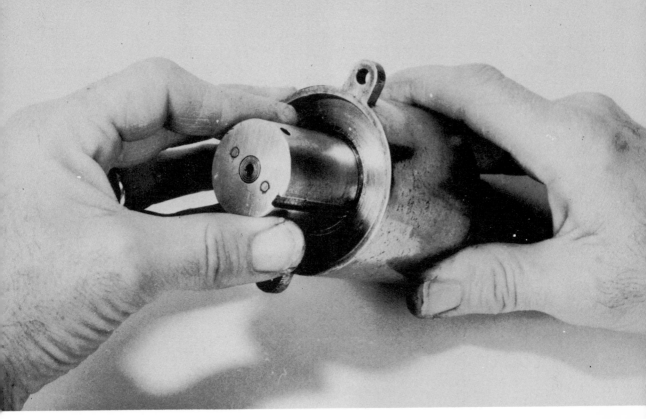

86   Testing the fit of
the piston in the dashpot
barrel of an SU carbur-
etter

The SU carburetter is used on all Morris cars, and a large number of other makes now under the Leyland group banner. Its working principles are covered in many books so I will concentrate on the aspects of overhaul where I have found many people have trouble.

The first thing is cleaning the barrel and piston of the suction chamber. I have seen instructions in some books that these can be cleaned with fine emery paper. Ignore them. These parts are machined to close tolerances and there is only one case where it is permissible to use anything other than petrol or a petrol solvent. I will come to that case in a moment. The large diameter of the piston should never wear because it should never touch the dashpot. What does wear after years of use is the smaller diameter, the steel

part at the top, and the small bore at the bottleneck of the dashpot.

Because of this you should always mark the body of the carburetter and the side of the dashpot so they go back in the same position. The piston cannot go back in the wrong position because there is a groove in the lower part and a guide on the body.

When you have the piston and dashpot clean turn the piston so it is in the same position as it will be when the carburetter is assembled, push it up and down and rock it from side to side. Check whether the large diameter touches the side of the dashpot. It should not, but on old worn carburetters it sometimes does. This is the only time it is permissible to use an abrasive. Ease both the bore and the rim of the piston where they have been touching until you have clearance. Use a strong metal polish such as Brasso, and clean out all traces of it afterwards.

Even if the jet and needle look unworn it

pays to renew them on a complete overhaul. The manual will probably give three sizes of needle, often labelled rich, normal and weak. Unless the car is run in very high altitudes where the weak needle might be needed to compensate for the thin air, or unless you are going racing where you might need the rich needle to give the last ounce of power and help keep the engine cool, always fit the standard needle. The weak needle is not intended as an economy alternative. On a fast run it will probably result in worse fuel consumption and, probably, overheating as well. Fit the new needle with its shoulder flush with the end of the piston.

The jet may be the older type with a number of cork packing washers under the gland nut — the later type which has a flexible pipe on it does not need gland packing — or it may be a diaphragm type usually fitted to higher performance cars. In any case it will need centralizing to meet the needle. On the first two types of jet centralizing can be carried out with the carburetter assembled, but with a diaphragm jet the float chamber has to be taken off in order to get at the jet locking nut under the diaphragm.

It often helps to lower the needle slightly in the piston so that its taper can be used as a guide to centralize the jet, but take great care not to bend the needle. A bent needle cannot be straightened satisfactorily. Remember to raise the jet to its correct position afterwards.

When the jet is centralized the piston and needle should fall down on to the jet bridge with a clean metallic click. On diaphragm jets mark the diaphragm with a pencil when you centralize it, and do it with the holes in the diaphragm and the body in line. If you rotate the diaphragm when you are bolting things together you may loose the centralization.

Check the level of the fuel in the float chamber by putting a bar under the float lever fork. A drill shank is suitable. On older carburetters the bar should be 3/8 in (9.5 mm) diameter, and on later models 7/16 in (11 mm). With the bar resting on the lid of the float chamber the needle valve should be shut when the fork rests on the bar.

When the carburetter is finally on the car, a check can be made on the fuel level by taking the dashpot off, pulling the jet down to its lowest, richest, position and looking down into the jet well. You should be able to see the bead of petrol about 1/8 in (3 mm) below the jet bridge. If the petrol flows over the bridge the level is too high, and if you cannot see it at all the level is too low. The car should be on level ground.

Some SUs are mounted with auxiliary solenoid controlled starting carburetters. Usually the solenoid is controlled by a thermostatic switch in the cooling system, but many owners convert it to control by a hand switch on the dash.

To set the starting carburetter bring the engine up to operating temperature, short out the solenoid switch and give the throttle a quick flip open to bring in the auxiliary carburetter. The only adjustment is the screw which acts as a stop for the needle. This screw should be adjusted so that the engine runs distinctly but not excessively rich. There should be a trace of black smoke in the exhaust but the mixture should not be so rich that the engine hunts with a marked irregular beat.

Solex carburetters have what amounts to an auxiliary starting carburetter built into them. It varies slightly in design between different models but they all work in a similar way. They have an air jet which must be kept clean, and a petrol jet which is varied by the position of a lever on the side of the body. On the opposite side of the body some Solexes have an accelerator pump which gives an extra

87   A typical Solex carburetter

squirt of petrol through an injector pipe for acceleration when the throttle is opened.

Apart from making sure all the parts are clean and assembled in the correct order with new gaskets, there are no snags in overhaul. The main cover lifts off after undoing five or six screws, and the float toggle and spindle can be lifted out. Be careful not to loose the

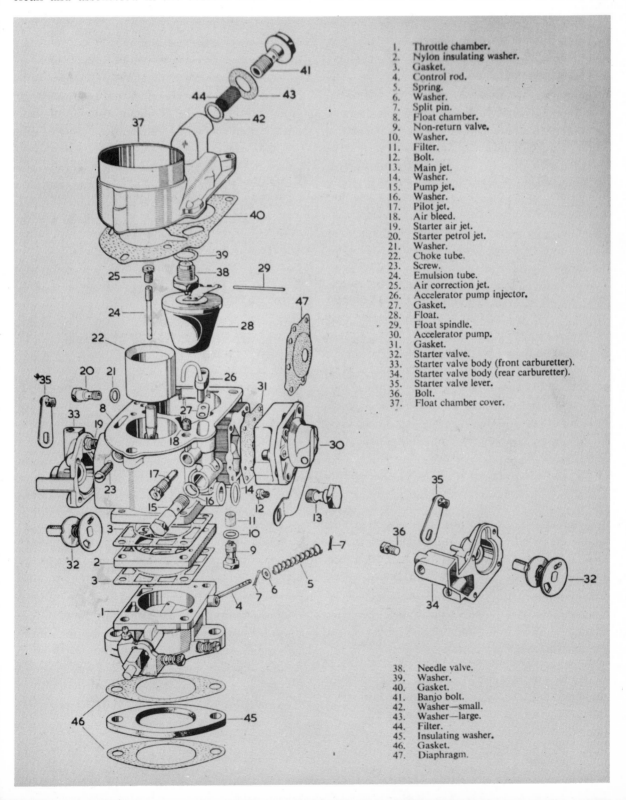

1. Throttle chamber.
2. Nylon insulating washer.
3. Gasket.
4. Control rod.
5. Spring.
6. Washer.
7. Split pin.
8. Float chamber.
9. Non-return valve.
10. Washer.
11. Filter.
12. Bolt.
13. Main jet.
14. Washer.
15. Pump jet.
16. Washer.
17. Pilot jet.
18. Air bleed.
19. Starter air jet.
20. Starter petrol jet.
21. Washer.
22. Choke tube.
23. Screw.
24. Emulsion tube.
25. Air correction jet.
26. Accelerator pump injector.
27. Gasket.
28. Float.
29. Float spindle.
30. Accelerator pump.
31. Gasket.
32. Starter valve.
33. Starter valve body (front carburetter).
34. Starter valve body (rear carburetter).
35. Starter valve lever.
36. Bolt.
37. Float chamber cover.

38. Needle valve.
39. Washer.
40. Gasket.
41. Banjo bolt.
42. Washer—small.
43. Washer—large.
44. Filter.
45. Insulating washer.
46. Gasket.
47. Diaphragm.

small spindle — it drops out very easily. All the jets unscrew from the outside of the body, as does the pump non-return valve and its gauze. At the centre of the choke tube is an air correction jet. When this is unscrewed the emulsion tube under it can be lifted out with a matchstick.

The auxiliary starting device comes apart for cleaning. The accelerator pump operates with one or two diaphragms depending on the model. These can be had as complete assemblies. The control rod for the pump has a spring held by a split pin and washer. There are a number of holes into which the split pin can fit, and make a note of the one on your engine because this setting tunes the pump to the engine.

Sometimes with a Solex heavy fuel consumption comes from someone with a heavy hand bending the accelerator pump injector tube. The bottom end of the tube should be 0.020 in to 0.040 in (0.5 mm to 1 mm) above the base of the block into which it is mounted. Trying to straighten it usually kinks the tube, so if it is bent it means a new one.

Always put a Solex together with new gaskets and fibre washers under the jets and a new gasket under the cover. The thickness of the fibre washers controls the height of the jets, so use genuine parts in a replacement pack from Solex.

Zenith carburetters are also quite simple to dismantle and clean. In this case the jets are in the base of the float chamber and are unscrewed with the square key on the end of one of the bolts holding the float chamber. The accelerator pump and its spring will lift out when a small screw is taken out. The pump should come up smartly under its spring pressure, but they sometimes stick with corrosion. If you find this, clean the pump plunger and housing with metal polish.

On the end of the float chamber where it fits in the body of the carburetter is an emulsion block held by six screws. It is not normally

necessary to take this off unless the accelerator pump jet under it is blocked. If you have to take it off always use a new gasket. The old one whiskers, and the whiskers find their way into the drillings in the block.

Stromberg carburetters have got themselves a bad name for being difficult to adjust because of their somewhat more complicated linkages. They suffer at the hands of home tuners who like to alter everything in sight to see if it cures their trouble. It is almost essential to have a manual for the car because of the wide variety of Strombergs, particularly the D series. The basic model is the DA which has a manual strangler and mechanically operated economy device. Type DBVA has a thermostatically controlled strangler with a vacuum operated economy valve. Then there is the DAA with a modified design of manual strangler, and the DBVC which is a special model for Rolls-Royce.

Because of these variations it is impossible here to deal with overhauling and setting Strombergs for all the different model cars to which they are fitted, but there are broad principles which apply to all models.

For some reason many home tuners suspect the float level setting on Strombergs. This is checked by removing the top of the float chamber, levelling the carburetter with a spirit level across the top of the chamber and measuring the depth of the top of the petrol from the edge of the bowl. The correct depth will be specified in the manual. As a guide, it should be ¾ in (19.1 mm) on Armstrong Siddeley Sapphires, 21/32 in (16.7 mm) on Austin Princesses and Sheerlines (the old Princesses, not the current ones) 27/32 in (21.5 mm) on Sunbeam Talbot 90s, and it varies between 21/32 in (16.7 mm) and 27/32 in (21.5 mm) on Humber Hawks and Super Snipes. The only way to adjust the level is by bending the float arm with two pairs of pliers.

To enable an economy main jet to be used,

a by-pass jet, sometimes called a power jet, has to come into operation for maximum power. With manual by-pass jets there is a tappet attached to the accelerator pump cross piece. As full throttle approaches, this pushes open a spring-loaded valve to allow petrol through the by-pass jet. To set this tappet the throttle has to be held at a particular position while the screw on the tappet is adjusted. The throttle is set by holding a drill shank between the throttle disc and the body. The drill size varies from car to car. With the throttle set the tappet is adjusted so it just touches the by-pass valve.

Some Strombergs have an automatic choke, or thermostatically controlled strangler, as Stromberg prefer to call it. This is a bi-metal strip wound like a clock spring in a housing bolted to the exhaust manifold. There are left hand and right hand thermostats, so called because of the position of the arm relative to a check pin. The ball joint at the top of the rod connecting the thermostat to the strangler flap should be in the centre hole for right hand units and the bottom hole for left hand. The top hole is for special applications. The thermostats themselves are often found in a corroded condition, so many owners disconnect them and fit a manual control, but it is sometimes possible to pick up new thermostats at autojumbles and swap-meets. Some Stromberg agents may still have them in stock for earlier cars. They should be set at about 21°C (70°F).

The bi-metal spring is set so many notches 'rich'. In other words it is given a slight pretension, the amount depending on the car to which it is fitted. The rod and lever connecting the thermostat to the strangler is adjusted for length so that the strangler is closed when a specified size of drill shank is held between the thermostat lever and the check pin. This use of drill shanks as setting gauges by Stromberg saves restorers a great deal of money and frustration searching for special setting gauges.

Setting of the fast idle cam screw is also made with a drill shank as a gauge, and by adjusting the strangler-to-cam-lever link, which has left and right hand threads. Once again obtain the correct size for the drill from a car manual.

Setting up a Stromberg linkage sounds complicated but only because there are different settings for each model of car. These settings are naturally lost when the carburetter is stripped for overhaul, but tackled in a systematic way, with a manual, there should be no difficulty. Once set, they remain so. The only tool required apart from a screwdriver and pair of pliers is a special jet key — and a selection of drills.

Once the carburetter is cleaned and its linkages set, all that remains is to set the slow running throttle stop and idling mixture. The idling is an air bleed screw on most fixed jet carburetters, and is made by adjusting the height of the jet on SUs. As a starting point, screw an air bleed screw fully home and back it off one and a half turns. With an SU, screw the jet fully upwards and back it down between one and half to two turns.

With these settings, and the throttle stop screwed open a little, start the engine and bring it up to operating temperature. Slow it down on the throttle stop to an even tickover and adjust the mixture till the engine speeds up. Slow it down again on the throttle stop and repeat this till no further adjustment of the idling mixture increased the speed.

In the case of twin carburetters disconnect the throttle linkage between the two so that each is adjusted independently. When you set the throttle stops hold a piece of garden hose to each intake in turn and listen to the hiss at the other end. To balance the carburetters adjust the throttle stops so that the hiss is the same at each intake. Do this for the initial setting of the stops, and again each time the engine is slowed after adjusting the idling mixture.

=18=
INSTRUMENTS

Most people like to have a well stocked dashboard, and adding extra instruments is a popular pastime. Whether you stick with the original instrument layout of your car or, if this was on the meagre side, add more, is up to you and your views about originality. My own view is that if they could have been ordered with the model as optional extras they are authentic. If you can find extra instruments that were on the market as accessories at the time your car was built, this, in my view is also keeping it original. What I do not care for are obviously modern extra instruments added to an old car. Whichever view is taken, all the instruments should be in working order.

Speedometers are obligatory on post-war cars in Britain. If the instrument itself is faulty there are a number of specialist firms who will repair and restore it even if it is an obsolete model. But before packing the head off for repair make sure the fault is not somewhere else. In many cases speedometers misbehave because of faults in the flexible drive.

Sharp bends are the biggest enemy of flexible drives. Smiths Instruments recommend that the minimum radius for a bend in a speedometer drive is 6 in (15 cm), but I like to keep a wider curve than this if possible. It is most important not to have a bend close to the gearbox take-off point, nor near the

instrument head. Smiths say not nearer than 2 in (5 cm), but try to make this more if possible.

Another cause of trouble in flexible drives is bad support along their length. The cable must be held so that it does not wave about, but many car makers seem to be happy with flimsy clips made from sheet steel, perhaps with a nut and bolt or self-tapping screw. Originally most of these clips had a rubber packing to protect the cable, but with the passing of the years many of these have passed as well. Some clips are kinked by past heavy-handed owners, and even if this has not damaged the cable it may have pulled it too taut. It must run in gentle curves.

Any of these faults can make the inner cable bind in its outer casing so that instead of rotating smoothly it winds itself up and comes free with a rush. This makes the needle waver over a range of about 10 or 15 mph so you are never quite sure what speed you are doing. If this wavering comes and goes it could be that the end of the inner cable, either at the gearbox or the instrument, is not engaging properly because the connectors are loose or because the outer casing has been stretched. There is no need to force the connectors tight with pliers, though I have come across many that were chewed and scored. Provided

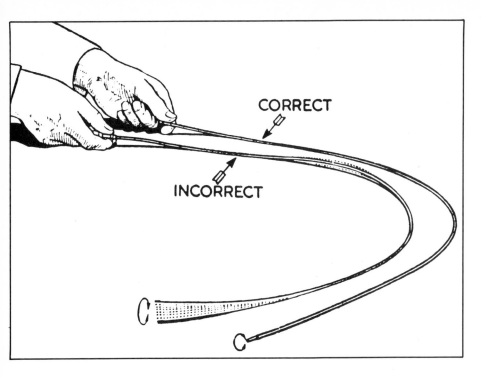

CORRECT

INCORRECT

the threads are clean, finger tightness is all that is needed.

Inner cables can also stretch. As a guide, disconnect the cable at the instrument and measure the length of inner cable protruding from the face of the flange on the outer casing. It need by only about 3/8 in (9.5 mm). If it is much over ½ in (13 mm) it has stretched.

Before reconnecting the cable jack up one of the driving wheels and, with the other wheels securely chocked, run the engine with the car in gear. The end of the inner cable should rotate smoothly and centrally in the outer. If it rotates in a cone check again for sharp bends in the run of the cable, but if this is not the fault you need either a new inner or a new complete drive.

The inner cable can be checked when it is out of the drive. Many pull out at the instrument end, but some have a brass ferrule with a C-shaped washer. In this case take the washer out and the cable will come out from the gearbox end of the drive. If you find a ferrule

with a groove for a washer, but no washer, this could be part of the trouble.

Wipe the inner cable clean, lay it on a flat surface in a gentle curve and twist one end. It should stay flat on the surface when you twirl it. If it kicks up at the end, or jumps in the middle, it needs renewing.

When putting the inner cable back, or fitting a new one, smear it quite sparingly with grease. Most people make the mistake of over-greasing speedometer drives. After feeding the cable in pull it back up again about 6 or 8 in (15 or 20 cm) at the instrument end and wipe the grease off. A speedometer cable should never be oiled. The rotation will feed oil up into the instrument and possibly ruin it. Oil can also get up the cable into the instrument if the seal at the drive gear is damaged.

The symptoms of oil in a speedometer head are sluggish operation, with possibly a slow swinging back and forth right across the dial. Sometimes this can be cured by washing the instrument out in petrol or benzine, but usually it means sending the head away to be stripped.

151

If you are looking for a secondhand head at a breakers or autojumble you need to know the turns per mile, usually abbreviated to TPM. The speedometer head from a similar car to yours may not have the same TPM because the rear axle ratio may be different. The TPM number is often marked on the dial, together with a code number for the instrument. The TPM number will be a figure such as 1180 or 1251, or something of that order.

If the speedometer is inaccurate, and you suspect that a previous owner has fitted one with the wrong TPM, it is quite easy to check. Disconnect the drive from the speedometer head and push a cardboard pointer over the inner cable so that its turns can be counted. Then mark one of the driving wheels at the bottom, and with the gearbox in neutral get a helper to push the car forward so the wheel makes exactly six turns, and count the number of turns the inner cable of the speedometer drive makes. The tires should be at their proper pressure, and the correct size of tire must be fitted.

Now the simple formula can be applied:

$$TMP = \frac{1680 \times N}{R}$$ where N is the number of

turns of the inner cable for six turns of the road wheel, and R is the radius from the centre of the hub to the ground, measured in inches. Try to count the last part of a turn of the cable to the nearest eighth of a turn.

As an example, if the inner cable turns $9\frac{1}{8}$ times, and the radius R is $12\frac{1}{4}$ inches, the TPM will be.

$$\frac{1680 \times 9\frac{1}{8}}{12\frac{1}{4}}$$

This, to the nearest whole number, comes to 1251. This figure should be within 25 either way the same as the TPM number on the dial of the speedometer.

To find turns per kilometre, measure R in cm and substitute 100,000 for 1680.

Many older tachometers, or rev counters, are driven from a cable on the back of the dynamo, and the same points apply here as to speedometer drives. A possible, though not very likely, cause of an inaccurate reading is a wrong-sized fan pulley or a wrong-ratio gearbox behind the dynamo. More likely, though, is a slipping fan belt.

More modern electrical rev counters are either moving coil instruments driven by a small generator somewhere on the engine — on Jaguar XK engines the generator is at the back of one of the camshafts — or they are pulse-counting instruments which measure the number of current pulses passing through the coil every minute.

If there is no reading at all from a moving coil type you can check whether the fault is at the instrument, the generator or the wiring by using an AC voltmeter. It must be an AC voltmeter; the more usual DC voltmeter is useless for this purpose. Check the voltage across the terminals of the generator. It should be in the order of 1 volt for every 100 engine revs. If all is well here try the voltage at the instrument end of the cables. No indication means a break somewhere in the cables. If there is a voltage reading here, and still no reading on the instrument, then the head itself is faulty.

Troubles with pulse-counting rev counters usually come from faults in the wiring. Either there is an open circuit somewhere, or the case of the instrument is not properly earthed, or it has been wired for the wrong polarity earth. The wiring also differs depending on whether or not there is a ballast resistance in the coil circuit. The only way to check all this out is from the car's wiring diagram. If it is an add-on instrument, and the maker's original fitting instructions are missing, write to the firm quoting the make, model and year of your car and any code numbers on the instrument.

There is one possible fault that can be checked on these instruments without a wiring diagram. Sometimes the feed cable in the back of the instrument is pulled so tightly it distorts a plastic former inside. The cable should pass through the iron core inside the instrument in an easy curve.

Most ammeters are robust moving-iron instruments and seldom give trouble from anything other than loose connections, unless they are completely burnt out. In that case there is little you can do except replace the instrument, or at least the insides. Trying to resolder a coil inside the casing is seldom successful.

The same goes for oil gauges of the Bourdon tube pressure type. These have a flattened tube in a curve that tries to straighten under pressure and moves a pointer through a gear wheel and sector. If the gauge is full of oil because the Bourdon tube is leaking it might be possible to repair it by soldering, but if the tube splits it usually splits all the way along and is useless. It is easier to get another gauge than repair it.

The copper pipe from the gauge to the engine should be mounted with freedom so it does not chafe as the engine rocks. Long runs should be secured in clips with plenty of felt or sponge rubber packing to stop vibration fractures. Remember there is a small washer at the end of the pipe where it fits on the gauge. If you forget this you get a nasty oily mess behind the dash.

Fuel gauges, and their wiring and tank units, are notoriously unreliable. Often the fault is in the wiring or the tank unit rather than the gauge. Always disconnect the battery before taking cables off because at the gauge end you could damage the instrument and at the tank end you could get a spark. If the tank unit is out the spark could ignite the petrol vapour. Never connect a live lead to the T terminal on the gauge; it will ruin it.

Most cars of the forties and fifties have the type of gauge that gives an instant reading when you switch on and fails to zero the instant you switch off. The wiring diagram might show three cables going to the gauge, and there are only two terminals, usually marked T and B. T stands for tank unit and B for battery. The third cable in the wiring diagram is an earth lead which usually goes to one of the fixing screws. With a metal dash erratic operation may occur if this cable is missing. With a wood or plastic dash you will get no reading.

The most usual fault with this type of gauge is that is remains at EMPTY when you know there is petrol in the tank. The first point to check is that the cable to the B terminal is live when the ignition is switched on. Then check that there is a good earth to the body of the gauge. If these are all right disconnect the T terminal, reconnect the battery and switch on. The gauge should read FULL. If it does, take a separate cable and run it from the T terminal to earth. If the gauge now reads EMPTY it is probably working all right and the fault could be a short to earth along the cable from the gauge to the tank unit.

If running a new cable does not cure the fault, check the tank unit. Disconnect the battery, take the tank unit out and take it up near the gauge well away from the tank in case of sparks. Use a pair of crocodile clips to connect the body of the tank unit to earth and run a cable from the terminal on the unit to terminal T on the gauge. Reconnect the battery, switch on and move the float arm up and down. The gauge should correspond. If it does, the fault is probably a bad earth connection either between the unit and the tank or between the tank and the chassis. On some cars the tank is rubber mounted and there should be an earth lead from one of the unit-holding screws to the chassis or body.

If the gauge does not move when the float arm is moved there is probably an open circuit somewhere in the tank unit. It could be a broken wire, or a burnt out resistance coil or a bad contact between the moving slider and

89   A beautifully
restored set of instru-
ments on a TC MG. Com-
pare this with the picture
in chapter 1

the coil. This is often the case when the unit
has been standing unused for years. It can be
cured by squirting switch cleaner on the coil
and moving the slider back and forth to remake
the contact.

If the gauge records but is hopelessly inaccurate it could be that someone has bent the

float arm or that a wrong tank unit or wrong
gauge has been fitted. Of the two, a wrong
tank unit is more likely. There will be a code
number on the tank unit if it is made by
Smiths, and either they or the car manufacturer will be able to say if it is the right one.

Most temperature gauges on cars from our
period are the Bourdon tube pressure type with
a capillary tube leading to a bulb at the radiator or engine block end. The gauges seldom
give trouble, the most likely fault being that
the tube has broken. The unit works on a
pressure principle by having a bulb full of

ether. This gets warm and vapourizes to build up a pressure that records on the gauge. It is fiddling, but repairing is reasonably easy at home.

You need two or three fluid ounces of ether. Commerical purity is suitable but you will probably have to buy medical ether from a chemist. You may have to sign the book for it, but if you explain why you want it there should be no difficulty. Remember that ether fumes are flammable so never attempt the repair near a naked flame.

The first job is to repair the break in the capillary tube. They usually go at the ends, and as they are nearly all of generous length the same tube can often be used again. If the tube is broken halfway along you may be able to get new tubing from an instrument suppliers. You need armoured tubing; plain capillary tubing as used in laboratories is easily kinked and broken. Alternatively you may be able to pick up a suitable length of tubing at a breakers'. Use an electric soldering iron rather than take the ether near a flame.

If you are fitting a new tube it will have to be soldered at the gauge end, and you need to get behind the dial anyway to refill the unit with ether. When you take the pointer and dial off be careful to pull the pointer straight up as the spindle is easy to bend.

At the block inside the gauge where the capillary tube is soldered there will be a second short length of tube closed with solder at its end. This is the filling tube. Unsolder the end of it, or nip it off if it is long enough. Then heat the bulb in boiling water to expand the air inside it. An electric kettle is advisable, again because of the fire risk. Hold the end of the filling tube under the surface of the ether and bubbles will start coming out. When these stop transfer the bulb to cold water and the contraction of the air inside the bulb will suck ether up the tube.

Repeat the process. This time there will be a mixture of air and ether gas. Keep repeating it till the bulb is full of ether. The flow of bubbles will never stop entirely but as the bulb fills the flow will get less and less as liquid ether comes out. Crimp the end of the filling tube with a pair of pliers and seal it with solder. It may be a little difficult to get the solder to take because the heat of your iron will blow ether gas out of the end that is being soldered, but with the bulb in very cold water it will seal eventually. Check the seal by heating the bulb again with the end of the filling tube under liquid ether. This time instead of producing bubbles the Bourdon tube should start to uncurl and the gear and sector should move. With the bulb in boiling water put the dial back and put the pointer on the spindle opposite the boiling mark.

Remember that as well as being flammable ether is also an anesthetic, so avoid breathing the fumes or you may wake up on the floor.

Most switches are fairly easy to repair if they go wrong. In most cases it is a matter of cleaning the contacts with switch cleaner. You may find trouble with the type of panel warning light which has a resistance wound round it and which takes a 2.5 volt bulb. If the resistance is damaged you can either short it out and use a 12 volt bulb — or 6 volt as the case may be — or else cut the resistance wire away and replace it with a resistor from a radio shop. To use a 2.5 volt bulb in a 12 volt system you need a 50 ohm resistor, and for a 6 volt system a 20 ohm resistor. Both should be half-watt rating. The normal resistor from a radio shop has a tolerance of plus or minus 15%. This is quite suitable; there is no need to ask for close tolerance components.

—19—
THE COOLING SYSTEM

Cooling system troubles come either from leaks or from sludge and scale in the radiator and engine. The coolant circulates from the top of the engine to the top of the radiator then down through the radiator where it cools. It follows that sludge carried round by the coolant is deposited in the radiator header tank and gradually blocks up the radiator tubes from the top. This is why flushing a radiator from top seldom does much good. The proper way to wash it out is to reverse flush it.

Before doing this it pays to loosen as much of the sludge and scale as you can. Use one of the proprietary cleaners. Then, to reverse flush it properly the radiator should come off. Leave the bottom hose connected and make up a wooden bung to fit it. Through this bung drill a ½ in (13 mm) hole and drive in a piece of copper tube to which a garden hose can be fixed.

Turn the radiator upside-down with the filler cap off, turn on the mains water and leave it to flush till the water comes out

90   When you get the radiator out it will probably look like this — dirty and rusted. The only way to flush it is to turn it upside down and reverse flush

clear. Every now and again turn the water off, turn the radiator the right way up and give it a shake to dislodge any sludge pockets the flow is not reaching.

Now if you stand the radiator the right way up and block off the top hose inlet, there should be a healthy flow through it when water is poured in the filler. If not it means that the sludge is too hard to remove by flushing. You have either to send the radiator to a specialist or try to clean the tubes yourself.

A specialist will take the top and bottom tanks off, but resoldering them without unsoldering the tubes is a skilled business. I feel most home restorers, if they are determined to tackle the job, would be better off cutting one or two holes in the tanks and soldering plates over them afterwards. If you can cut a panel out right across the tank it makes cleaning easier, but if the bottom tank has a reinforced section in the middle, or a hole for the starting handle, you will have to cut either side. Similarly the filler may mean cutting two holes in the top tank.

The tubes in the core of the radiator are quite narrow and it is not easy to find strips thin enough to push through them. I have had success with the binding straps used on packing cases which I got from a warehouse. Alternatively get someone with a guillotine to cut you some thin strips of 20 gauge steel.

To avoid kinking the strips as you run them through the tubes hold them with a pair of pliers and push in only an inch (or a couple of centimetres) or so at a time. If the strip goes solid draw it out, wipe it clean and try again. It may not be possible to get every tube free but most cars have radiators of generous size to cope with hot climates, so unless you are in a hot climate the radiator will probably manage with a few blocked tubes. If you tow a trailer, the radiator should be perfectly clear.

After cleaning and washing through, solder

19 or 20 gauge brass plates over the holes you cut. The plates should overlap the holes by about ½ in (13 mm) all round. Flatten and file the edges of the holes till the plates fit properly flat.

Tin both the plates and the tanks. A flame is much better than even a large soldering iron for this job. The only danger is of melting the solder where the tubes are fixed in. There are two ways round this. One is to put wet cloths round the tank, the other is to stand the radiator in a bath of water.

Use the flame, and a good flux, to spread solder all round the holes in the tanks and on the plates. Apply more flux, put the plates in position and press down on them with a block of wood while you play the flame over the edges to melt the solder and fuse them together. There should now be an even bead of solder all round the joint. If not, feed in more solder and flux and play the flame along the join. Any surplus solder can be wiped off while it is hot with a rag dipped in flux. As with any soldering job the secret is to get the parts to be joined clean and in close contact. If the job is done neatly the plates will hardly show when they are painted.

If there is sludge in the radiator there will also be sludge in the water passages of the block and head. Reverse flush the engine in the same way as the radiator. In this case the normal flow is upwards, so put the hose and wooden bung at the top of the head and flush downwards.

Reverse flushing will not reach all the small water passages at the back of the block and head. The only way to clean these is to take out the core plugs. Most core plugs are the domed welch type. The way to get these out is to drive a sharp centre punch through the middle. The plugs will dome inwards and come out skewered on the punch. When putting new plugs in smear a little jointing compound in the housing, put the plug in position and give its centre a sharp blow with a hammer to spread the edges into the dovetail recess of the housing. If the setting is badly corroded and the plug weeps, seat it in glass fibre resin.

Instead of welch plugs there may be screwed-in core plugs with a square hole for a key or two holes to take a peg spanner. Normally the threads can be cleaned and the plugs used again, but if they are very tight it is as well to make sure that new ones can be obtained before damaging the square or holes. If in doubt, play safe and leave them alone.

One other type of core plug, used on Ford engines, looks like the lid of a boot polish tin and fits with its hollow side outwards. It is put in with a special jointing compound that can be obtained from Ford dealers. The plugs are driven in with a length of rounded hardwood.

While flushing out remember the other small radiator, the heater. This should also be taken off and reverse flushed with a hose.

After cleaning out everything fit new hoses. If the car maker used tiny little pieces of twisted wire, or flat strips with a split pin through them, to hold the hoses, throw them away and use proper worm drive clips. Thermostats do not last for ever, and as they are inexpensive fit a new one.

Water pumps either work or they leak. If they leak it is because the gland seal has gone. Usually this is because worn bearings put an uneven load on it. Water pumps vary greatly in design, and it may or may not be easy to get a replacement pump or a new seal. If you cannot exchange the pump you may be lucky enough to get a repair kit complete with seal and bearings. If not, and you can get only a seal, it should be possible to get new bearings from any good bearing supplier as they are standard size. As a last-ditch effort you can try cutting down the nearest size seal you can get.

This is none too easy, but with carbon seals it can be done with a fine file, emery cloth and several tons of patience. Rubber seals are almost impossible to adapt if they are moulded to fit the pump gland, but the spares secretary of a one-make club might know of a way out.

Dismantling water pumps varies with the design. In some cases after taking off the pulley the shaft and impellor can be driven out. In other cases there is a circlip, and still others have the impellor held by a taper pin which has to be driven out. In yet others the pump body is in two parts, one holding the bearings and the other holding the impellor and seal. Unless you have a manual inspect the pump very carefully before starting to use force to get it apart. Sometimes it is worthwhile getting a secondhand pump, even in bad condition, to find out how it takes apart. If you break the spare one you are no worse off, but you have found out how to do the job.

Pack the new bearings in water pump grease when putting them in. Between the two bearings there is often a small drain hole so that any water which finds its way past the seal drains away instead of corroding the bearings. This hole being blocked is a frequent cause of bearing corrosion and failure, so make sure it is free.

On some high-performance cars the fan is a balanced assembly. Mark the position of any balance weights carefully before undoing the fan; sometimes they fall off when you undo the holding bolts.

The last item in the cooling system to receive attention is the radiator filler cap. Make sure it is the correct pressure rating for the car, and if the spring or seal looks worn renew it. Most garages keep stocks of pressure caps in various pressure ratings.

=20=
A ROUND-UP OF ODDS AND ENDS

This last chapter is by way of being a rounding-up operation to cover some of the problems that may be met on a restoration but which do not readily fall into any of the previous chapters.

I will start by tackling something that can be very annoying; when you have a perfectly good barrel lock and no key for it. On older cars the code number for the key, at least for the ignition and sometimes for the door as well, is stamped on the face of the barrel to make it easier for you, or a thief, to find a key. That, however, does not help much today if the key series is obsolete and unobtainable. You might also want to alter the lock so that the original key will not open it in case the key is not so unobtainable as all that.

Provided a key with the right grooves can be found to slide into the barrel, the code number does not matter because tumblers can be cut to suit. It may be feasible to re-arrange and cut the tumblers already in the lock. If not, the tumblers from any similar lock will suit.

When the barrel is taken out of the lock the tumblers, which have small coil springs under them, will pop up and can be lifted out. When the key is put in, the tumblers line up flush with the barrel so that it will turn. If the tumblers are reassembled at random at least some of them will still stick out of the barrel when the key is put in because they will be the wrong length to suit the serrations on the key.

If the key is held in place, the protruding parts of the tumblers sawn off and filed to the profile of the barrel, you will have a lock to suit whatever number key is being used. Check when withdrawing the key that enough tumblers pop up to lock the barrel, and you now have a lock that will fool anyone because it will operate only with the number key that was used to cut it, and not with the original key of the number stamped on the barrel.

From keys, on to doors. On a restored car the doors should all shut sweetly with a firm click, but unfortunately on many otherwise well-restored cars I have seen, this is not the case.

The first step in getting a sweetly shutting door is to position it accurately in the opening. With wooden doors the frame may have dropped and want rebuilding, but with steel doors which have not been damaged the fault is probably in the hinge setting. Some people manage to improve things by packing out the hinges, but the proper way on flap hinges — the sort that stick out from the door — is to be relatively brutal and set them physically.

Take the lock and striker plate off and close

the door. Either it will close without touching the side of the aperture or it will touch at points A, B, C, D or E in the diagram.

Fouling at point A means that the top hinge has opened out, and possibly the bottom hinge has closed. A foul at point B means the bottom hinge has opened out. At C it means the top hinge has closed, at D it means the bottom hinge has closed, and at E it means the bottom hinge has closed and the top hinge opened out but not enough to cause a foul at point A.

To close a hinge that has opened, close the door and put an adjustable wrench over the hinge to stop it opening. Then try to open the door. There is no need to strain, only moderate force is required.

To open a hinge that has closed, open the door and put a small block of hardwood in the hinge. Then try to close the door. Once again only light force is needed.

Once the door closes freely in the aperture it may stick out at A and B. If so, put a felt covered block of wood in the aperture level with the lock plate, close the door on it and lean gently on points A and B to strain it back into line. Lean only gently or you might raise a bump at the block.

Now you can have a go at the lock and striker. Refit them and close the door. Depending on the type of lock, a number of maladjustments can cause bad shutting. I have laid them out in the following table from information from Wilmot Breedon's service department.

Quite a number of cars from the forties and fifties are fitted with Jackall built-in hydraulic jacks, not many of which are still working.

Fault	Reason
Shut edge of door is inside body profile when closed	Striker parallel to hinge line but set too far in
Shut edge of door proud of body profile when closed	Striker set too far out
Shut edge of door drops when closed	Striker set too low, or on slam locks dovetails set too low
Shut edge rises when closed	Striker or dovetails set too high
Door fits properly but rattles and can be lifted when shut	Top of striker inclined to car interior, or dovetails badly worn
Door closing is hard and door slips to First Safety position (Rotary cam and rotary locks only)	Top of striker inclined to outside of car
Door slips to First Safety position (Slam locks only)	Remote door control lever bent, or striker tilted. Set striker at an angle so that only its inside edge is in contact with the lock bolt
Jerky closing and stiff opening (Rotary cam and rotary locks only)	Striker stud not pointing at hinge pivot

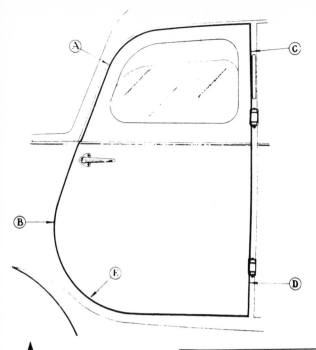

They are quite easy to overhaul except that the rubber valve plate which carries the cone valves to select Front, Rear or All is now difficult to obtain. Even so, the unit can be made to work.

The main body of the pump comes apart, but watch out for non-return balls in the drillings which may pop out as it is being dismantled. The wire gauze filter in the side plate may be blocked, and this may be half the trouble.

If the rubber valve carrier has hardened and the cone-ended valves to control Front and Rear operation have pulled out, the pump can still be made to work all four jacks at once. Take out the cone-ended valves and patch the rubber plate either with self-vulcanising patches or get a tire repair shop to vul-

91 Checking the fit of a pressed steel door with outside hinges

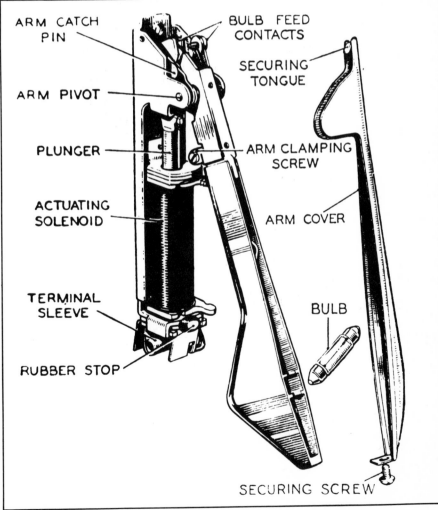

92 There may be semaphore indicators on your car. Most troubles come from corrosion on the plunger or on the bulb feed contacts

ARM CATCH PIN

BULB FEED CONTACTS

SECURING TONGUE

ARM PIVOT

PLUNGER

ARM CLAMPING SCREW

ACTUATING SOLENOID

ARM COVER

TERMINAL SLEEVE

BULB

RUBBER STOP

SECURING SCREW

canise the patches. The laminated leaf spring is a safety valve to prevent something bursting if you continue to pump when the jacks are fully down, so make sure it operates properly.

The jacks come apart for cleaning by gripping them in a vice with wooden clamps to save squashing the barrels, and unscrewing the bottom caps. The copper sealing washers can be softened for further use by heating them to a bright red and quenching them in plain cold water to anneal them. If the gland seal is perished (though this is not a common fault) try a factory for industrial hydraulics for a replacement. Repiping, preferably with non-corroding copper pipe or Kunifer 10, is straightforward.

On engines, hydraulic tappets (or hydraulic valve lifters as they are more correctly termed in America) have never been very popular on British cars, though American-designed units were fitted to some Armstrong Siddeleys just after the war, and the latest Rover 3500 and Range Rover has them in what is an American-designed engine.

There is not a great deal that goes wrong with them that cleaning will not put right. Their big enemies are dirty, oily sludge, and carbon on the plungers — which make them stick. On Armstrong Siddeleys the oil is fed from the tappet block, which is different from the American General Motors design where it is fed down hollow push rods from the overhead valve rocker.

The plunger cylinders can be lifted out of their housings with a piece of hooked wire. Twist the plunger and spring to release them and pull them out. You will need pliers for this, but wrap some tape round the jaws to avoid damaging the plunger. If the plunger does not want to come out push a wooden stick, about matchstick thickness, up the oil inlet tube at the bottom of the cylinder to release the ball check valve and allow any trapped oil to drain out. If the plunger can now be pushed down but still does not want

to lift out it is being held by old dried oil and carbon. Soak it in petrol for a time to loosen it. Though the complete plunger and cylinder assemblies are interchangeable in the tappet blocks, individual plungers and cylinders are lapped together and must stay together.

When the unit is clean and dry test it by putting the plunger back in and pushing it down sharply with your finger. If the check valve is working properly there will be a resistance as the plunger compresses the air inside the cylinder. If the plunger is stabbed down quickly it should kick back under this air pressure. If it is completely dead, put a finger over the oil inlet tube at the bottom of the cylinder and try again. If the plunger still feels dead the cylinder is so worn that air is escaping past the plunger and the assembly will never work properly because the oil will do the same.

If putting a finger over the inlet hole restores the springy feeling the fault is in the check valve. It may be that there is still some dirt stopping the ball seating properly, but if the ball or its seating are corroded or damaged, once again the unit needs replacing.

To reassemble the plunger push it down in the cylinder and twist it to lock the spring in the counterbore. (If the units are going straight back in the engine they should be put in dry, but if they are being stored while other parts are being reconditioned, wipe an oily rag over the parts to prevent rust.)

When the units go back on the engine set the dry valve clearance at the valve stem between 0.03 in (0.75 mm) and 0.075 in (2 mm). This will be taken up when the hydraulic lifters operate. To avoid a clatter when first starting up leave the oil feed pipe off the connection at the tappet block and crank the engine over to get rid of the air in the pipe. When a full stream of oil comes out, connect the pipe and continue cranking to fill the lifting cylinders before starting the

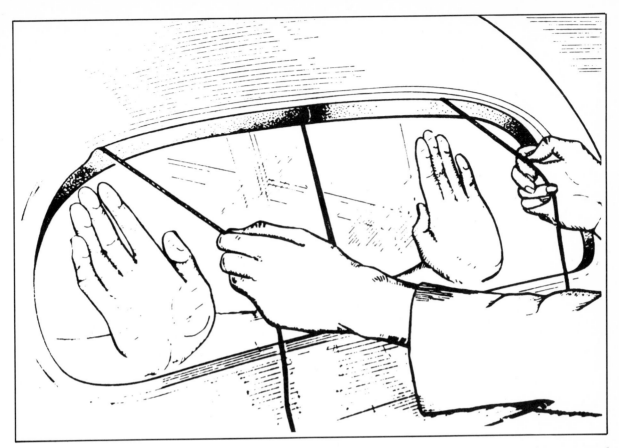

93   A helper is necessary to hold a window in position while you pull out the rubber fixing surround with a length of string previously threaded round it

engine.

The last item in this chapter is the Trico vacuum operated wiper motor. This has been completely overtaken by electric wipers because of the big failing that when you accelerate, and probably need the wipers most, the manifold depression drops and the wipers slow to a crawl or stop. A reservoir helps, but on a long hill it is inclined to run out.

Even so, if you want to keep the car original the vacuum wipers should be retained — if only for concours. An alternative to the reservoir is a vacuum booster pump, often coupled with the mechanical fuel pump and driven by the camshaft. This was popular on some American cars but never caught on in Britain.

The popular half-moon vacuum motors have a paddle inside. The paddle wiping seals should not be taken off as they were put on in special jigs to form the lip at the paddle edges. If the wiper linkage is free and operating properly, and if the vacuum pipe connections are not leaking, the main points of attention are the check valve on the inlet side of the reservoir and the valve assembly on the motor.

Most troubles with the valve come from old grease stopping it working, or burrs on the stamped-out parts. These can be filed flat. Take the lid off the vacuum chamber to clean it out, and smear the paddle with grease when you put it back. Use a new gasket on the lid to be sure of an airtight seal.

94 And, for the last picture in the book, this is what it's all about. The owner of this 1948 Jensen, of which only about 15 were built, found it in a field under a tree where it had stood with the doors open for over two years. He has painstakingly and carefully rebuilt it from the ground up

So now we have come to the end of the book. I have not been able to cover everything you will meet in the course of a complete chassis-up restoration, but I hope I have been able to point you along the right roads, save you a few heartaches — and maybe a little money as well.

Good luck, and enjoy your car restoring — and your motoring when the job is finally gleaming and ready to go.

Index

Page numbers referring to illustrations appear in *italic* type

Relevant United States Publications

Publisher	Address
Cars & Parts	P.O. Box 482, Sydney, OH 45367
Classic Motorbooks	729 Prospect Ave., Osceola, WI 54020
Crank 'En Hope Publications	450 Maple Ave., Blairsville, PA 15717
Hemmings Motor News	Bennington, VT 05201
Old Cars	Iola, WI 54945
Skinned Knuckles	175 May Ave., Monrovia, CA 91016
Woodgraining Secrets	Neal Rodgers, 6214 Lynbrook, Houston, TX 77027

Suppliers

Name	*Address*	*Service or Product*
Abingdon Spares, Ltd	1329 Highland Ave. Needham, MA 02192	MG parts
Bassett's Jaguars Restoration & Supplies	P.O. Box 14514 Peace Dale, RI 02883	Jaguar Restoration and supplies
Big T Parts Co.	19337 Greenview. Detroit Mich. 48129	Thunderbird parts
California Mustang Parts	1249 E. Holt. Pomona, CA 91767	Mustang parts
Cambria Metal & Furniture Strippers	900 W. Commerce St. Cambria, WI 53923	Metal and Furniture stripping
Chernock Enterprises	P.O. Box 134. Hazelton, 18201	Lexol for leather, Armorall for rubber
Classic Auto Supply Co.	P.O. Box 810. Coshocton, OH 43812	Parts
Classic Chrome	2430 Washington St. Boston, MA 02119	Chrome
Classic Muffler	23 North Center St. Orange, NJ 07050	Mufflers
Condon & Skelly	P.O. Drawer A Willingboro, NJ 08046	Insurance
Stan Coleman Supplies	320 South St., Bldg 12-A Morristown, NJ 07960	Parts
Warren Cox	P.O. Box 216K Lakewood, CA 90713	Covers
M.H. Diels	12005 Tulip Grove Road. Bowie, MD 20715	1956 and 1957 Continental Mark II parts
Diverco	P.O. Box 277. Oak Forest, IL 60452	Gear Sets
Harold Drake	20035 Bellemare Ave. Torrance, CA 90503	1955-1958 Chevrolet supplies
Ralph Dunwoodie	5935 Calico Dr. Sun Valley, NV 89431	Appraisal service
EGGE	8403 Allport Santa Fe Springs, CA 90670	Parts
The Fibre Glass-Evercoat Co., Inc.	6600 Cornell Road Cincinnati, OH 45242	Fibre Glass
Gaslight Auto Parts, Inc.	P.O. Box 291 Urbana, OH 43078	Parts
Graves Plating Co.	P.O. Box 1052C Industrial Park Florence, AL 35630	Plating
Greenland Company	P.O. Box 332. Verdugo City, CA 91406	Accessories
Hibernia Auto Restorations, Inc.	Maple Terrace Hibernia, NJ 07842	Restoration
Bill Hirsch	396 Littleton Ave. Newark, NJ 07103	Leather, upholstery and convertible top material, carpets, Packard parts
Hoffers, Inc.	201 Forest St. Wausau, WI 54401	Automotive Glass
Hydro-E-Lectric	Paul B. Wiesman 48-B Appleton, Auburn, MA 01501	1966-1697 Lincoln parts
J & J Chrome Plating & Metal Finishing Co.	168 Peabody St. West Haven CT 06516	Chrome plating
Jahns Quality Pistons	2662 Lacy St. Los Angeles, CA 90031	Pistons for old cars

Jake's Restorations	Farrington Machine Services Route 4. Lebanon, MO 65536	Restoration
Fred Kanter	76R Monroe St. Boonton, NJ 07005	MG and Mercedes upholstery kits, tops, and carpet sets
LeBaron Bonney Co.	14 Washington St. Amesbury, MA 01913	Fabrics, carpets, vinyls, toppings, weltings, trims, leathers
The Lester Tire Company	26881 Cannon Road, Befor Heights, OH 44146	Tires, brass moldings, magnetos
Mark Auto Company, Inc.	Layton, NJ 07851	Parts and accessories
Dean McDonald	R.R.3., Box 61	1932-1948 Ford parts
Metro Moulded Parts	3031 Second St., No. Minneapolis, MN 55411	Moulded parts
Mid-Continent Leather Sales	P.O. Box 4691 Tulsa, OK 74104	Upholstery leather
Mitchell Motor Parts	1037 Parsons Ave. Columbus, OH 43206	Chrysler, Plymouth, Dodge and DeSoto parts
Moss Motors, Ltd.	7200 Hollister Ave. Galeta, CA 93017	British spares connection- - mechanical, electrical, rubber, chrome, trime and accessories
Muscle Parts	2793 Schaefer Hwy. Dearborn, MI 48121	1965-1970 Mustang parts
P.R. O'Connor & Co.	290 So. Elm St. Windsor Locks, CN 06096	1923-1959 Chevrolet parts
Old Time Auto Parts, Inc.	2741 CTH #N Cottage Grove, WI 53527	Parts
Pulfer & Williams	Robbins Road, R.D. #1 Rindge, NH 03461	Thunderbird parts
Ricks	Box 662. Shawnee Mission, KS 66201	1928-1948 Ford parts
David N. Rosen	364 Tompkins St. Cortland, NY 13045	Power brake units
Jack Rosen	Reliable Auto Parts 1751 Spruce St. Riverside, CA 92517	Continental Mark II parts
Schaeffer & Long, Inc.	210 Davis Road. Magnolia, NJ 08049	Restoration
Shadetree Automotive Restoration Supplies	P.O. Box 59406. Dallas, TX 75229	Restoration supplies
Special Endeavors, Inc.	2416 South 101 Ave. Omaha, NE 68124	Trailers
Special Interest Cars T-Bird Sanctuary	15055 Weststate Westminster, CA 92683	1955-1966 Thunderbird parts
Lynn H. Steele	Rt. 1, Box 71W Denver, NC 28037	Rubber reproduction parts for all American makes except Ford
Alfred C. Stone	223 Summer St. Somerville, MA 02143	Cadillac and LaSalle parts
Swirin Plating Service	535 Indian Road. Wayne. NJ 07470	Chrome plating
Terry's E Type Jaguar Parts	Rt. 2 Benton, IL 62812	Jaguar E parts
TIP Sandblast Equipment	17 Kenmore. Youngstown, OH 45407	Sandblasting
Western Hide-Tex	Box 2133 Encinal Station Sunnyvale, CA 94087	Cloth, leather and carpets
Wheel Repair Service, Inc.	176 Grove St. Paxton, MA 01612	Wheel repair
J.C. Whitney & Co.	1900-24 So. State St. Chicago, IL 60680	Parts